TIN HOUSE

MAGAZINE

Mothers of America
let your kids go to the movies!
get them out of the house so they won't know what you're up to
it's true that fresh air is good for the body
but what about the soul
that grows in darkness, embossed by silvery images . . .

—Frank O'Hara

Volume Two • Number Two

Tin House is published quarterly by McCormack Communications. Vol. 2, No. 2, Winter 2001. Printed by Edwards Brothers, Ann Arbor, MI. Send manuscript subscriptions (with SASE) to: P.O. Box 10500, Portland, OR 97296-0500. ISBN# 0-9673846-5-6

Subscription Service: Basic subscription price: 1 year $39.80. Send subscription requests, inquiries, and change of address to PO Box 469049, Escondido, CA 92046-9049, or e-mail to tinhouse@pcspublink.com Newstand Distribution through Independent Press Association/Big Top Newsstand Services. If you are a retailer that would like to order Tin House: please call (415) 643-0161, fax (415) 643-2983, or e-mail jesse@bigtoppubs.com. Please visit the IPA on the web at www.indypress.org

Volume Two Number Two

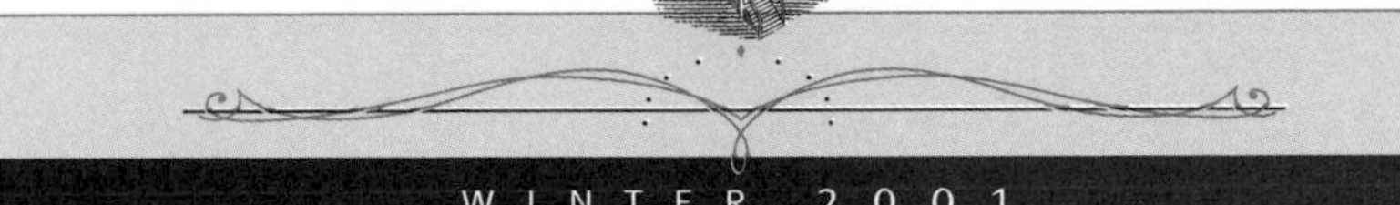

WINTER 2001

FEATURES

FICTION

POETRY

INTERVIEWS · PROFILES

EPISTLE

SCREENPLAY

LOST AND FOUND

THE LAST WORD

EDITOR'S NOTE

Hemingway once suggested that the best way to deal with Hollywood was to drive to the California border, toss your book over, take the money, and run. Things have changed since the days when studios sequestered authors in bungalows, filled them with rye, and cracked the whip until they produced. While whip cracking never goes out of vogue, writers today are no longer always viewed as necessary inconveniences. More than ever before, authors are seeing their work done justice on the big screen.

And that's why *Tin House*'s first theme issue is devoted to the movies, specifically to the intersection of writing and filmmaking. Oh, sure, we had an ulterior motive: the desire to rub sloped shoulders with fat cats who might want to float our project—a *Tin House* musical: *Lumberjacks, Highballs, and Tin*. We're thinking *McCabe and Mrs. Miller* meets *Breakfast at Tiffany's*, with gratuitous water ballet scenes. Actually, putting this mammoth issue (our biggest yet) together was something like a big budget special-effects extravaganza—good money after bad, our regular columns and good sense tossed out the window, mistaken identity, betrayal, cryptic e-mail, heartbreak, a stick of butter, plagiarism exposed, a bicycle chase, a flood, and a small fire.

We aren't sure exactly what a Best Boy does, but the mighty Rachel Resnick, brass-knuckled-guru, and consulting editor for this issue, is our Best Gal. She gets credit for casting the lineup of literate movie people, from András Hamori, the producer of *Crash* and *The Sweet Hereafter*, to Alex Cox, the outlaw director of *Repo Man* and *Sid and Nancy*. Scene One: The tone of the issue is set by the great Russell Banks who holds forth on the new intelligence in films and how filmmakers have creatively adapted his own uncompromising novels into movies. Scene Two: Party Scene with Mysterious Parlor Game, in which a dashing and bewitching array of writers, producers, and directors answer five questions, brilliantly dishing about the film adaptations they love and hate. We would like to invite you, after reading what nimble-witted folks such as Carrie Fisher, Buck Henry, Rick Moody, Benicio Del Toro, and Alison Maclean have to say, to please register your own loves and love-to-hates on our spanking new website at www.tinhouse.com. Scene Three: The Final Battle Scene and The Kiss. A twenty gun salute to our new art director, Bill Stanton. Despite our insistence that he read every account of the making of *Apocalypse Now* before taking the job, he pressed bravely on into the heart of darkness and came back alive—if a bit bloodied and bruised—but deserving of medals of valor and a Purple Heart for taking all manner of shrapnel. Lucky for us, Bill, like the rest of us here at *Tin House*, loves nothing more than sneaking into a movie in the middle of the day. Oh, it's starting now . . . Shh. Pass the Milk Duds.

No, but I Saw the Movie

For many years, or maybe not so many—for some years, anyhow—I'd be out on the book-tour hustings and after a reading would be signing books at a table in the lobby, and a lovely thing would happen. A stranger, a total stranger, would appear in line and volunteer that he or she loved one of my books (one other than the book that I was at that moment signing, of course, and was now embellishing with endearments and fawning declarations of lifelong gratitude). There is, of course, nothing more satisfying to an author of serious literary fiction or poetry—which is to say, an author who does not write for money—than to be told by a stranger that one's work has entered that stranger's life.

HAS HOLLYWOOD FINALLY BECOME HOSPITABLE TO SERIOUS FICTION WRITERS?

BY RUSSELL BANKS

Hollywood Theater in Portland, Oregon

And whenever a person told me that he or she had enjoyed *Affliction*, say, or *The Sweet Hereafter*, I assumed the reference was to my book, and I might say in a surprised way, for it was, after all, to me still somewhat surprising, "Oh? You read the book?" As if the reference were possibly to another affliction, like cholera or extreme poverty, or to a different Sweet Hereafter, a designer drug, maybe, or a chic new soul-food restaurant on Manhattan's Upper West Side. Inviting, I suppose, what usually followed, which was a description of the circumstances or conditions under which the book was read—a book club, my brother-in-law gave it to me for Christmas, a college course, I read it in prison, in the hospital, on a train/plane/slow boat to China, et cetera.

It's what we talk about when we talk about a book that one of us has written and the other has read. We're inevitably somewhat self-conscious, at a loss for the appropriate words, in a bit of a blush, both of us. Writing and reading literary fiction and poetry are activities almost too intimate to talk about. Literature is intimate behavior between strangers, possibly

Alberta Watson and Bruce Greenwood in *The Sweet Hereafter*

more intimate even than sex, and it occurs between *extreme* strangers, who sometimes do not even speak the same language and thus require the services of a translator. Sometimes one of the strangers (the writer, usually) has been dead for centuries; sometimes he or she is utterly unknown, anonymous, or someone, like Homer or the author of the Upanishads or the Song of Solomon, whose individual identity has been mythologized and absorbed by an entire people.

My point is simply that this activity of writing involves at its center the desire on the part of the writer to become intimate with strangers, to speak from one's secret, most vulnerable, truth-telling self directly to a stranger's same self. And it's so central to the impulse that it actually does not work when one's readers are *not* strangers, when one's readers are one's friends, lovers, or family members (it's well known, after all, that no writer takes pleasure from the praise of his mom or kid sister, and we're all conditioned from our apprenticeship on not to take seriously the critiques offered by our husbands and wives and best friends). Either way, people who know us personally have motives and knowledge that disqualify them as readers. No, it's only the kindness of strangers that counts, that shyly offered gift, "I have read your novel." (With the clear implication, of course, that it was not an unhappy or unrewarding experience.)

I know this, because I am a reader, too. I am other writers' intimate stranger, and I have sat next to an author at dinner and have felt the same odd, embarrassing need to declare, as if revealing a slightly illicit or inappropriate interest in baseball cards or negligee mail-order catalogs, that I have read his or her novel, and I know that, in saying so, I am confessing that I have traveled out-of-body deeply into that stranger's fictional world and have resided there, dreamed there, hallucinated there, and have been moved, comforted, and frightened, have laughed aloud there and maybe even wept. The author, I can always tell, is slightly embarrassed by my confession, but pleased nonetheless—the more so inasmuch as he or she and I have never met before and never will again, and he or she has never read anything of mine and, if the author wishes to preserve our beautiful relationship as it is, never will, either. Reader and writer from two different solar systems, our orbits intersect for a second, and we reflect back the flash of each other's light, take brief comfort from the actual physical existence of the other, and then speed on, safely back in our own imagined universe, as if the other were not circling far away in another universe, around a different, possibly brighter sun than ours.

In the last few years, however, there has been a subtle but important change for me in this exchange between writer and presumed reader. Nowadays, when at the book-signing table, I'm often approached by a person carrying a copy of *Affliction*, for example, the paperback with the picture of Nick Nolte and James Coburn on the cover, or maybe the Canadian edition of *The Sweet Hereafter* with Ian Holm and Sarah Polley staring mournfully out, and the person will say, "I loved *Affliction*," or, "*The Sweet Hereafter* meant a lot to me," and pleased and slightly embarrassed, as usual, I will say, "Oh? You read the book?" And the person will look at me somewhat quizzically, and say, "Uh ... no, but I saw the movie."

I honestly don't know how that makes me feel, how I *ought* to feel, or what I ought to say in response. What *do* we talk about when we talk about a book I wrote whose movie version you saw? Or a book I wrote that you know of solely because you heard about the movie and saw the clips on the Academy Awards television show? What is the relationship generally between literary fiction (that relatively esoteric art form) and film (the most popular and powerful art form of our time), and in particular between my literary fictions and their film adaptations?

These are not simple questions, and literary writers have historically been reluctant to discuss them, except in dismissive ways. Hemingway famously advised novelists to drive (*presumably* from the east) to the California-Nevada state line and toss the novel over the line, let the movie people toss the money back, then turn around and drive away as fast as possible. Which is what most novelists have done, and is what most producers, directors, screenwriters, and actors have wanted them to do. Let us buy your plot, they say, your characters, setting, themes, and language, and do whatever we please with them, that's what the money's *for*, Mr. Shakespeare, so we can leave dear old Lear happily ensconced at the Linger Longer Assisted-Living Facility in Naples, Florida, with his three daughters, Melanie, Gwyneth, and Julia, living together in adjoining condos nearby, heavily into Gulf Coast real estate, romance on the horizon, fadeout and hit the credits soundtrack, "Stayin' Alive" by the Bee Gees, and let's get Newman for the old guy, and for his pal, whatzisname, the guy with glaucoma, get Jack—we'll keep the title, sort of, only we'll call it *Shakespeare in Retirement.*

The story is that Hollywood is like Las Vegas—if you have a weakness, they'll find it.

Writers who didn't, or couldn't, afford to take Hemingway's advice almost always paid for it dearly with their pride, their integrity, often their reputations, and sometimes even their whole careers. The story is that Hollywood is like Las Vegas—if you have a weakness, they'll find it. Everyone knows Fitzgerald's sad tale of depression, booze, and crack-up, and there are dozens more. Faulkner seems to have managed only by staying solidly drunk from arrival to departure. Nelson Algren sold the film rights of *The Man with the Golden Arm* to Otto Preminger, contingent on Algren's being hired to write the screenplay; later, safely back in Chicago, he said, "I went out there for a thousand a week, and I worked Monday, and I got fired Wednesday. The guy that hired me was out of town on Tuesday." S. J. Perelman said of Hollywood, "It was a hideous and untenable place when I dwelt there, populated with few exceptions by Yahoos, and now that it has become the chief citadel of television, it's unspeakable." A native of Providence, Rhode Island, and a great writer about boxing and horse racing, you'd not think of Perelman as especially fastidious, but Hollywood he saw as "a dreary industrial town controlled by hoodlums of enormous wealth, the ethical sense of a pack of jackals, and taste so degraded that it befouled everything it touched." (Sort of the way I see Providence, now that I think of it.) More or less in the same vein, John Cheever said, "My principal feeling about Hollywood is suicide. If I could get out of bed and into the shower, I was all right. Since I never paid the bills, I'd reach for the phone and order the most elaborate breakfast I could think of, and then I'd try to make it to the shower before I hanged myself." Strong statements, but not at all atypical, when serious literary writers found themselves obliged to work in, for, and with the makers of movies. Ben Hecht put it in depressingly simple terms, "I'm a Hollywood writer; so I put on a sports jacket and take off my brain."

And yet, one is forced to ask, was that then and this now? And how do we account for the difference? Because, when one looks around today, one notices an awful lot of very respectable fiction writers having what appears to be a very good time in bed with Hollywood, both as authors of novels recently adapted to film, like Michael Ondaatje's *The English Patient*, Toni Morrison's *Beloved*, Peter Carey's *Oscar and Lucinda*, David Guterson's *Snow Falling on Cedars*, and Mona Simpson's *Anywhere but Here*, and as fiction writers turned screenwriters, like Richard Price, John Irving, Amy Tan, Jim Harrison, and Susan Minot. Paul Auster has even *directed* his first film and is planning to try a second. There are others waiting in the wings. And we're not talking about the Crichtons and the Clancys here, whose fiction seems written mainly to fit the template of blockbuster movies—a respectable line of work, but not one I myself identify with.

Ralph Fiennes and Cate Blanchette in *Oscar and Lucinda*

No, we're talking about writers whose fiction aspires to the somewhat more Parnassian heights where literature resides, work composed without consideration of financial reward and meant to be compared, for better or worse, to the great literary works of the past. And there is a growing phalanx of such writers, whose often difficult, morally ambiguous novels, complexly layered books with unruly characters, have been eagerly sought out and adapted for film. I honestly can't remember a period like it. We could easily make a very long list of novelists and story writers, serious, literary writers, almost none of whom actually lives and works in Hollywood, as it happens (thanks to fax machine, modem, and e-mail), but all of whom are making a fairly good liv-

Sigourney Weaver in *The Ice Storm*

ing from the film industry these days, a much better living, certainly, than they could make on the sales of their books alone or than many of them used to make teaching in university creative-writing programs.

I now must add my own name to that list, and confess that in the last few years, not only have I made a pretty good living from the movie business, I've had a heck of a good time doing it, too. And furthermore, I'm not ashamed or even slightly embarrassed by the movies that have been adapted from my novels. Well, that's not altogether true: there are a few moments in each that make me cringe and crouch low in my seat when I see them. But overall I am delighted to have been associated with the making of those two films, *Affliction* and *The Sweet Hereafter*, and am grateful to the people who made them and to the businesspeople who financed them. I think they are interesting, excellent films on their own terms, and I feel they honor the novels on which they are based. And I don't believe I'm alone in having had such a delightful experience—most of the writers I listed earlier, if not all of them, feel the same about the films adapted from their works. Oh, Rick Moody might grumble about aspects of *The Ice Storm* and William Kennedy might quibble with some of the decisions made in the making of *Ironweed*, but unlike the Faulkners, Cheevers, Perelmans, and Hechts of previous generations, none of the writers mentioned here feels demeaned, exploited, or deceived. The contrast between my experience and that of so many of my colleagues on the one hand, and the experience of our predecessors on the other, is so great as to raise an interesting question. Simply, has the movie industry in the last ten or fifteen years, and especially in the last five years, become uncharacteristically hospitable to serious works of fiction, or have the sensibilities and needs of the writers of fiction been coarsened and dumbed down to such a degree that they no longer feel offended by Hollywood?

Obviously—since, rightly or wrongly, I feel neither coarsened nor especially dumbed-down—I believe it's the former. It's Hollywood that's changed. And it's possible that my own experience there, since it hasn't been especially uncharacteristic, can illustrate how it has changed, if not suggest why. Although *Affliction* was not released until December 1998, and *The Sweet Hereafter* was released a year earlier, in December 1997, both movies were shot within weeks of each other between January and March of 1997. Both were filmed in Canada, *Affliction* in Quebec, less than two hours' drive from my home in upstate New York, and *The Sweet Hereafter* in Toronto and British Columbia. The most salient aspect of this (other than the fact that, because they were nearby, I got to hang around the sets a whole lot) is merely that neither movie was filmed in Los Angeles. A far more important fact, however, is that the director of *Affliction*, Paul Schrader, and the director of *The Sweet Hereafter*, Atom Egoyan, although a generation apart, are both auteur-style, independent filmmakers, serious cinematic artists with highly developed artistic imaginations. Crucially, they are men with no studio affiliations, who finance their projects by hook and crook, pasting together support from half a dozen sources, foreign and domestic, risking their mortgages, their kids' college educations, and next summer's vacation every time out, in a game that for them is high stakes and personal, but leaves them with maximum control over what ends up on the screen. Final cut, in other words, all the way down the line. And this is only possible because of budget size. Paul Schrader likes to point out that somewhere around fourteen million dollars you have to put white hats on the good guys and black hats on the bad guys. It's practically an immutable law of filmmaking. Fourteen million dollars, adjusted to inflation, is the point where you're told by the person with the checkbook: no more shades of gray, no more contradictions, no more ambiguities. *Affliction* cost a little over six million dollars to make, *The Sweet Hereafter* cost about $4.7 million, and you can be sure that Nick Nolte, Sissy Spacek, James Coburn, Willem Dafoe, and Ian Holm did not receive their usual fees. These actors, movie stars who command salaries equal, in a couple of cases, to the entire budget of the movie, worked for far less because they admired the director and the other cast members and wanted to work with them, they were excited by the screenplay and the source material for the film, and they wanted to portray characters who were colored in shades of gray, wanted to inhabit lives made complex and believable by contradiction and ambiguity, dealing with serious conflicts that matter in the real world. They believed in film as an art form and in their craft and the abilities of their colleagues, and were trying for that rare thing, a collaborative, lasting work of art.

Two important factors, then, contributed mightily to getting these rather difficult and, some might say, depressing films made: the directors, both of them artists with strong personal visions of the world, were independent filmmakers free of studio affiliation, with track records that attract great actors; and both films were budgeted low enough to keep down the debt service, so that an investor could recoup his money and even make a profit without having to sell tickets to every fourteen-year-old boy and girl in America. Without, in other words, having to turn the movie into a theme park or a video game. Also, there may have been a third factor, which underlies both of these first two: technology. The technology of filmmaking has changed considerably in recent years. From the camera to the editing room, from the soundtrack to the projection booth, filmmaking has gone digital, as they like to say, so that it's possible, for instance, as in *The Sweet Hereafter*, to send a school bus careening over a cliff and skidding across a frozen lake to where it stops, then slowly sinks below the ice, a horrifying sight—all composed in a few days in a dark room in Toronto, pixels on a computer screen, a *virtual* school bus, cliff, frozen lake, et cetera, for one-tenth the price and in one-quarter the time it would have taken to stage and film in 35 millimeter an *actual* bus, cliff, lake, et cetera. The enormous and incredibly expensive technological resources and hardware available to a studio will soon be available to almost any kid with a credit card or an indulgent uncle, and that kid can set up shop with a laptop anywhere—from SoHo to Montreal to Toronto to Seattle—and compete with the Lucases, Disneys, and Hensons of the world.

Atom Egoyan, director of *The Sweet Hereafter*

American independent filmmaking seems to be entering a truly brave new world, and it will create a transition comparable, perhaps, to the transition between silent films and talkies, one in which, thanks to technological change, the old controlling economic structures undergo seismic shifts and rearrangements, with the result that the prevailing aesthetic and thematic conventions will have to give way. The boom in recent years of independent movie-making is just the beginning. The trend toward multinational corporate bloat and gigantism will no doubt continue, if for no other reason than, thanks to that same technological change put to other uses, it *can*—unifying theme parks, professional sports, retailing, and gambling under one all-season stadium roof, so that the distinction between shopping and entertainment eventually disappears altogether, and Las Vegas and Orlando become our national cultural capitals, the twenty-first-century Model Cities of America. But at the same time, thanks to the very same technology, the equivalent of a cinematic *samizdat* is beginning to evolve right alongside it. This is where the real filmmaking is being done; the rest is little more than consumer advertising, tie-ins, and product placement. And this is where we'll see the bright young directors, screenwriters, cinematographers, and actors going to work. The Atom Egoyans and Paul Schraders of the future will be making their films rapidly and cheaply, editing them as fast as they're shot, and releasing them as independently as they're made, by the internet or on video and DVD. Films like *The Blair Witch Project* and *Being John Malkovitch* and *The Celebration* and the recently-released *Last Night*—inventive, unconventionally structured, freshly and bravely imagined movies, are not anomalies in today's film world, although five years ago they would have been. Five years ago they probably would not have been made at all. Nor, for that matter, would *Affliction* and *The Sweet Hereafter.*

This is why I think you're seeing so many serious novelists hanging around the filmmakers these days. They sense there's something marvelous happening here, and, if it doesn't take too much time away from their fiction writing and pays reasonably well, they'd like to be a part of it. Just consider the writing itself—until fairly recently, the conventions of screen-

> *American independent film making seems to be entering a truly brave new world, and it will create a transition comparable, perhaps, to the transition between silent films and talkies.*

writing were, from a late-twentieth century novelist's perspective, moribund, stuck in linear time, glued to the old Aristotelian unities of place, time, and character, a three-act tale as anachronistic and predictable as... well, as a late-nineteenth century novel. What self-respecting post-modernist fiction writer would want to work in a form so limited and so inappropriate to our times? Yet for the writers of screenplays, until recently, it was as if, five generations after Faulkner, Joyce, and Woolf, modernism never existed, or if it did, that it had no relevance to narrative except between the covers of a book. No wonder Ben Hecht felt he had to take his brain off when he went to work in Hollywood. No wonder Hemingway couldn't be bothered even to cross the state line. And no wonder there was such a fuss a few years ago when Quentin Tarantino in *Pulp Fiction* pushed the envelope a little and played with narrative time and point of view. At the time, it was a radical move for a screenwriter, perhaps, but all he was doing was employing a few of the tools that practically every second-year fiction-writing student keeps at the ready, switchback and replay, and a *Rashomon* split point of view.

It is amusing to imagine pitching the stories to an old-time studio executive... The door, Mr. Banks, is over there.

Consider, again, our two examples, *The Sweet Hereafter* and *Affliction*, not just how those screenplays were written, but the (to me) amazing fact that the novels got adapted for film at all. Never mind the subject matter—although it is amusing to imagine pitching the stories to an old-time studio executive. "Mr. Warner, I've got this very dark story that starts with a school-bus accident in a small north-country town, and a large number of the children of the town are killed, and the movie is about the reaction of the village to this mind-numbing event." Or this: "An alcoholic, violent, forty-five-year-old small-town cop tries and fails to overcome the psychological and moral disfigurement inflicted on him as a child by his alcoholic, violent father." The door, Mr. Banks, is over there.

Let's look at just the narrative form and structure of the two novels. *The Sweet Hereafter* is told from four separate, linked points of view, four different characters, each of whom picks up the story where the previous narrator left off and continues for seventy-five or so pages before handing it off, in the process remembering and recounting his and her past, offering reflections, ruminations, observations, and grief for the lost children. *Affliction* is told from the point of view of an apparently minor character who is gradually, indirectly, revealed to be an unreliable narrator and thus by the tale's end has become the central figure in the story, displacing the person we *thought* the story was about. Neither form lends itself to a conventional three-act screenplay with the usual plot points and fixed unities of time, place, and point of view, and if for no other reason than that (never mind subject matter), I was amazed that anyone even wanted to *try* to make a movie from them. Happily, both Atom Egoyan and Paul Schrader did, and they both felt free to invite me into the process of adaptation from the start and allowed me to look over their shoulders, as it were, all the way through to the editing room and beyond. It was fascinating and very instructive to see the liberties they took, not with the books, but with the old conventions of filmmaking, from screenplay to casting to camera placement to editing and sound.

For instance, to preserve the multiple points of view of *The Sweet Hereafter*—in the novel one can think of them as being structured vertically, like four columns of type, or four members of a mile relay team, which in the "real-time" constraints of a movie (as opposed to the more interactive "mental-time" freedoms of fiction) would have resulted in four separate, consecutive, thirty-minute movies—Egoyan essentially tipped the story onto its side, ran the several points of view horizontally, as it were, almost simultaneously, the relay runners running four abreast instead of sequentially, so that the story moves back and forth in time and from place to place with unapologetic ease. Egoyan trusts his viewer to reconstruct time and place and reunify point of view on his or her own, just as one does when reading a modern novel. No big deal. Similarly, Schrader with *Affliction* felt no compunctions against letting the narrator of the novel, a minor character, it seems, one outside the action, function in the film as the witness and recapitulator of his older brother's deeds and misdeeds. This is the character who would surely have been eliminated at once from a studio production of this film, but Schrader makes him slowly, subtly, become the center of the story, using voice-over to establish his presence at every crucial juncture and giving us explicit, dramatized inconsistencies, conflicting versions of events, to establish his unreliability, so that Willem Dafoe's voice-over at the end, "Only I remain . . . ," can be heard and felt with a terrible chill of recognition by all of us in the audience, we who—unlike poor Wade Whitehouse, the ostensible and long-gone hero of our story—*also* remain. And in that way, the story of *Affliction* becomes our story, Wade's affliction becomes our culture's affliction.

Working closely with Egoyan and Schrader, I received a crash course in filmmaking, and what I learned *can't* be done in film was just as interesting and instructive to me, the fiction writer, as what I learned *can* be done in film was interesting and instructive to me the neophyte screenwriter. A particularly useful, and typical, insight, for instance, came to me early on in the writing of *The Sweet Hereafter* screenplay. Egoyan had told me that one of the aspects of the novel that most excited him was the final scene, a demolition derby. We even drove to the Essex County fair in upstate New York and videotaped one. It was the most cinematic scene in the book, Atom said. But when it came time to write it into the screenplay, he just couldn't. It was too big, too loud, crowded, too crammed with action. What to do? He asked me, "What's the underlying function of the scene in the *novel*?" I explained that it served as a social rite, a familiar but strange, rigidly structured ritual that could embrace, embellish, and reconfigure the roles of the various members of the community. With the devices and artifices of fiction available to me, I could keep the noise down, thin out the crowd, slow down the speed—distancing the demolition derby, so that it could function in the novel as an emblem for everything else in the story. He got this. Also, all along I'd told him that, to me, the novel only *seemed* realistic; that actually it was supposed to be experienced as a moral fable about the loss of the children in our culture, an elaboration on a medieval fairy tale. That's when he proposed cutting into the film the whole of the Browning poem "The Pied Piper of Hamelin," inserting a literal reading of the book. At first I said no way, too literary. There's barely a mention of it in the book, one or two passing allusions, maybe. But the more I thought about it, the more I realized—too literary for a *novel*, maybe, but not for a film. Just as the demolition-derby scene was too cinematic for a film, maybe, but not for a novel. Film, I was discovering, is in your face; fiction is in your head.

Here's a further example: something I learned a full year after *The Sweet Hereafter* was released. In Toronto one night, Atom and I gave a presentation to benefit a small theater group there and decided that I would read scenes from the novel, and he would show a clips of the film version of the same scenes, and then we'd discuss why we'd each done our respective work the way we did. One of these scenes was the incest scene, which a number of people who had, and some who hadn't, read the book complained about in the film. "It was like a dream," and "I thought maybe I'd imagined it," the fourteen-year-old Nichole tells us over and over in the novel—distancing us from the actual act, the incest, by placing her account of her *response* to it between it and us, so that we simultaneously imagine the act and the girl in two different time frames, both during and after. Egoyan tried to find a cinematic way to show that from Nichole's point of view it was like a dream, maybe something she imagined, et cetera, and as a result he presented it as if it *were* a dream, i.e., dreamy, with candles, music, a father who almost seems to be her boyfriend, which has the effect, not of distancing the incest and allowing us to pity the victim and fear for her in an appropriate way, but of romanticizing it, making the victim seem way too complicit and fear and pity nearly impossible.

These lessons don't suggest to me that fiction is in any way superior to film. Merely different, in fascinating and challenging ways. Furthermore, the freedom to make movies this way, to be inventive, imaginative, and complex in the formal and structural aspects of the screenplay, and to deal with life-and-death issues that affect us all in our day-to-day lives, this is what attracts novelists like Paul Auster, Peter Carey, John Irving, and so many others like them to the movie business. It's not, as in the past, merely the business of the movie business that attracts; it's the movies that can be made there. It's certainly what has attracted me. And as a direct result of my experience with *The Sweet Hereafter* and *Affliction*, in the last few years I've become a screenwriter myself. I'm a dues-paying member of the Screenwriters Guild of America, having adapted two of my novels: *Rule of the Bone*, for Chris Noonan to direct, with Chris, his partner Barry Mendel, and me to produce; and *Continental Drift*, with Willem Dafoe and me to produce. I am also now at work on an adaptation of a novel by a different novelist, *On the Road*, by Jack Kerouac, for Francis Coppola, and am planning soon to write an original screenplay, too. And the people I'm working with, the directors, actors, producers, even the agents, are smart, and they are exceedingly skilled at what they do. They know all kinds of things that I don't, and in no way do they make me feel that, to work with them, I've got to put on a sports jacket and take off my brain. Quite the opposite.

In no way do they make me feel that, to work with them, I've got to put on a sports jacket and take off my brain.

Eudora Welty once said, "The novel is something that never was before and will not be again." That is the reason why we write them. When it begins to appear that a film can also be that new, that uniquely itself, then, believe me, men and women who otherwise would be writing novels will want to make films, too. We are fast approaching that point. Oh, sure, it is a lot of fun to hobnob with movie stars and go to Cannes and Sundance and ride to the Oscars in a limo the likes of which you haven't seen since your senior prom, but the thrill fades faster than cheap cologne. The thrill of becoming intricately and intimately involved in the process of making a true work of narrative art, however, and the chance to make that work of art collaboratively in the most powerful medium known to man, that's as thrilling as it gets; at least for this old storyteller it is. And, too, as Peter DeVries once said, "I love being a writer. What I can't stand is the paperwork."

But I don't want to leave the mistaken impression that I or any of the other novelists I've mentioned, my blessed colleagues, is likely to give up writing fiction to devote him- or herself to film. Despite the paperwork. That's inconceivable to me. These dalliances with film—however thrilling, remunerative, and instructive they are—can't replace the deep, life-shaping, life-*changing* response one gets from creating a fictional world, living in that world for years at a time, then sending it out to strangers. *Perfect* strangers. A novel, like a marriage, can change your life for the rest of your life; I'm not so sure that can be said of a movie, any more than it can of a love affair.

What, then, *do* I say to that very kind stranger who tells me, "No, but I saw the movie"? I can answer, "Ah, but that was in another country, friend, and in a different time. If you read the book, you will now and then be reminded of that country, perhaps, and that time, but only dimly and incidentally." For when we open a novel, we bring to it everything that we bring to a film—our memories and fears and our longings and dreams (our secrets, even the ones we keep from ourselves)—all of which the film either displaces or simply disregards as it unspools in the dark before us. All of which—our memories, fears, longings, and dreams—the novel engages and utilizes wholly as it takes us out of our lives into another that's as much of our own making as it is of the novelist's. That intimacy, that secret sharing among strangers, is what no novelist and no reader can give up. No matter how remarkable it is, a film is what it is, regardless of our presence or absence before it. The darkened theater can be empty, and it won't affect the essential nature of the film being shown there. But a novel simply does not exist until it's read, and each time it's read, even if it's read a second time by the same person, or a third, even if it's read a thousand years after it was written, it's just as Eudora Welty said, it is "something that never was before and will not be again."

Above Sunset

by

David St. John

All the hippest ghouls are out tonight
Along the boulevard the day calls "Sunset,"
& she's the loveliest dead girl in sight,

Her skin powdered blank as China White,
A torn red bustier & kohl leather jacket;
& all the hippest ghouls are digging it tonight,

Amazed that she's stepped out beneath these bright,
Piercing klieg lights . . . & in all this neon racket
She's the loveliest dead girl in sight—

& she's walking right beside me, holding on tight
To balance spiked heels & spiked hair (black-jet)
& the hippest ghouls parading Sunset tonight

Turn as she passes, some weeping in delight,
Though the tourists look clearly appalled. Fuck it—
She's mine: the loveliest dead girl in sight.

Now, on her bedroom balcony, the dawn light
Sifting down these lush hills above Sunset,
I know we're the happiest ghouls of the night;
& she's still the loveliest dead girl in sight.

Naked PORTRAIT OF A PRODUCER

ANDRAS HAMORI

An Interview with András Hamori in Fifteen Phone Calls and One Bathtub

Please do not bend

INTERVIEWED BY RACHEL RESNICK

András Hamori is a successful Hollywood producer, but not in the studio mold. He favors a silky T-shirt and jeans, rather than the regulation Armani, has carved out a niche in the independent film world with such daring and critically acclaimed successes as Atom Egoyan's *The Sweet Hereafter*, David Cronenberg's *Crash* and *Existenz*, and, most recently, Istvan Szabo's *Sunshine*. Recently he split off from AllianceAtlantis and started his own production company, H_2O. His production slate is full of literary properties, ranging from heavyweight to offbeat to classic to lightweight, which is why *Tin House* thought he would be the producer to talk with for this special issue.

Rachel Weisz as Greta (left) and Molly Parker (right) in Istvan Szabo's *Sunshine*

Some of those properties are: *The Bird Artist*, by Howard Norman; *Morvern Callar*, by Alan Warner; *The Notebook*, *The Proof*, and *The Third Lie*, by Agota Kristof; *Running Wild*, by J. G. Ballard; *Are You Experienced?*, by William Sutcliffe; *Ivanhoe*, by Sir Walter Scott; *Willie Hogg*, by Robin Jenkins; *White Clouds*, a screenplay by Dennis Potter based on Tim Parks's *Cara Massimina*; *People Who Knock on the Door*, by Patricia Highsmith.

Once a scathingly outspoken theater critic in his native Budapest, András Hamori follows a long line of Eastern European, Hungarian and Russian Jews who made their way to Tinselburg, people whose names are synonymous with the birth of Hollywood: Samuel Goldwyn nee Goldfish, Louis B. Mayer, Carl Laemmle, and Adolph Zukor. The Hungarian Zukor became president of Paramount Studios and invented the feature-length film. In 1981, at the age of twenty-eight, Hamori defected from Hungary, first to Canada, and then to Los Angeles. For the past twelve years, he's lived in L.A., and for the last eleven, he's made his home in the Hollywood Hills with his longtime girlfriend. The house they share looks like a stark white ship adrift in the hills, the deck floating against the foreground of the Sunset Strip. It is here that Hamori throws his famed dinner parties, beguiling many an actor and director with his savory home-cooked

Hungarian-style meals, where the supply of sausages and fine wines is inexhaustible, and a bottle of mouthwash-green absinthe is always at the ready to complete the delirium.

We meet in person to kick off the interview at one of his favorite restaurants—Ristorante di Giorgio Baldi.

It is a haven for film moguls, record execs, celebs, and dot-commers. No one else can afford it. Strictly expense account. I have never set foot in here before. I arrive first and do as Hamori has instructed, informing the maître d' that I am meeting two people and the reservation is under "András Hamori." The name is magic. I am immediately seated at a large round table in the very crowded restaurant. People look over, trying to place me. Everyone looks vaguely familiar. I pull out a cheap yellow legal pad and start scribbling, which further confuses them. Five, ten, twenty minutes pass. I steel myself for getting kicked out, politely. I risk ordering a bottle of bubbly water.

Hamori finally arrives. With his thick crop of punk-cut salt-and-pepper hair and mischievously lively face, he radiates energy and intelligence. He scopes the restaurant with birdlike stop-and-start intensity. "Let me sit here," he says, pulling out a chair near me and gesturing with his head toward a couple one table over, "so I can look at that woman's tits." Hamori orders a mildly expensive bottle of Campaccio Riserva Speciale, Terrabianca, truffle carpaccio and deep-fried shiitake mushrooms with pecorino to start. "Are you sure you can see well enough?" I say. "Oh, I don't care. They're not so good after all," he says. "I always ask for a table for three. I hate small tables. Even though they know the third person never comes. The ghost. We'll just say they're late," he whispers mock-conspiratorially.

Hamori has requested I don't bring a tape recorder. He wants the initial interview to be informal. Hamori is an engaging raconteur, funny, with a charming Hungarian accent and dramatic intonation. He loves his food, and the enjoyment is infectious. Just after the meltingly fresh grilled branzini arrives, garnished with artfully arranged sprigs of rosemary, Hamori excuses himself. "I have to go shoot up in the bathroom," he winks. Hamori is a severe diabetic. He has to inject himself with insulin four times a day. Despite doctors' warnings, he persists in driving himself relentlessly in his work, and in consuming sumptuous foods and wines. I ask him why he makes films. Art? Money? Kicks? And he says, "The easiest way to get laid . . . and besides, I am like a junkie. The best is both—getting money and making something satisfying." The conversation ranges from Hungarian theater to his career history to recent books to Hollywood gossip. I ask him how he knows when an adaptation is final, and he says, "The same way with a book. Adding or losing a word at a time. Then it's suddenly done. Like when you pull the hairs off the tail of a horse hair by hair until it's poof! not a tail anymore—except the other way around." We finish off the evening with fresh peach sorbet packed into a scooped-out frozen real peach.

The next day Hamori jets to Europe on business. I will have to contact him through his assistant or by international cell phone for the rest of the interview. So I do. I sink into reading the books he's developing, and the script adaptations. I think about how, as a fresh-off-the-plane defector, he sprang up from an assistant at Canada's Alliance Entertainment when he barely spoke English, to visionary film producer in little over a decade. I track him down in London, Liverpool, Ibiza, Budapest, and the Hungarian countryside near Lake Balaton. I tape-record our conversations in cars, taxis, restaurants, airports, country homes, Soho lofts, hotels, and bathrooms. I am even, in Budapest's airport, sent through the X-ray machine in the body of his cell phone. In this series of recorded phone calls, Hamori is variously glib or thoughtful, bored or lively—and usually late and distracted. He has many of the mannerisms of the consummate Hollywood producer. Always cavalier, always wielding the upper hand. But, he is refreshingly un-self-obsessed, never dull, and full of surprises. Especially on the telephone, where Hamori improvises a bizarre form of living theater.

Phone Call #1: London, Soho loft, 12 A.M. Greenwich Mean Time

Hamori is champagne-drunk after a night glam-pubbing. I take advantage of his bubbliness.

András Hamori: I love Soho. Everyone is a "twat" here. A "cunt," a "twat." Kate Moss gave me a lighter tonight in the shape of a cigarette. You flip the filter. I love Kate Moss. Mmm.

Rachel Resnick: Hey, what the hell is a producer?

AH: The definition of a producer? Someone who can always find a better writer, actor, director than himself. Producers are matchmakers, matching the material with the artists. Call me a movie yenta.

RR: Where do you read?

AH: I read everything in the bathtub. I always have. Or lately, on planes . . . the best two places to have sex by the way.

RR: Does that help your irreverence toward the text?

AH: No, it's 'cause you can combine masturbating with reading.

J. G. BALLARD

18 March, 1996

To David Cronenberg

Dear David,

Your film of Crash absolutely stunned me! It's the most powerful and original film I've seen for years. In many ways it takes off where my novel ends, and is even more erotic and mysterious.

The actors are superb. Holly Hunter as the avenging angel, James Spader and Deborah Unger as the husband and wife drawn into this violent and sensual world, Rosanna Arquette as the voluptuous cripple and Elias Koteas as the hoodlum scientist together help to create a masterpiece of cinema that will be the film sensation of the 1990's.

Thank you for a brilliant achievement!

Very best wishes,

Jim Ballard

Letter from *Crash* author J. G. Ballard to *Crash* director David Cronenberg

RR: And so masturbation plus reading in the bathtub equals filmmaking?

AH: Equals ultimate pleasure. And filmmaking is ultimate pleasure.

RR: When you're adapting a book, do you come at it with reverence or disrespect? Is adaption akin to cannibalizing?

AH: Disrespect. I might respect the spirit of the book, or certain elements. But I don't consider respecting the book my duty when I'm developing adaptations. It's a different media. Different things work in film and novels. You might catch something in a novel which is why you decide to make the movie, but by the time you

finish the adaptation and the film, a new creature is born. Remember when I told you about my very first adventure in the film business when I arrived in America, with Mordecai Richler? *Joshua Then and Now*? That was a case where we were totally faithful to a wonderful novel, and the end result is flawed. Then sometimes you move away from the novel, like David Cronenberg did from *Crash*, and the film is better than the novel. I think Jimmy Ballard agrees. He's had so many of his books made into films. Cronenberg's *Crash*, Spielberg's *Empire of the Sun*, and now David Leland doing *Running Wild*. He'll be the first to admit sometimes the adaptation is better.

RR: So are you saying the book is a corpse and the producer is a vulture who flaps down, and drags the printed carcass over to the auteur, who in turn shreds it up and vomits something entirely new onto the screen?

AH: No. How disgusting. You should have met Dennis Potter. You two are soul mates. I have to go. My head hurts.

RR: Can a bad book make a good script? Like *Disturbia*, which I thought sucked. Even though I couldn't stop turning the pages.

AH: Sometimes it can. You throw it away, and keep the basic thought. In this case, the cat-and-mouse game that takes place over the course of one night in London. And there can be a fascinating movie around that, even though the title bugs me.

RR: Why did you buy it?

AH: We bought *Disturbia* for the Jude Law-Ewan McGregor-Johnny Lee Miller-Sadie Frost-Sean Pertwee company Natural Nylon. They want to do it. I'm not buying it for myself. I don't want to take this to a totally practical level, but I think I have to because that's what a producer does. It's not always an aesthetical decision when you buy something. Sometimes you buy it because, maybe it is not so brilliant, but you have a group of people who could make it brilliant.

Phone Call #2: London streets, Taxi cab, Morning over there, Hellishly late for me

AH: Oh, this is great. We're passing the Blind Beggar, where Ronnie Kray shot Cornell for calling him a "big fat poof."

RR: What's the parallel between the worlds of theater and film?

AH: When you watch Shakespeare's *Hamlet* in 2001, you don't give a fuck about Shakespeare, you don't give a fuck about this stupid Danish prince who's screwing around and playing with his meshugenah stepsister. What you really care about is what the director today in 2001 has to say using Shakespeare's *Hamlet*. If you go to a director like David Cronenberg with *Crash*, you don't care about J. G. Ballard's *Crash* anymore, you care about David Cronenberg's *Crash*.

RR: Are you a hands-on producer?

AH: Absolutely, but it depends on who my director is. Because if you want David Cronenberg's take on life through J. G. Ballard's *Crash*, you don't force your own vision on him. You discuss it with him and criticize it and point out certain flaws and that's it. Midwife it along.

RR: Barth drew a distinction between Windexed windows of prose and stained-glass windows of prose. It seems you pick properties where there's a simplicity, a transparency of prose, like *The Bird Artist*. Do you avoid language-based work?

AH: Huh? Who? I don't know what you're talking about. Nope. Doesn't matter. It's all about the story. I always know the text will change. It goes through scriptwriters, directors, actors, dramaturgs, producers. Good luck if there is one line left from the original book once the film gets made. The last line from the book gets thrown out when the actor on the set says, "I can't say this, who the fuck wrote this stupid line?"

RR: How do you find the books you option? Do you hang around in bookstores or do you depend on publicists?

"Jude Law will be perfect in this role! We bought it for him. It's like in theater, you have a company of actors, and you pick some projects because you know what they'll bring to it."

AH: The bookstores are too late. Most of the time we get the manuscripts from the writers' agents before they're published. One time I found a book in a second hand store for ninety-five cents Canadian. It was a detective novel by Laurence Saunders, but under a pseudonym. No one even knew it existed! I got the rights for nothing! Never made the movie.

Phone Call #3: Sometime over a weekend, At Roman Polanski's summer beach house

RR: So what drives you to buy a literary property?

AH: I don't know. I can't think. I'm sitting on the deck boiling. My brain is boiling.

RR: What was the experience of reading *Cara Massimina*, the book, after Potter's script?

AH: Wait. There's some sand in the cell phone. (Pause.) What was the question? *Cara Massimina*. I was happy that I didn't read the book first, because I probably wouldn't have bought it. The script addressed what the book was lacking. Humor. Even though the script is pretty fucking grim as well because he bludgeons this girl to death. In Potter's hands, it's a really black comedy. Jude Law will be perfect in this role! We bought it for him. It's like in theater, you have a company of actors, and you pick some projects because you know what they'll bring to it.

RR: How did Dennis Potter get attached?

AH: This is a very unusual situation. Dennis bought the book himself, which scriptwriters very rarely do. I asked him why he bought it. He said, because this guy is more vicious than I could ever be. Which is a great line, because Potter was one of the most vicious people I ever met in my life. He was a fucking monster. He was rude, suspicious, vulgar. When I first met him, he shook my hand; except he had that skin disease which shrunk the nerves in his hand, so instead of shaking my hand, he was scratching my hand. And while he was scratching my hand he looked into my eyes to see how I was reacting, and he said, "Aren't I disgusting?" And he didn't let my hand go. Then he said, "I haven't been with a woman for five years." Then I introduced him to my partner at the time, Schultz-Keil. "Hmm, Schultz-Keil, your people bombed my country." And Schultz-Keil said, "Dennis, I was born in 1945." And Dennis said, "That's what they all say." So mean. I remember we wanted to do a rewrite, and we had a question about switching around two scenes, and the director called Dennis and said, "What would you say, Dennis, if I switched scenes thirteen and fourteen," which you quite often do even when you're in editing. "What would I think?" "Yes, I'm really curious." "I would say you were a fucking moron, that's what I'd say." And he wasn't joking. He hung up the phone. So it's completely understandable that he buys this book. He was so impressed someone else wrote meaner than him.

RR: *White Clouds* sounds like a character study, or a sketch. That might work for a short story, but for a whole film?

AH: I think *White Clouds* is actually a very small movie. Some movies are like full theater, or a circus with all the acts in it. This one's just a one-man show. *White Clouds* is like an acrobat. A tightrope walker. You watch it and you're amazed by that one character only. You know in the first sentence he's going down the wrong road, and you want to see how he fails. Like in puppet theater when the kids scream, "Oh, please, don't go there, the witch is behind you!" That feeling where you want to stop the character from fucking up? Not every movie has to have a grand scope.

RR: How has starting out as a theater critic fed into being a producer?

AH: The only direct link is you value the material.

Phone Call #4: Al Fresco Restaurant, 11 P.M.

RR: Hello?

AH: I can't talk right now. I'm having dinner with Polanski, and this crazy man keeps asking Roman to hold his kid so he can take a picture. Call me in London on Monday after work.

Phone Call #5: Liverpool, A Chinese restaurant, Monday evening

RR: Mr. Hamori?

AH: Can't talk. I'm in a meeting with six other people. My mouth is full of Peking duck. You should come to Liverpool! I'm taking the train back to London. Call me at two a.m. at the loft.

Phone Call #6: London, Soho loft, 2 A.M., Greenwich Mean Time

RR: Hello...

AH: (Yawns.) Aren't we through yet? I'm too tired tonight. I have meetings all day tomorrow, Sam Jackson is in town. Let's try later in the week. Okay? Nights are the best. Or come to London. You can stay with me.

PHONE CALL #7: LONDON, SOHO LOFT BATHROOM

Sound of spigots. Or is it streaming piss? Toilet flushing. Jesus. He was pissing. I think. I feel *this* big.

AH: I'm just splashing water on my face! I'm sleepy and I have an enormous hangover. Can you call me later? Give me a couple hours.

PHONE CALL #8: LONDON, SOHO LOFT, LATE MORNING, REALLY LATE IN L.A.

Three A.M. PST—a dangerous time to try and come off lucidly.

RR: I hear you're a huge fan of *Bridget Jones.*

AH: When Lynne Ramsay said she wanted to do *Morvern Callar,* I said yes, this is the subculture's answer to *Bridget Jones.* I hate *Bridget Jones,* that stupid British twat. It's a piece of shit. And yeah, it's probably going to make $200 million dollars, but it still pisses me off.

RR: Why do you look to books for films anyway?

AH: One reason I go for books is there are not grand enough ideas in scripts. Books still take on grand ideas. Also it's like a chain reaction. Get a great book, pull in a great writer, then a great director, then great actors, then the critics pounce. The critics can't say much about studio films. They need quality work to respond to. As an independent producer, you can't afford to bribe the actors with a twenty-million-dollar fee, nor can you bribe the audience with a forty-million dollar P&A (prints & advertising), so all that's left is to bribe the director with a great novel, to bribe the actors with a great director, and bribe the critics with a great story. Look at *Crash.* Someone calculated that the scandal in the U.K. alone, where they wanted to ban *Crash* for being a "car-crashing sex movie," generated twenty-five to thirty million dollars free advertising.

RR: What's the difference between the films you make and what the studios make?

AH: Studios don't have the taste and the patience to do these kinds of unformulaic films. Studios develop events, roller-coaster rides. I find intelligent movies more interesting. Taste is the most important thing.

RR: Can you define taste?

AH: No. But you can buy it. Look at David Puttnam. He didn't have taste. He imagined what taste he should be having.

That's what studio heads do.

RR: How did you develop your taste?

AH: I didn't grow up watching Mickey Mouse. I grew up watching *Battleship Potemkin.* I loved it. It was obscene. I had to watch it seventeen times a year while I was in kindergarten. It's a different start from Americans growing up on comic books. I read Thomas Mann and Bulgakov as a kid. I was reading four to five hours a day as a child. I loved reading.

RR: Why is Hollywood so crazy about book options?

AH: The original Hollywood guys, East European Jews, wanted to tell great stories and had an ability to attract New York writers. No longer. So we use books. Lately the studios are buying up everything. Then there are the novels that nobody can crack. Like *The Master and Margarita.* There are novels on the studio shelves, like *The Diceman* at Paramount. They've spent five million dollars or something already, but they can't crack them. Also *Perfume,* by Patrick Susskind. Scripts and scriptwriters don't deliver you the kind of scope of story and emotion that novels do, so, this is why the recent hysteria (last fifteen years) of book-buying. They used to have it, that scope and emotion. Lately they don't because 99 percent of the film industry doesn't, so why would the scripts? It's even rare to find in books, but at least you have a chance. Half of Hollywood is eating bad and having bad sex, and that's why they're making bad movies.

"Half of Hollywood is eating bad and having bad sex, and that's why they're making bad movies."

RR: How is this affecting screenwriters?

AH: Bad sex?

RR: (Silence.)

AH: I spoke to a scriptwriter just the other day—he's a brilliant scriptwriter, I think he was nominated for an Academy Award for one of his scripts—and he said, I'm going to start to write novels instead of scripts. Why? Because you want to write full characters? No no no, I just want to make more money. Because I guess I'm writing the same story and I'm getting paid for it twice.

RR: Didn't David Leland say that?

AH: I was hoping you didn't remember.

Phone Call #9A: Budapest hotel, Sometime later

?: (Thick British accent.) What? Who's this? No. No he's not.

Phone Call #9B: Budapest hotel, Sometime a few minutes later

AH: (Gleefully.) You woke up Ralph Fiennes. I switched rooms with him.

RR: Do you consider you have an overall vision?

AH: No. Listen, every single project has some kind of a reason why it's on my slate. Some of the reasons are disgustingly practical, like *51st State*, which I'm doing right now. It's not its literary value which caught me. It's not the brilliant dialogue written by a North London liquor-store clerk in vulgar English. "Cunt, cunt, cunt, cunt, that's what they all are, cunts," that's the first sentence. But, what caught me is that I knew that it's a great movie of attitudes colliding, and if you think about Samuel Jackson and Robby Carlyle, it's perfect. That's the movie. It's nothing to do with literature. Whereas, for instance, *The Bird Artist* is simply a great novel and a great story to tell, with great characters and I can see brilliant actors in it. So is Agota Kristof's *Notebook*, and I really want you to read the whole thing... you will have an erection. I read that in one fell swoop.

RR: So that's the book you think is most literary? Most stands on its own?

AH: That's an interesting one, because I actually believe it's a poorly written book. I actually believe Agota can't write her way out of a fucking paper bag, but the end result is amazing. I can't even describe it to you. It's like a whirlwind, it's like being hit by lightning to read that book. It's not like *The Bird Artist*, which you enjoy every page.

RR: Where does *Morvern Callar* fit in?

AH: I think it's a great subculture novel, about a generation which unfortunately I'm not a part of anymore.

RR: There's no second half, there's no end...

AH: David Cronenberg told me someone wrote a reader's report on *Crash*, they had problems with the third act, and David said, What the fuck is the third act? Who cares about the third act? Who says that?

RR: Robert McKee.

AH: Fuck Robert McKee. I think Sophocles, not Robert McKee. Does literature always have a third act?

RR: Why'd you match Vinterberg with Agota?

AH: She's crazy, he's the cinematic equivalent.

RR: What's he like?

AH: He's beautiful and smart. He looks like Brad Pitt. He's totally gorgeous and totally paranoid. And married.

Phone Call #10: Driving through Budapest in a rented diesel Mercedes that's dangerously low on fuel

RR: What are you eating now?

AH: I am eating fresh strawberries, driving through Budapest. The first time I went back to Hungary after five years, I had a piece of tomato and cried. Listen, in Hungary you're not allowed to drive and talk on the cell phone, so if I see a cop, I may have to drop you or shut you off without warning. Oh shit, I'm going

> "Two Hungarian Chihuahas walk on the main street in Toronto, and one looks at the other and says, 'Ah, in Hungary, I was a rottweiler.'"

the wrong way down this street. Fuck. Hold on. (Long pause. Sound of tires.)

RR: Why did you defect? How?

AH: I can't give you anything spectacular. A Toronto writer once told the joke: Two Hungarian Chihuahas walk on the main street in Toronto, and one looks at the other and says, "Ah, in Hungary, I was a rottweiler." Everyone talks about, Oh it was so romantic—bullshit. I just hitched a ride with a friend to Paris. I wanted to produce movies and there was no such job as "producer" at that time in Hungary. Money came from the state.

RR: And no sense of oppression?

AH: It was part of my daily life, so it didn't bother me. I mean, I didn't leave for

Agota Kristof and Thomas Vinterberg

political reasons. I needed new enemies. And new friends. And, it was just boring, totally boring. Predictable.

RR: You started out as a critic. Do you believe in criticism?

AH: I do, but I don't want to be the one doing it.

RR: Is there a link between producing and criticizing?

AH: They're both about power.

RR: Why is producing preferable?

AH: The power's more active, because you actually bring together something as opposed to just making faces at what other people are doing. It's more fun. Let's not fuck around. Uh—cop. I'm putting you down. (Long pause.) Okay. I hid you under my ass.

RR: Don't you think most critics are frustrated creators?

AH: Probably. I just couldn't address it and make the jump from there to actually creating. So I started this department of cinema in Budapest. It was about making movies about filmmakers. Like, The Making of . . . a Milos Forman film, *Ragtime*. Then there was another film, *Escape to Victory*. A John Huston movie. And that's that. And then I left.

RR: Do you have any producer idols? Like Saul Zaentz (*The Fellowship of the Rings, The English Patient, The Unbearable Lightness of Being, At Play in the Fields of the Lord, One Flew Over the Cuckoo's Nest*)? Do you see yourself as a particular kind of producer?

AH: I don't know Saul Zaentz, but I would like to be Saul Zaentz, because he spends two or three years on one project and nothing else. That's the ultimate luxury. But I see myself in the tradition of the European and Eastern Jews, like Alexander Korda in London, and those others in Hollywood, who wanted to tell stories. Of course it was good money, as well. But they loved stories. And if you think about it, with great old movies there's always a great story. If you want to tell the story of *Judge Dredd*, good luck. If I think about it, the common denominator in all my projects is they're all great stories. Shit, I'm out of gas. I've got to go.

Phone Call #11: Budapest hotel, Morning there, bathroom, bathtub

(Constant sound of gentle splashing. Scrubbing. Dribbling water. Occasionally some kind of squeaking—a shampoo bottle? A Hungarian rubber ducky?)

"AUTHORS ARE TOTALLY ANAL AND WHEN YOU DON'T RESPECT SOMETHING IN THEIR BOOK, WHEN YOU EMPHASIZE SOMETHING ELSE, THEY GET HYSTERICAL, THEY DON'T GET IT."

RR: How would you compare novelists and screenwriters? Do you cut novelists out of the process completely?

AH: The simple answer would be yes. But, not always. With J. G. Ballard, we do have a dialogue if we don't understand something, if I have problems. Jimmy's very smart. I have problems with *Running Wild*, and once you read the script you will see that there are some questions which one has to ask. Why why why? And I don't dare to make the movie without having answered this question. Then we got a great letter from Jimmy where he explains how and why this is. But there are very few times when you have really a serious dialogue with the author. Ordinarily you don't.

> "I have another call."
>
> (Long pause. One minute. Five minutes. Ten minutes.)
>
> "That was my secretary. My third one this year."

RR: Because?

AH: Because authors are totally anal and when you don't respect something in their book, when you emphasize something else, they get hysterical, they don't get it, and you have to explain to them time after time that it is a different medium when you adapt a novel into a book.

RR: So they're insecure too. Unlike Ballard.

AH: I think J. G. Ballard is so sure that he delivered something in his own medium that he's generous. He can afford to be generous.

RR: Are you close with any of the other writers in your stable?

AH: We met Agota. That was really interesting. We're doing this adaptation with Vinterberg and he's writing with his partner Mogens Rukov, who also wrote *The Celebration*. They said, it's a very difficult adaptation, so let's meet the author, and I said fine. We met in Switzerland in a small town near Lausanne where Agota lives. She's crazy, a total eccentric. She lives in this very small apartment. She talks very little. And she sort of tricks you with her eyes, and she doesn't have answers. To anything. We started to ask questions: Why is this, and How is this, and she said, I don't know, it's on the paper, I don't know, I don't know. And Thomas asked her, "So, why did you break it into three parts, this novel? Obviously you wrote it in one fell swoop." She said, "No, I wrote novel number one first, and then I started to write something else but I couldn't, and I just had to continue and write it again, and then I wrote part two." And Thomas said, "You must have had this in your mind when you started writing?" And she said, "Absolutely not. I wrote one book, then I wrote another book, then I wrote a third book. And I couldn't write anything in between. I tried, but it just didn't work." Then she asked if her daughter could play the lead in the movie.

RR: So the meeting was useless?

AH: Totally useless. Though it might turn out to make sense later. But now that I think about it consciously, I do try and attempt to have a relationship with the author. Because I talk to Jimmy and I went to see Agota for her opinion. Just a minute. I have another call. (Long pause. One minute. Five minutes. Ten minutes.) That was my secretary. My third one this year.

RR: What about the other writers, Howard Norman, Highsmith, Sutcliffe, Alan Warner. . .

AH: Who's Alan Warner?

RR: *Morvern Callar.*

AH: I never met her.

RR: No, it's a guy. The writer.

AH: That's like the typical development story. Lynne Ramsay, who is a brilliant director, wanted to do that book, and we bought it for her. It's not that we bought the book and are looking for a director. Which we're doing by the way with William Sutcliffe. I just thought it was really really fun, commercial subject matter—backpacking teenagers trying to find their soul and meanwhile lose their virginity. It's not a great book, *Are You Experienced?* But it's a great title. And I hope we get the song. And it's three characters, and you take people away to a fun location in India, but without being pretentious like Jane Campion.

RR: Sutcliffe wrote the first draft?

AH: If the author brings it up we have to let them sometimes. Brian Moore always wanted to write the first draft because he wanted to save the integrity of the novel. Of course he lied. Everyone knows they're going to be rewritten. Brian used to tell me, I know I will be rewritten, so why not get another quarter of a million dollars? And if you get a credit you get royalties.

RR: He wasn't untalented.

AH: No, he was a brilliant writer. His last novel makes no attempt to be literary; it's written almost in scenes.

Phone Call #13: Lake Balaton, Hungarian countryside, Andras's parents' summer home he bought for them with money made from film biz, (in actuality a flimsy two-bedroom cottage on a scummy lake in which swimmers have been known to get vaginal infections), Afternoon

Hamori tells me he is the only son, that his parents are obsessed with him. The whole time we talk, his mother watches him surreptitiously from the kitchen window, with the curtain parted.

AH: Wow, this is scary. I'm walking up and down in the garden and there are suddenly two branches on the ground in the shape of a perfect crucifix. How scary. It is totally scary. I'm not kidding you. Maybe I should find Jesus.

RR: Which brings us to, why did you respond to *Willie Hogg*? The book doesn't seem to fit.

AH: I have no fucking idea. It's one of those things where I like the three characters, I have no idea why. From time to time we want to make a movie for our parents, and I just felt this was. There is something it tells about that generation which a scriptwriter would never do because it's so fucking uncommercial. Yet, if you think about it with Dame Judi Dench and Albert Finney, and Angela Lansbury playing the missionary, it's such an unusual casting that people might go into the theater for that. Wow. My mother's watching me. She's wondering who I'm talking to for the last ten hours, walking up and down the garden. I can see her eye at the window.

RR: Why these books, these films?

AH: We always want to impress a lot of people. We want to impress the people who are the closest to us, then we want to impress our enemies, and then we want to impress our parents, then we want to impress our future lovers, and people who we don't even know yet. With movies, I believe it's all personal. And I was so fucking amazed that for the first and only time—after twenty movies or whatever I was involved in and two hundred hours of television, and the only time I could impress my father was with *Sunshine*. He came out of the screening and he said, "I had no idea that you know so much about life." What a feeling. Of course, I said it's not me, it's Istvan Szabo who knows so much about life. And he said, "Yeah I know, but it's your movie as well." I can name you exactly what film is for who—and *Willie Hogg* is for my parents.

RR: Tell.

AH: No, then I have to get into my future lovers! My future young love lovers.

RR: Who's *The Bird Artist* for?

AH: I think it's for me. And I think *The Bird Artist* is for my girlfriend as well, 'cause she's about that scope and... I think it's one of the most brilliant ones. Actually one of my most brilliant ones is not based on a literary work. It's called *The Murder of Madame Lafaye*. Bill Condon is directing. The scriptwriter's a New York writer who's never written scripts. This is his first one, and actually, it's not a script—it's what he imagines a script would be. His name is Brooks Hansen. I don't know who he is actually. I don't care, I just read this so-called script and it amazed me.

RR: Okay. When you read books as a producer, does it detract from your reading pleasure or completely change it?

AH: It does change it. I miss reading for pleasure. But you're right, it's a disease that you take a book and my first question is, Find out if this book is available. I used to read a lot back in Hungary, and it was never purpose reading. Now it's always purpose reading

Phone Call #14: Budapest airport, Sound of foreign bustle, foreign language over speakers.

RR: You're not intentionally picking less commercial, more controversial material.

AH: No, I have only one criterion—it has to attract a director.

RR: Ah, all goes back to chain reaction. Curious,'cause *Crash* experienced censorship.

AH: When we did *Crash*, we knew we needed a niche distributor, and luckily we found one. *Crash* is a great example, because you pick something up which does not fit the mold, and there's room for you because there's no way a studio would develop *Crash* with Thomas Vinterberg after *Festen*, after *The Celebration*. They're still offering Thomas two or three scripts a week, but they just don't get it—this is not where his head is. Our way to get these directors is to find the right material and to match them, with the right material and the right artists.

RR: So you subscribe to the auteur theory since directors are the linchpin.

AH: Yes, they are. Really, I think the

"If you work with auteurs, it's like inviting a chef to cook at your house, you don't give them a ready-made meal to reheat, you just get them the ingredients."

only book which I acquired without a director or any major talent attached is *The Bird Artist*. My reasons are practical. You develop a script, then you pick a Roman Polanski and he is not going to say, Oh, excellent, that is exactly how I saw it and how I want to do it. No. Of course he would rewrite it and rework it and then you start the whole thing again. If you work with auteurs, it's like inviting a chef to cook at your house, you don't give them a ready-made meal to reheat, you just get them the ingredients. Wait, I have to give my passport—in ten seconds you will go through an X-ray, because I'm checking in at the gate. (Much babbling in what I guess to be

Hungarian. Then silence. Long pause.)

RR: Didn't you own a restaurant in Canada?

AH: Yeah, that's the ultimate show business, to own a restaurant and have thirty to forty people every night happy with what you're creating for them. That was a time when I was trying to find out what on earth am I going to do, because I had to realize that the film business and show business is business in North America, even in Canada. I really did feel that was the ultimate show business.

RR: And do you still?

AH: Oh yeah, I love to go to restaurants. Actually I still do believe it. Some restaurateurs are artists, aren't they? You cause more pleasure with Giorgio's restaurant with the truffle carpaccio than with *Battleship Earth*—Hungarians are so fucking amazing. This guy is standing beneath a No Smoking sign, like a cigarette crossed, and next to it a garbage can with a huge cigarette crossed with the red, and smoking there. These Hungarian bastards. My people.

PHONE CALL #15: LONDON, SOHO LOFT

RR: Last question. I swear! What's the secret ingredient to the films you make?

AH: The first movie I produced was *The Gate*. It was a children's special effects movie. I met with an executive producer and made the financing deal for the sequel in ten minutes. "You must have really liked my first movie," I said. "I've never seen it." "But this is the sequel." "Yeah, I looked at the numbers. They were good." Then he admitted he never watched movies because they confused him. He worried he might like them and then he'd get emotional about them. (Pause. Ear-splitting scream.) There's a huge bee in here! There's a bee! Go away. Go away! He's trying to kill me! (Sound of smacking. Chair moving.) Let me wave this magazine with a picture of Elizabeth Hurley. That will scare him.

RR: Are you allergic to bees?

AH: I hate bees. (Pause. Another bloodcurdling scream.) This bee is out to kill me!!! It's crazy. Wait, there, wait, okay, he's gone out the window. That bee was trying to kill me!

RR: You were saying, about filmmaking, and how for this exec producer he avoided getting involved . . .

AH: Right. To me, it starts with getting emotional and then trying to figure out how to finance. Because in movies like *The Sweet Hereafter*, even *Crash*, or like *Sunshine*, you have to fall in love with and be emotional about it.

Finis

Rita Moreno from the book *Hollywood Candid*

Nabokov and **Hitchcock**

Imagine Lolita and Humbert Humbert Checking into the Bates Motel

BY
DAVID GATES

It might never have rocked the culture quite the way the Coleridge-Wordsworth *Lyrical Ballads* did in 1798; still, the Hitchcock-Nabokov *Frenzy* might at least have been up there with the Stanley Kubrick-Stephen King-Diane Johnson collaboration on *The Shining*—if it had ever happened.

What little I know about Alfred Hitchcock's brief dance with Vladimir Nabokov comes from *The Dark Side of Genius*, the Hitchcock biography by Donald Spoto, who got his information from a *Film Comment* piece by Nabokov's friend, critic and annotator Alfred Appel Jr. Here goes. In late 1970, Hitchcock was shopping for a high-class writer to adapt Arthur La Bern's crime novel *Goodbye Piccadilly, Farewell Leicester Square*. He phoned Nabokov, who said "Yes, of course I know who you are," and begged off because he had too many irons in the fire. (Among them, as I've gathered from Brian Boyd's biography of Nabokov, were his novel *Transparent Things*, his second volume of memoirs, *Speak On, Memory*, and revisions on both his *Poems and Problems* and a translation of his Russian novel *Glory*.) After Nabokov turned him down, Hitchcock got Anthony Shaffer (the author of *Sleuth*) to write the screenplay; the 1972 movie made some money, dazzled contemporary critics, moved just about nobody and in the long run had no effect either on Hitchcock's reputation or on the culture at large. End of story.

Though not exactly the beginning, it turns out. While browsing in Nabokov's *Selected Letters*, I learned that Hitchcock had made a similar call six years earlier, in November 1964, and followed it up with a letter pitching Nabokov a couple of movie ideas. The first ("based upon a question that I do not think I have seen dealt with in motion pictures, or, as far as I know, in literature") was about a woman married or engaged to a defector; this eventually turned into Hitchcock's 1966 film *Torn Curtain*, written by Brian Moore, in which a double agent pretending to be a defector (Paul Newman) is followed by his girlfriend (Julie Andrews) to East Germany. The second ("Now this next idea I'm not sure will really appeal to you but, on the other hand, it might") had to do with "a gang of crooks" running a "large international hotel"—a place, though Hitchcock didn't say so, like Montreux's Palace Hotel, where Nabokov was then living. "As you will see, the hotel setting—especially the 'backstage' part—would be extremely colorful, especially when the bulk of the story would take place, not only backstage, but in the public rooms and even in the night club section. In other words, I was looking for a film that would give us the details of a big hotel and not merely a film played in hotel rooms. . . . Well there it is, Mr. Nabokov. I sincerely hope you could be interested in one or the other."

Both of them seemed to have forgotten the whole thing when Hitchcock got back in touch in 1970.

Nabokov promptly wrote back. He didn't know enough about "American security matters and methods" to make the first idea work, but the second was "quite acceptable to me." Trouble was, he was "at the present very busy winding up several things at once"—we know from Boyd's biography that he was translating *Lolita* into Russian and working on a novel that would turn out to be *Ada*—and couldn't start thinking about a screenplay until the following summer. But in return, he pitched a couple of ideas to Hitchcock. In the first, "a girl, a rising star of not quite the first magnitude is courted by a budding astronaut" who comes back from a space expedition strangely changed ("I have more than one interesting denouement for this plot"). In the other, a defector from a Soviet-bloc country takes shelter with an apparently benevolent American couple on their western ranch ("I have in mind some marvelous scenes at the ranch and a very tragic ending").

Hitchcock wrote back that the astronaut story wasn't in his line, that something like Nabokov's defector idea had been used in William Wellman's 1948 film *The Iron Curtain*, and that he couldn't wait until summer: "My needs are immediate and urgent." Both of them seemed to have forgotten the whole thing when Hitchcock got back in touch in 1970; at any rate, they never met and neither of these more-or-less desultory exchanges came to anything. A waste of breath for us to wish it otherwise.

Both liked to tip self-referential winks: Hitchcock with his blink-and-miss-it cameos and Nabokov with his anagrammatic alter egos.

But if you've got a minute, let's consider how tantalizingly Hitchcock's and Nabokov's lives, work, and sensibilities echoed each other. They were both born in 1899 and both left behind already formidable careers in Europe—Hitchcock in 1939, Nabokov in 1940—to create their masterpieces in the United States. At the age of 63, the once-lanky Nabokov ruefully acknowledged their physical resemblance: when he arrived for the premiere of Kubrick's 1962 *Lolita*, he noted that fans peered into his limousine "hoping to glimpse James Mason but finding only the placid profile of a stand-in for Hitchcock." (I like to think that three years earlier Nabokov might have seen Mason, whom Kubrick would choose to play Humbert Humbert, as the suave Euro-heavy Philip Vandam in Hitchcock's *North by Northwest*. But probably not. Nabokov told Appel he "fondly" recalled one Hitchcock film, "about someone named Harry"; if *The Trouble with Harry* gave him fond recollections—I remember almost nothing about it but its wonderfully garish autumn colors—you'd think *North by Northwest* would've blown him away.) Both men humorously (or not) affected a mandarin persona, and each plumed himself on the disparity between the fever dream of his imagination and the respectable quietude (so each of them said) of his private life.

Beyond these gee-whiz affinities, they seem to have had enough in common aesthetically to have worked well together. Both liked to tip self-referential winks: Hitchcock with his blink-and-miss-it cameos (schlepping a bull fiddle onto a train, trying to board a bus) and Nabokov with his anagrammatic alter egos (Vivian Darkbloom, Adam von Librikov). Both toyed with secrets, obsessions, doppelgangers, murders. Both loved in-your-face artifice: Hitchcock with his preposterous plots and notoriously fakey back-projections; Nabokov with his equally preposterous plots and the scrim of jokes, puns, allusions, and figurative language through which we discern them. *Lolita* and *North by Northwest*—my personal favorites—both combine wide-eyed American travelogue with mysterious pursuits involving the main character and his shadow double: Humbert Humbert and Clare Quilty, Roger O. Thornhill ("What does the O stand for?" "Nothing") and the nonexistent George Kaplan. You can almost imagine a put-upon Hum and a bored Lo among the tourists at the cafeteria near Mount Rushmore—"these gay surroundings," Vandam calls the mise-en-scène, with Humbertian snottiness—where Eve Kendall (Eva Marie Saint) pretends to kill Thornhill (Cary Grant) with a small handgun like the .32 caliber pocket automatic "Chum" in *Lolita*. Both Nabokov and Hitchcock mixed the comic and the murderous with Shakespearian double-mindedness—the opera buff shooting of Quilty, the deadly assault on Thornhill with bourbon and Mercedes—and propagated memorable minor characters in Dickensian profusion. And both ruled their created universes with the benevolent despotism of a Prospero. Hitchcock storyboarded every detail of every scene in advance; actually shooting the picture he considered mere dogwork. Similarly, Nabokov planned and elaborated his novels in his head: "There comes a moment when I am informed from within that the entire structure is finished. All I have to do now is take it down in pencil or pen." And neither welcomed any outbreaks of wayward spontaneity that might disrupt the shape of the work he'd so meticulously imagined. Hitchcock called his actors "cattle"; Nabokov called his characters "galley slaves."

Hitchcock called his actors "cattle"; Nabokov called his characters "galley slaves."

But in spite of all this, I can imagine a Hitchcock-Nabokov film ending up like, say, the 1961 Louis Armstrong—Duke Ellington recordings: two masters, in late middle age, not quite connecting and producing something perfectly okay and perfectly unnecessary. Much as they both revered craftsmanlike detail and loathed "messages," Hitchcock saw himself as an entertainer, trading in "the customary

Hitchcock suspense" (as he said in his 1964 letter), while Nabokov saw himself as an enchanter. Hitchcock was a far darker spirit, more nakedly compulsive, almost sadistic—especially in *Psycho* and the films that came after—in his urge to put his (more than willing) audience through the wringer. Yet his cozy self-definition as movieland's Master of Suspense left him free to give us his deepest gift; his fears and obsessions, made safe for consumption, even beautiful, by his rigorous shaping power. Similarly, in *Lolita*, Nabokov's so potent art sea changes a story of pedophilia and murder into something rich and strange; but although he gives us lust, bliss, remorse, grief, and transcendence (none of which much interested Hitchcock), he never comes within a mile of dread, psychosis, hellishness.

It's impossible to imagine Nabokov reveling in Frenzy's *necktie murders and audibly snapped fingerbones.*

Well, who says he had to? And would Hitchcock's films have benefited from a "saner," more inclusive view of human possibility? The point is that when you peel off enough layers, these are radically different sensibilities; ultimately, it's impossible to imagine Nabokov reveling in *Frenzy*'s necktie murders and audibly snapped fingerbones. Hitchcock's idea about crooks fronting as high-class hoteliers might have given the two of them common ground in which to amuse themselves, but could Nabokov really have stayed interested in the nuts and bolts of hotel management? Who knows? And really, who cares? It's like, what if MGM has been able to borrow Shirley Temple for *The Wizard of Oz*? Or, you know, what if the person from Porlock hadn't showed up? But since we're just talking here, I've got one. How would it be if Humbert *doesn't* die of a heart attack, escapes from jail, kidnaps Lo away from Dick Schiller, and the two of them put up for the night at a run-down motel overlooked by a gothic manse? (I have in mind a marvelous scene in the shower and a very tragic ending.) I can see Hitchcock maybe cracking a smile before telling me to go peddle my papers, but I can only picture Nabokov getting huffy; he had a sense of humor about his appearance, but not, as far as I can tell, about his art. Whereas Hitchcock, in that famous trailer for *Psycho* (where he keeps interrupting his tour of the set just as he's about to let slip a plot point), played for laughs his darkest work and his defining practice as an artist, the manipulation of suspense. Each took just the right attitude toward his work. And it's surely just as well they never found each other out. ☗

[A countinuity shot from *Modern Hero*, 1934]

[A continuity shot from *The Public Enemy,* 1931]

we are not friends

fiction BY FRED G. LEEBRON

When they're not sailing their boat or hiking in places where nobody recognizes them, the two take their friends with them to Tuscan villas, where everybody cooks, drinks good wine, and stays up late talking and waiting for something unexpected to happen.

"We fly them in if they don't have money," she says of her mates. "One of the hard things about dealing with wealth is that you don't want to lose your friends. And a lot of that is saying, 'We happen to be very fortunate and very lucky—so let's all enjoy it.'" (From a profile of Nicole Kidman, in *Vogue* magazine, June 1999.)

There is something about the way the phone rings that lets you know it's Them—a kind of glitter in the chime, a certain *je ne sais quoi* to the cadence, which seems to skip a beat as if it can't quite believe that They are calling. You pick up, heart throbbing, getting ready to move your mouth, a sly frisson of sweat striking your palms.

"They asked me to call," Their assistant says. "They want you at the house next Thursday. And then you'll all go somewhere. A plane will be involved. You'll want to bring a passport. Until Monday, let's say. Can I pen you in?"

Of course, you say. Because, really, you know no other response. And you want to. And you like Them.

All week you attend to dropping everything—meetings at work, the children at your mother's, the cats at the kennel, your own self-involvement into the basement of your brain. You feel a wonderful tingle at the top of your head—someone likes you and it is Them. You shop for clothes, scout the itinerary that will get you to the house on time, and concentrate on biting your lip when anyone asks you if you have any special plans. One of your attributes is discretion, another is your wry or winning or self-deprecating humor, a third the fact that your personality doesn't change when you drink. Beyond that, you're not sure. It's certainly not your looks or your bitterness or your propensity toward self-pity—which They simply will not tolerate. Maybe it's just you. You're a special friend, a member of the inner circle, a trusted one. You have watched Their back and They have watched you watch it. Together you've skinny-dipped, drunk too much expensive single-malt, fallen down stairs and off trampolines. You know things about Them that you've made yourself forget, so fearful are you of being quoted by anyone who hounds you for tidbits.

At Their house—an ascetic zen bowl sink in the bathroom, ten-thousand-dollar rococo couches opposing each other on the hardwood floor, flames roaring in the marble fireplace even though it is spring outside—you sit dazed with the other friends, some of whom you don't know at all and others whom you know too well. "I'll tell you," a loud brunette whispers, "the most surprising thing in my life is that I am Their friend." You nod politely—you've been on many such junkets with her, you know her for the starfucker she is and you believe you are not—and yet your face saddens and you cast around inside yourself for some kind of truth—what does this summoning really feel like, this performance of friendship?

They saunter down the steps, smiles dazzling, eyes secreted behind sunglasses, the room growing brilliant in the light that great success can shed. "We set?" He says, in that muscular grunge way. "Shall we?" She offers, with that sweet slope of her voice. A tinted Mercedes van instantly pulls up. The assistant shoos you in, calling, "Disposable cameras are in your favor bags. I've made sure dinner is vegan." And you drive off, people clicking off cell phones, everyone grinning as if in on a great secret, terrifics and excitings strewn about the interior like petals in the aisle at Their wedding. You're not even sure where you're going.

At the airport in the descending darkness waits a camp of paparazzi. Within the plush hush of the van you listen to His instructions: all friends off first, meet in the celebrity lounge. You open the door to the frantic glare.

"Who's that?"

"Is it Them?"

"Don't shoot, don't shoot! It's no one."

Needlessly grinning, you hurry inside. From behind the heavy glass you can't

Finally, it is Her. Dressed in white. Bright red lipstick. Sunglasses off. Smiling with élan.

help turning and watching. Eventually, He descends, stands smirking for an instant as flashes pop and spray, agreeably removes his sunglasses momentarily, mouths some ironic remark you cannot hear, and shoulders his way through. Finally, it is Her. Dressed in white. Bright red lipstick. Sunglasses off. Smiling with élan. Then they let Her go.

In the lounge you're all panting hard from the near-celebrity exertion. The flight is called. Wait, you're told. You sip a seltzer. The clock turns. "That time at Moomba," one friend says. "What a bitch," someone sneers. "Then Kenny did that thing to her." Uproarious laughter when She laughs, solemn nods when He is pensive. There is industry chitchat that you cannot follow, names tossed out like so much parade candy. Five minutes before departure, you all rise. Those of you who have sunglasses put them on. At the wordless direction of the oldest friend, a multimega exec in a double-breasted suit with an electronic device in each pocket, you form a phalanx of escorts around Them and stride through the dark airport onto the dark plane.

"Should I know you," an older stewardess nervously giggles to Them, taking the new dress on its hanger that She has somehow managed to purchase as She charmingly entertained in the airport. "I know I should know you. I'm sure my son would know you."

You sit back in your seats, marveling at how hard it must be to be Them, to be commented to and on at every available turn, to surrender any iota of private embarrassment or pain or joy, to have all elements of life cut up into smaller and smaller pieces to be chewed and emitted by the bulimic media, to pose and play in full nudity in scenes that can be viewed and reviewed until everyone everywhere knows just where the coifed curl of pubic hair gives way to scraggly fur. To be so exposed. You shudder honestly and sip your cocktail as the plane lifts and lifts.

Of course, you understand, this will all come to an end.

In Italy there are ten times as many paparazzi and their hands beat at the metal flanks of the Volvo bus as you sail by and away and the shutters stop, the road empties, and you are up past olive trees and lines of vineyards into the tender hills. The eight or ten of you who have made it this far beam radiantly and when a relative newcomer offers cigarettes you dismissively decline as you wisely await further instructions on protocol. Up front, by the driver, the Two who've brought you hold hands across the aisle. In the distance a white compound with red tile roofs rises, destined peaks of emotion and indulgence fronted by the tiny heads of many ingratiating servants and the bursting frills of bougainvillea and hyacinth.

Of course, you understand, this will all come to an end. Someday you will arrive late for a command appearance, flustered by a rough business lunch and the fact that you will have performed too much beforehand, and one of Them will tease you and you will tease Them too much in return, perhaps you will even talk back, perhaps you will even be rude. The assistant will snap her carnivorous jaws at you, He will look away in disappointment, She will wait you out in silence until you recognize that you must leave. You will stumble at the door, unwilling to apologize, unable to sense anything but the exhilaration of yourself unmasked as a person. Their look has lit you in a thousand different ways, at gala benefits and in cozy restaurants, on Page Six of the *Post* and in a dozen weekly magazines, on the beach and in lift lines, but now the gold has gone out of it. Is it something you have done to Them, or They have done to you, or you have done to yourself, or—incredibly—They have done to Themselves? What has this friendship meant if, in the instant you watch it slip from your hands, you feel both relieved and regretful, nostalgic and enraged, redeemed and vilified, negligible and tangible? Who knows, but in this long moment of first and last betrayal—Their impatience, your indiscretion; your transgression, Their dismissal—shines the only time that They will ever remember that you were there.

Viva Vamp, Vale Vamp

by

Ogden Nash

Oh for the days when vamps were vamps,
Not just a bevy of bulbous scamps.
The vintage vamp was serpentine,
Was madder music and stronger wine.
She ate her bedazzled victims whole,
Body and bank account and soul;
Yet, to lure a bishop from his crosier
She needed no pectoral exposure,
But trapped the prelate passing by
With her melting mouth and harem eye.
A gob of lipstick and mascara
Was weapon enough for Theda Bara;
Pola Negri and Lya de Putti
And sister vampires, when on duty,
Carnivorous night-blooming lilies,
They flaunted neither falsies nor realies.
Oh, whither have the vampires drifted?
All are endowed, but few are gifted.
Tape measures now select the talent
To stimulate the loutish gallant
Who has wits enough, but only just,
To stamp and whistle at a bust.
O modern vamp, I quit my seat,
Throw down my cards and call you cheat;
You could not take a trick, in fact,
Unless the deck were brazenly stacked.

JERRY STAHL

PART ONE

INTERVIEWED BY ANN MAGNUSON

The first time I spoke with Jerry Stahl was as a fan. I mustered up the courage to approach him at a Silverlake cantina to tell him how much I enjoyed a live reading he had recently given from his then-unpublished novel *Perv*. He was gracious, self-effacing, and very, very funny. The next time we met was when we shared a stage together at another spoken word event. I did a piece dramatizing a recent real-life humiliation; he shared one of his. Again,

Jerry Stahl with Ben Stiller, who portrays Stahl in *Permanent Midnight*

he had me in stitches. I gushed and got an autographed copy of *Permanent Midnight* in return. Now, having read *Perv*, I am again reassured that I'm not the only freak in town. "It's all research," Jerry repeatedly reminds me whenever I relay yet another no-one-would-believe-it-if-I-wrote-about-it misadventure in Hollywoodland. Needless to say, I jumped at the chance to interview him for *Tin House* about those strange bedfellows, movies and books.

[with an assist from an old friend]

Ann Magnuson: What did you think of the film they made of *Permanent Midnight*?

Jerry Stahl: Well, like I always say, you haven't lived till you've seen the worst moments of your life reenacted by celebrities nine feet high. It's like being a fly on the wall and having your wings plucked at the same time. That said, I think Ben Stiller was beyond brilliant, as was Owen Wilson as "my best friend"—a character, oddly enough, that didn't exist in real life. (Being a junkie, I didn't have friends, I just had people I could be nice to long enough to rifle their wallets.) Maria Bello, who played my girlfriend, was also great. Strangely enough, she looked exactly like

the original, which cranked things up to a whole new level of existential weirdness: there I am, watching some guy, as *me*, rolling around in bed with a woman I loved, but whom I can't actually touch, because she's really just an actress. I was in the surreally odd position of being jealous of myself.

AM: That brings up the idea of novelization, when people write the book after the movie. With the twist that your book is a memoir. Has there been any public confusion? About character identity, fact versus fiction?

JS: Funny you should bring that up. I think at this point my book has become a novelization. I think that just happens. It flips on you. Because a lot of people haven't read the book before seeing the film, or they didn't even know there was a book. That's when you know you've really arrived. When people think you've written the novelization of your own life based on a movie.

AM: I was in a coloring book for *Small Soldiers*.

JS: Beautiful. You must be so proud.

AM: Was the movie a lot different from the book?

JS: Let's just say, in some ways, I was a different kind of asshole on-screen than I was in print. David Veloz, the director, who also wrote the screenplay, took things in directions I might not necessarily have gone, but that's why they hired him. He was one of the original writers of *Natural Born Killers*, which is one of the few movies I've actually watched nine times. So he seemed like a great choice. And the producers, Jane Hampsher and Don Murphy, produced *NBK* with Oliver Stone. But it is, as they say, a process. In the first draft of the script, for example, the writer had me tying off with toilet paper, which was slightly problematic. Apparently, they don't teach the dos and don'ts of heroin abuse at USC Film School. I ended up as kind of an on-set needle wrangler, teaching Ben how to find a vein, get a register, cook up Mexican tar, and vomit like a man. Thank God I'd done the research.

AM: I think Ben did a good job. I enjoyed his drug-addled pitch to the TV execs.

JS: His pitch was good. Yeah, I was never that smooth, actually. What I strived to communicate to all involved, though, was that the book wasn't really about drugs. It was about being a stranger in your own skin, about fear of sunlight, mailman-dread, slow-motion suicide, and that soul-deep need to simultaneously obliterate awareness of what you're doing and yet be constantly aware so you can keep on doing it ... But don't get me going.

Miss Magnuson collects herself after interviewing Stahl

There's a flavor of solitary desolation inherent in addiction that can't be described, only experienced. And in some ways film was a better medium for that. There's one moment in *Permanent Midnight* when the camera zeroes in on Ben's eyes after he's fixed in his neck. He's

{ I ended up as kind of an on-set needle wrangler, teaching Ben how to find a vein, get a register, cook up Mexican tar, and vomit like a man. Thank God I'd done the research. }

Stahl on the set of the as-yet-unreleased *Down with the Jones*, directed and written by L.A. novelist and screenwriter Arty Nelson (right).

sitting in the front seat on some shit street in downtown L.A. with his baby wailing beside him and the night whirling around outside and Tony Robbins babbling out of the car radio.

For me, that scene embodied the mundane trauma inherent to junkiedom. I mean, Tony Robbins! *Perfect*! Because, you have to understand, this was *normal behavior*. You reach a point where geezing speedballs and spraying bloody tulips on the ceiling of a Burger King bathroom while the cops pound on the door and you're hearing dogs bark in Guatemala is totally ho-hum. But sitting down to chicken à la king with your wife and child seems more extreme than leaping out of a burning 747... This was the quotidian surrealism the film needed to capture. The addict's reality stands out as the negative image of everybody else's.

Happily, the director was gracious enough to let me put my own stamp on Ben's dialogue and character (i.e., me), so that by the time we got to a final cut, Big-Screen Jerry became more recognizable to the off-screen version. While the specifics diverge hugely from those of my book—not to mention my life—the emotional reality, at certain moments, was spot on. And that's what ultimately matters.

AM: What's that line from Hemingway? That anyone who sells their book to the movies should just stop at the border of Hollywood, throw the manuscript as hard as he can, and run like hell in the other direction?

JS: My line would be slightly different. I'd say, once you take the money, you should just shut the fuck up.

AM: But you are happy with how it turned out?

JS: I'll tell you a story. The first day of shooting interiors, I walk through the studio door, and one of these tool-belt-and-donut guys kind of puts out his hand and tries to stop me. He wants to know who I am, and I say something genius like "Oh, I'm, uh, the guy the movie's about." To which he replies, with this creepy smile, "Oh, man, you must feel so lucky. They don't usually make movies about losers!" So why wouldn't I be happy? Who knew that ending up an ass-to-the-curb dope fiend, destroying my liver, trashing ten years of my life, and carpet bombing the lives of friends and family would be such a great career move? I think there's a lesson here for all of us.

AM: You also acted in *Permanent Midnight*. In fact, I thought you gave a fine performance as the doctor in the methadone clinic.

JS: Right, I'm the guy who tells me I'll never get clean. To tell you the truth, I love acting in movies. I've actually worked a couple of times since. My last role was as a DEA agent in *Gun Shy*, with Liam Neeson and Mitch Pileggi. The film was written and directed by Erik Blakeney, a hipster I knew from my TV days. He ran this *21 Jump Street* spinoff I worked for called *Booker*, starring Richard Grieco. Not to brag. At the time, my marriage was falling apart, I was strung out like a lab rat, and my eyes hadn't uncrossed in months. A not-uncommon situation in Hollywood. But Erik was very cool about it. In fact, when I ended up homeless, not long thereafter, he let me live in his garage, where I ultimately ended up kicking, for the second to last time, during the L.A. uprising.

But I digress. This is why I have such a hard time writing movies. I always want to move the story sideways instead of forward. I can't get to the second act because I have eleven first acts. Which works great in novels, but really throws the young people who grow up to be studio readers off their feet.

Anyhow, I also did a day on an as-yet-unreleased indie called *Down with the Jones*, written by this terrific L.A. novelist and magazine writer, Arty Nelson. I play

{ Who knew that ending up an ass-to-the-curb dope fiend, destroying my liver, trashing ten years of my life, and carpet bombing the lives of friends and family would be such a great career move? }

a minimall grocery-store owner ripped off by Josh Leonard, one of the actors from *Blair Witch Project*. Again, Arty was a friend, which is how I got the gig. I haven't progressed to the eight-by-ten glossy stage. Which is just as well, because, once they saw my head shot, the only thing I'd be offered are those really prestige-y "Jew thug" roles. *"We need some Hebe muscle to play the guy who whacks the Colombian—hey, look at this Stahl mook!"*

Next up, I'll be playing a bodyguard in *Zoolander*, Ben Stiller's male-model epic. Mind you, these aren't exactly featured roles. But what the hell. It gets me out of the house. Plus which, as a writer, actually being on set with actors—let alone trying to function as one yourself—you get to see and, more importantly, hear, up close, their approach to dialogue, the incredible range a gifted actor can bring to a given stream of words. When I write dialogue, whether in book or screenplay, I always hear the words coming out of a particular person's mouth. The height of this, for me, was working on the adaptation of Budd Schulberg's *What Makes Sammy Run?* with Ben Stiller. To literally sit in the room, banging out lines, then have some genius actor sitting across from you saying them when they're hot out of the printer, is an incredibly mind-expanding experience. You get to where you can hear their rhythms in your own head, and write accordingly. Like a composer writing for a particular instrument.

AM: I'm just thinking more about adaptations, and acting. Ironically, the reason I got a chance to act in *Clear and Present Danger* was because my character was different in the book; she figured prominently there, and had that been the case in the movie, they would've had to cast a big-name star. But it's interesting that, as a writer, you enjoy acting. I would think there would be conflicts.

JS: There are a lot of reasons for that. The most obvious, of course, being that writing is such a heinously lonely and unnatural pursuit, I'd probably jump at the chance to fill in as brisket man at Canter's if anybody asked. But acting, forget it. The idea of a job where you hang out with other people, get fed great food, and work about fourteen minutes a day is fucking heaven.

More than that, though, it's one of those skills a person can hone without knowing it. I remember, years ago, interviewing Samuel L. Jackson, and I asked him how he learned to act. I've never forgotten his answer. He said, basically, that he learned by being a drug addict. That when you're a junkie, you have to learn to say just what people want to hear to get what you want from them; or say exactly what they don't want to hear, so they'll give you what you want just to get rid of you. All you have to do is look at

{ Adapting one's own book packs its own set of pitfalls. But, for better or worse, I've lived and breathed these characters. I was there when they popped out of my forehead. }

his role as the crackhead in *Jungle Fever* to see what he was talking about. When you break it down, that's not the worst approach in the world to acting—or creating characters. And God knows, back in the proverbial day, it was a craft I had plenty of time to practice myself.

AM: I want to go back to *What Makes Sammy Run?* That never got made, and I wonder why.

JS: I think the lesson here is, no matter who you are, it's a struggle. I mean, here's a major actor and director, Ben Stiller. And we're talking about a modest budget, from a book that's an absolute giant of the genre. And we could not get a fucking green light. I mean, this was such a classic situation. People I'd never met in the business would call up to say how much they loved the script. Blah-blah-blah. . . . But when push came to shove, it was one brick wall after another.

We heard all kinds of explanations for this: that it was the "Jew" thing—on the most surface level, *Sammy* is a story of Jewishness—or that the industry rarely likes to make movies about itself. Who knows? This was a book that people have been trying to adapt for forty years, and they'll probably be trying for another forty.

Still, the chance to collaborate with somebody as accomplished as Ben, the opportunity to dig down to the heart of the book and come back up with what's shootable and what isn't, to find that through line on which to hang the particulars—which is what adapting a book ultimately boils down to—was worth the hell of seeing the thing end up in the *Fucked Again* pile. Or almost.

AM: Are you going to be adapting your last novel, *Perv—A Love Story*? I'd love to see that film.

JS: Oddly enough, Showtime has said they want to do it. Negotiations have been going on for a while—not, as was widely reported, because I insist on playing the roles of both sexually psychotic killer hippies myself—but I'm nothing if not hopeful. Adapting one's own book packs its own set of pitfalls. But, for better or worse, I've lived and breathed these characters. I was there when they popped out of my forehead.

AM: Will they censor you? Can you dramatize the scene involving Michelle's shaved pudendum?

JS: Can a shaved pudendum go on cable? I don't know. It's hard for me to even say "shaved pudendum" without having to take my teeth out or put them in, one or the other.

AM: What I like about your books is your voice, but that's a problem in films. Unless they use narration, they can't capture that voice. And sometimes narration works to great effect, and sometimes not. How would you handle that with *Perv*?

JS: In *Perv*'s case, the entire story is told—and seen—through the eyes of a slightly drug-addled sixteen year old. And I'd want the screen version to capture that. I love point-of-view movies, like *Jesus' Son*—an amazing adaptation—where the action on-screen exists as the ongoing projection of what's going on inside the main character's head. In books and movies, I love when a character's psyche serves as filter for reality. The more questionable the character, the more fascinating the reality.

Most often, you're right, this is done with voice-over, where the character comments on the action as it's happening, or as it's about to. A lot of people hate voice-overs. If the writing sucks, there's nothing more cringe-inducing. You can almost see the screenwriter sitting there thinking, *"Hey, now I'm really WRITING ... Watch me work!"*

When you think about it, the VO is the one chunk of a movie that really stands or falls on what's on the page. Obviously, if there's some kind of grab-you-by-the-throat action going on around the actor, you can get by with bunk dialogue. But when you're hearing what's inside a character's brainpan, it's hard to fake it.

For me, voice-overs convert a movie into the visual equivalent of a first-person novel. It all comes down to voice. In *Permanent Midnight*, I banged out a voice-over after the film was already shot, to try and inject the flavor of the book into footage that was already there.

When voice can be preserved in the transition from page to film, as it was, so beautifully, with Denis Johnson's work, that's when both genres—text and celluloid—come together to create something more intense and gratifying than the sum of their parts. A great example of this, for me, is Martin Sheen's voiceover monologue at the beginning of *Apocalypse Now*—another monster adaptation—when Sheen is shown sweating in his Vietnam hotel room, talking about how he needed "a mission." Right away, that tone of off-balance obsession and weirdness is set for the rest of the movie. Jack Nicholson's opening monologue in *The King of Marvin Gardens* does the same thing. While not a voiceover—he's an all-night talk-show host, sitting alone in the booth and telling a story about how he and his brother let their grandfather choke to death at the dinner table—it's almost like a little psychic trailer for the madness to come.

INTERMISSION:

At this point, ladies and gentlemen, our interviewer, Ms. Magnuson, had to leave the premises, and the country, to head north to Canada to shoot a movie with the aforementioned Samuel L. Jackson. While some may question her sense of priorities—interview with Jerry Stahl or love scene with Samuel Jackson? You decide!—none, we hope, will question the possibility that there was more info to mine on the whole literature vs. film, book vs. screenplay, prose vs. big-screen adaptation front. Happily, we were lucky enough to find another willing, if unlikely and—to be honest—slightly hostile volunteer to step in and continue the exchange. His name is Alf, and we don't think he needs any introduction.

JERRY STAHL INTERVIEW: PART TWO

The first time I met Jerry Stahl, he was a callow and green-skinned strung-out sitcom writer. Even then, he was unable to grasp how lucky he was to come on my show and crank out the snappy patter. I was a star, Stahl was nothing but a no-name failed novelist and magazine writer who'd done some kind of treacherous art-porn film in the eighties called *Café Flesh*. Unbelievable! Where they dug him up, I still don't know. But I'm not here to make this about me. Stahl used yours truly to jump-start his own questionable career—and don't ask me why I'm not on the cover of *Permanent Midnight*—while I am now relegated to forgotten novelty items like Alf mugs and KISS ME, I'M AN ALIEN! T-shirts. But never mind. Let's get started.

Listen, ace, Ann's not here to toss you softballs any more, okay? I want the truth. Why didn't you write it? It was your life, wasn't it?

Alf: I hate you.

JS: Excuse me?

Alf: Don't give me that. Why didn't you use my name in your movie? Don't lie to me, I saw it. They called me "Mister Chompers, the TV puppet." What's up with that?

JS: Well, as I said in the interview with Ann, I didn't write the screenplay.

Alf: Listen, ace, Ann's not here to toss you softballs any more, okay? I want the truth. Why didn't you write it? It was your life, wasn't it?

JS: Yes, but.

Alf: But nothing! You sold out, plain and simple. Isn't that what happened? You figured, *Hey, they'll probably make Alf look stupid, they'll probably get a lot of other shit wrong, but so what? I'll take the money. It's only my name, only my reputation. What do I care? I've already hurt everybody near and dear to me in life, why not drag them through the mud all over again?*

JS: That's not how it was. Not at all. I actually liked the guy who wrote the screenplay. I liked his work.

Alf: Yeah, yeah. If it was such a great movie, how come there were no action figures of *you*, huh?

JS: Action figures?

Alf: Sure! Little Jerry Stahl action figures. You know, *"Shoots real blood! Steals money from his child's piggy bank for drugs!"* You were sitting on a gold mine, my friend.

JS: I really don't think—

Alf: Of course you don't. But you're wrong! Action figures are where the money is. Trust me, there are half a dozen different Alf dolls. You can still scoop 'em up on Ebay! And if you don't think they're gonna make some heavy cake on the Harry Potter tchotchkes, you're a fucking idiot.

JS: Do they have antidepressants for puppets? Because, I have to say, your hostility level is way, way out of proportion to the situation. I'm sniffing a cry for help here.

Alf: Spare me the faux compassion, needle-boy. I'm asking the questions. I bet your mother wasn't too thrilled either, was she?

JS: *What?*

Alf: Don't act surprised. You killed her,

didn't you?

JS: What are you talking about? My mother is still alive.

Alf: No thanks to you. Imagine how she feels walking into the beauty parlor, having all the old biddies lift up their *Ladies' Home Journals* in front of their faces and snicker, *"Oh Marge, there she is... Her son's the CELEBRITY JUNKIE!"*

JS: Hey—

Alf: Don't interrupt. If writing the damn book didn't do the job, you had to go and do a movie where you pretended she was dead. Oh yeah, I bet that really made her day. I bet that really made her glad she bothered to suckle your ungrateful ass when you clawed your way out of the room. Don't deny it. There was that big funeral scene. Ben had to fly home and clean up all the blood. And I'll tell you something else. You didn't just kill Mom, pal, you killed Lainie Kazan, who happens to be one of the finest actresses of her generation.

JS: Oh, man. Is this thing on?

Alf: You better believe it.

JS: Okay. Well, uh, like I say, the movie took some license with the facts of my life, but, uh, it wasn't actually my decision to—

Alf: You killed her! You killed her! *YOU KILLED YOUR OWN MOTHER FOR MONEY!*

JS: Jesus, calm down! Let me explain. Sometimes, when a work gets translated to the screen, there's a certain amount of streamlining that takes place. Other times, for reasons that have nothing to do with the actor, certain scenes have to be cut, and you have to rework the story. It wasn't intentional... For Christ's sake, I didn't know they were going to kill my mother when I sold them the book. Don't you get it? Once they bought the damn book, they could have made her a nine-year-old Chinese girl if they wanted to.

Alf: Uh-huh. Why don't you look *whore* up in the dictionary? See if your picture's there and get back to me.

JS: You know, I'm not sure I like the way this interview's going. This is the film and literature issue, okay? This is a high-toned literary magazine. I don't see what's so literary about—

Alf: Okay, okay. Stop whining. You wanna talk literary, how 'bout your newest book, what's it called, *Pancake Vapid*? That gonna be a movie?

JS: Actually, the title is *Plainclothes Naked*. It's coming in fall 2001. They're holding it 'cause *Perv*'s coming out in paperback in January.

Alf: Whatever. What's this masterpiece about?

JS: Since you asked, it's about these two

{ There's a weird phenomenon when it comes to having your book rejected for being "too dark." After the suits pass on your book, they call up your agent and say they want to invite you into their office to tell you how much they loved it. }

crackheads who stumble on a photograph of George Bush Junior's testicles with a happy face tattooed on them. And then there's a sexy rest-home nurse who murders her husband by putting Drano in his cereal, and the bent cop who falls in love with her. These two manage to get the photo themselves, so then the two crackheads—

Alf: Yeah, yeah, I get it. Sounds uplifting as hell. I bet the studios are falling all over themselves to get their mitts on that one, huh?

JS: Yes and no.

Alf: Meaning?

JS: Well, a lot of people in, uh, non-buying capacities liked it.

Alf: Who, the parking valets at Sony?

JS: No, no. I swear, half a dozen VPs and such at production companies told me they really, really dug it. But then, you know, when they had to go to their parent studios, who actually shell out the money, the people there thought it was too dark. So...

Alf: So they hauled your depraved butt right out of the office, didn't they? They called security and had you dragged out past the guard gate and dumped.

JS: Well, that's the funny thing. There's a weird phenomenon when it comes to having your book rejected for being "too dark." After the suits pass on your book, they call up your agent and say they want to invite you into their office to tell you how much they loved it. It's really odd. I finally asked one guy at a major studio, If you love it so much, how come you don't just make it anyway? And you know what he said? The guy just looked at me, dead in the eye, and kind of whispered: *"Because I want to have a career!"* Which is actually kind of endearing. It's like, they stick a knife in your heart, then they ask if they can buy you lunch. *"You're really sick,"* another VP told me, *"but in a really good way!"*

Alf: I'd have to agree with him.

JS: No, listen, this is amazing. Here's how it goes. After they fill you in on all the reasons they can't make your book into a movie—even though, you know, *they really want to*—they tell you about some lame-o teen splatter film or that big-screen version of the eighties TV show *they don't like at all*, but absolutely *have* to make...

It's insane. But you can't dislike these

people, because they're totally honest. They know all the money's on their side of the fence, but they really appreciate the fact that you're on the other side, working your deluded artistic ass off. It's like, if they're stuck in a limo in the middle of a traffic jam, nibbling caviar, somehow it reassures them to know that, somewhere on the planet, half-naked pygmies are crawling on their bellies through the rain forest looking for dead slugs to feed their children. It just gives everybody involved a warm feeling.

Alf: Aren't we sounding just a teensy-weensy bit bitter?

JS: Not at all. I'm just stating a fact.

Alf: So why do you even care if they make a movie out of your book or not?

JS: What can I say? That's the dirty little secret about the whole book-to-movie thing. I mean, *Permanent Midnight* didn't hit the best-seller list until the movie came out. And when Artisan pulled the movie, to slap all their money into *Belly*, the book disappeared from the list.

Alf: Boo-fucking-hoo.

JS: Would you shut up? You don't fucking get it. It's not like your publisher *wants* to sink any cash into promoting your book. Publishers feel a lot more comfortable promoting authors who are already huge, so they can stay that way. But if Hollywood's got a piece of the action, then the publisher can sit back and let *them* shove your work down the public's throat. All they have to do is rush out that $5.95 movie-tie-in paperback and count the receipts.

Alf: I thought this was supposed to be a literary discussion. Here you are talking about money.

JS: Don't kid yourself. If you're talking about Hollywood, you're talking about money.

Alf: Hey, that gives me an idea. I think you should write another memoir.

JS: About what?

Alf: What do you think? About how, after you kicked dope and got productive, you actually had less dough than when you were a drug-addled maniac. It's the American dream turned inside out. Horatio Alger on smack. Work with me here!

JS: Forget it.

Alf: Don't be a schmuck, I'm serious. I guarantee there'll be a six-figure floor for the movie rights.

JS: Oh yeah? So what do I call it?

Alf: How about *Relapse*?

JS: (indecipherable)

Alf: What?

JS: I have to get out of here. ☗

Maurice ("The Pope")

A Celebration of Professional Celebrity Look-Alikes

In the film business, there exists a professional subculture of body doubles, stunt doubles, and stand-ins. Body doubles, when contractually allowed, may be used for sex scenes but more often appear via inserts when a celebrity can't perform—dancing, say, or playing a musical instrument—on the level required to make his or her character believable. Stand-ins save production time by acting as mannequins during camera and lighting rehearsals while stars are busy in makeup or wardrobe; they're usually expected to be the same general coloring and physicality

BY **BRUCE WAGNER**, PHOTOS BY **WILLIAM EGGLESTON**

You see them on TV talk-show sketches but their bread and butter is corporate trade shows, mixers, and private parties. Conventiongoers like the novelty.

of the designated celebrity, hair length included, though facial resemblance isn't strictly required. Same goes for stunt doubles; the brain doesn't need the real item in order to build a seamless bridge between a star and his or her substitute.

The preceding naturally excludes thousands of countrywide "non-pros" (*Variety*speak for those not in the Business)—the friend, relative, or passing stranger who bears casual, even uncanny resemblance to a major or minor icon; the legions of gawky high-school royalty known through their districts as Gwyneth or Leonardo types; nor the white and blue collared men and suburban housewives long ago tagged as broken, morphed, or nascent Natalie Woods, Tammy Wynettes, Gig Youngs, Mary Tyler Moores, Joe Namaths, et alia. When I was a boy, my mother told me people said she looked like the French film star Corinne Calvet; walking through the halls of Saks, where she works, she's still frequently mistaken for Texan socialite and *W* magazine mainstay Lynn Wyatt. What does a person do in his or her head with such public affirmations? Most sweetly let it slide. Some pursue a niche called "celebrity look-alike."

Frequently, look-alikes are neophyte actors who stumbled into the trade for fun and extra dollars. They network through Web sites or ads in showbiz trade rags; some of these specialty-agency owners are look-alikes themselves. Look-alikes are usually gregarious, with a sense of humor about what they do. You see them on TV talk-show sketches—Leno or Letterman—but their bread and butter is corporate trade shows, mixers, and private parties. Conventiongoers like the novelty.

One person whom I wanted to include in these pages turned me down. A dead ringer for a legendary singer long dead (the singer in his youth), he told me he just didn't like the way he photographed. I had heard through the grapevine he'd become romantically involved with the actual daughter of the man he impersonated, and even "helped her stop drinking." I don't know how recent any of that was—I can't even attest to its accuracy. It didn't seem far-fetched; to what extent the look-alike positively or negatively insinuated himself into the singer's "real" family, I'll never know.

LISSA ("Cher"): I was ten when I saw Sonny and Cher's first album. I rushed to a store in Brooklyn with my cousin and got a version of Cher's outfit: an emerald-green poorboy. Walking down 9th Street in Brooklyn any time I do Cher, I think of that *kid* singing "Alfie" in her bedroom to the mirror. Cut to: singing "The Way of Love" at the Mirage in front of a thousand high rollers. It's strange. † My partner, Curtis, and I do events at the Bellagio and Mirage. They treat us royally—limousines, flowers in the room, messages delivered by hand. And sometimes I look around and say, "Wait a minute. I'm an actress and an entertainer. This is what I *wanted*, this is what I *worked* for—but not like this. Not as a Cher look-alike. We do these private parties at the casinos. We did "Gone with the Wynn"—you know, because of Steve Wynn—or we'll do "Cash on a Hot Tin Roof" or "The Whole Enchi-Slot-A." People crowd around after a show because they want to take pictures. I always wonder what they think about when they look at the pictures on the plane on the way home. Does the moment come where they say, "Hey! this isn't Cher"? I mean, what are they thinking? † After a show last week, a couple was clamoring for a picture and I hid my head. Curtis was dressed like

Lissa ("Cher")

Rip Taylor and kept grabbing at me to be in the shot; he didn't realize the couple was Billy Bob Thornton and Laura Dern. So we took the photo and Billy Bob grinned and grinned and I was mortified. † I got a call the other day from an agency to do a party; we get calls like that all the time. Not to perform; just to mingle. When I got to the house, it was very sedate. I went inside and there was Marilyn Manson—his girlfriend, Rose McGowan, was throwing it. Marilyn talked to me. He said Cher had called

Joe and Marti ("Clint" and "Sharon")

him to ask for advice on her videos. I guess that's why Rose wanted me there, that's why it was funny, because Cher had called. † I was in Malibu once, walking with a friend. A car pulled up and this woman shouted out the window: "Fuck you! Fuck you! Fuck you!" Then the car pulled off and I stood there with my mouth open. I mean, it's one thing if you're in Hollywood and someone shouts that from a car. But this was Carbon Beach. I said to my friend, "What was that about?" And he said, "Well, you'll get a chance to find out because the car's coming back." My friend split; I think he thought they might have a weapon! But I really wanted to talk to this person. They pulled up and the same woman said, "You're shitting on your chakras!" Then she split. The police were down the street and we caught up to them and told them what happened. I told them if they happen to see the car, to let the people know that they weren't yelling at who they thought they were. It turned out everyone in Malibu was pissed at Cher for what she was doing to her house; a lot of extra building or whatever. But even if the person knew it wasn't Cher, she probably would have gone off on me just the same—that's the weird part. People will stop me on the street and start crying and tell me they slept with Sonny but when they see it's just me, they keep talking. † I did this Swedish television thing once, in front of Mann's Chinese. They taped me as I greeted tourists. Most of them knew I wasn't Cher but I wasn't supposed to say anything. Some old guy from Daytona Beach shook my hand and I heard his wife say, "Good, you *touched* her." I felt skeevy; I'd been bullshitting people all day! I'm gonna be in someone's home movies, in Wales! And yet, how weird it is to be someone who matters that people touched you. I came home, threw my wig in the closet and said, *Uh, don't take bookings for a while.* † It's been a dry spell, for men. My ex died recently; Pierre and I were together for thirteen years. After we split, we were the best of friends. He moved in with me the last two years. He had melanoma; he was only fifty when he died. One of my best friends is a Marilyn impersonator. She was the Marilyn in *Pulp Fiction*—she does really well. We were in Palm Springs doing a show. Usually, bookers separate the "dead" (celebrities) from the "alive." And everyone's hitting on us. But then we go back to our little hotel rooms with our costumes and our wigs, and I knocked on her door—her room was a tumult—and she's in her nightgown, watching CNN. I said, "Oh, Suzie, we're tragic!" No guys would ever *think* of calling. The *cast* won't even call—everyone assumes you have the life Cher has. And she's probably at home watching herself on Larry King, thinking, My phone's not fuckin' ringing! † Last night I dreamed I was with Curtis and this force of people had come and taken all our blood out and replaced it, and from that point in time we were supposed to become robotic people who still *looked* like us, but were doing their bidding. And after the operation or whatever it was had happened, my friend and I were side by side doing some kind of work, without speaking. And I looked at him and he looked at me and we both realized that we hadn't yet been fully taken over.

MARTI ("Sharon"): I'm an only child. My mother's second husband (I called him Dad) died when I was eight. I found the body, in the basement den. He said he was going to take a nap and when my mother and I came home, I found him. That was hard. He had a blood clot in his spine. . . . I went to the University of New Hampshire. I was VP of my sorority, pledge educator, *lots* of parties. Right out of college, I entered the Miss USA pageant. I was Miss Bedford, placed top ten in the prelims. Did some prelims for Miss America but was bored to shit. The girls were all too back-stabby. I needed a job but I *hated* to work. My mother suggested I apply to be a flight attendant. She said they only worked three days a week, and the longer you worked for them, the less you had to fly. So I applied to Delta—flew down to Atlanta and was drug-tested the same day. Started flying out of Boston and *loved* it. I had friends in L.A. from Delta training. I came out for a wedding and said, "This is *it*." Rented a U-Haul on La Brea, picked up my stuff from Delta cargo, and hauled it to my new apartment in Redondo Beach. Beach life was like college life—I *loved* college—I was in heaven. Redondo's like the after-college life you grow out of. I was there about seven years, then moved to the Hollywood Hills. Then I said, "L.A.—*acting*—of course!" Hey. Fine. Got my head shots. Did some commercials—Ford Explorer—and bit parts on soaps. † Back then, during the *Basic Instinct* time, I didn't really look like Sharon. My hair was red. When I went back to blond, I heard it all the time—in elevators, on the street. I mean, the open-mouth stares. My friend Linda—she's a typical back-East Pennsylvania Jewish girl, deep voice, smoker—one day Linda said, "Hey, Marti, I gotta talk to you! I met this guy Brian in a print shop who represents celebrity look-alikes." I thought she was crazy but I gave him a call. He said, "Well everybody thinks they look like someone." So I sent my head shots in, met with him, and he booked me on a CBS show that same day. It was *Vibe*, with Sinbad—they were doing a spoof on the Academy Awards. They had a Clint and an Elizabeth and they wanted us to get into a big fight. It was fun. † I mostly do conventions: you know, two thousand Japanese, *swarming*. I like to make people smile. People like to pretend—it's an escape. We did one on a yacht, where we met the buses as they pulled to the dock. The people who hire you don't like it, but if the folks ask, I just tell 'em I'm a stewardess and an actress. I don't have anything to hide. Hey, I'm not Sharon Stone! I don't know what floats her boat. Though I'd love to meet her. Maybe she'd say, "Oh my God! Come help me on my next movie!" † There was a woman at a convention who was extremely obese. And I don't like to judge people. She said, "It must be nice to look like Sharon Stone—even for a day." I thought that was so sad and so sweet. I like my hair short; I didn't cut it to look like her. And I *never* had plastic surgery. You can quote me. † I went to a party in Brentwood, on Rockingham—near where O.J. lived—with my fiancé and future mother-in-law. I was dressed up and my hair was spiked and the hostess saw me and made a beeline. She introduced herself and when I said, "I'm Marti Faron," her face just *dropped*. Well, I didn't see it, but Mike did. † People say you can't have everything. I say you *can* have everything—just not all at once.... My fiancé acts too. He's on the board of directors of Hollywood Park racetrack. He's also a director of his family's foundation—the Ornest Family Foundation. His father, Harry, was a great patriarch. He owned the St. Louis Blues hockey team; built an arena there. Owned the Toronto Argonauts. He was a Friars Club member—that's where we're getting married. All of Harry's old friends still belong: Red Buttons and Monty Hall. He passed away last year, in July. I

Loren ("Barbra")

love Mike because he doesn't tell me not to fly. He respects and loves me for who I am—if I'm skinny or gaining weight or without makeup—he lets me be *me*. I'd love to be a mother. I have seniority now; at ten years, they let you fly just twice a month. That's when a lot of stewardesses become moms. Though sometimes, I say, Gee, I wonder if I'm going to die today?

LOREN ("Barbra"): I'm doing the Burbank Parade on April 12th—that's Barbra's birthday. It's my grandma's birthday too: her ninetieth. I was born April 30—we're all Tauruses. In *The Mirror Has Two Faces*, Barbra's character's name is Rachel Rose. Those were my grandmothers' names: Rachel and Rose. That movie meant so much to me. My sister was always the pretty one, just like in the

They'll say, "Why do you wear your hair like her?" Well, I've always had gay hairdressers. Who do you *think* they're going to make me look like?

movie. † I looked like her from an early age. When I was a waitress in Cleveland, my college years, word got around: *you gotta go in and see this girl who looks like Barbra.* Even when I had my kids—I had them seventeen months apart—the doctors and nurses came to check me out. Sometimes people aren't so nice. They'll say, "What's your problem? Are you trying to look like her? Why do you wear your hair like her?" Well, I've always had gay hairdressers. Who do you *think* they're going to make me look like? I say, "I do this for a living." I know *exactly* who I am—it's everyone else who's mixed up. I could be in a mental hospital too. My mother used to worry about that. People said I looked like her when I was *eleven.* I started to wonder: who *is* this person? My uncle Benny mentioned it one day, in Florida—then the floodgates opened. People started pointing wherever I went. The paramedics came for my grandma once and saw a picture of me on the table and asked if she was "related"—she was coherent enough to later tell me that story. † I worked on a TV show based on that movie magazine, *Photoplay.* They were doing a celebrity mom segment and I got assigned to call Barbra's mother. I couldn't believe it. Here I was, chatting with the woman who gave birth to the person I'd been told I looked like all my life. A few days later, I got a call—it was Diana. She asked me to lunch. That was totally unexpected. I went up to the house—I was *so* excited, a *wreck.* Roslyn, Barbra's sister, was living there. At the time, Barbra was dating Richard Baskin. It was so *strange.* There were all the family pictures, and the one that stood out was of Barbra and her son, Jason. I remembered seeing that photo in a magazine years before at Leader Drugs in Cleveland! It was the first time I said, *"Oh my God, I really look like her."* Here it was in the house and I said to myself, There it is! That's the one! The first thing Diana did—Diana Kind, Barbra's mom—the first thing she did was offer me a bagel, which is what *my* mother did with guests. We went to lunch somewhere on Fairfax. I'll never forget what she said—she said her daughter was so busy that "I'll have to cart *you* around with me." I saw her a lot after that for awhile. We went shopping at Robinson's-May for Barbra's brother's wedding present. We used to talk on the phone, and she'd tell me how to make chicken. How you have to *clean* it, how careful you have to be of the *germs*, how you have to let it *soak* and wash your *hands*. And the fact she was Barbra's mother gradually kind of disappeared—she was just a person. She gave me oriental teacup things for my wedding, you know, the tops that you put on to keep the tea hot? I think they were her personal things. I had a feeling that, to a point, she *liked* the idea people thought I was her daughter. A missing link. But when people occasionally said things—well, once I was waiting in the car for her and some girls walked by and said, "It's Barbra Streisand!" I think *part* of her liked that, but part of her didn't. Maybe she was thinking: But this isn't my daughter. Where is my daughter? This is an impersonator. Then one day, I got a call from Diana saying she'd won an award from the Jewish National Fund. She asked me to go and I took my fiancé. I thought Barbra might be there but she was in Europe at the time. It was a luncheon; there weren't a million people there. I got stared at in the elevator; I wasn't really introduced. We didn't sit at the family table but people were looking, I think, and wondering: Who is she? Roslyn was there and we took a picture: me, Roslyn, and Barbra's mom. It was a little weird. I called to thank her and she said, "People didn't know if you were *Barbra*, if you were a *relative*—" My feeling is it got to the point where it was uncomfortable for her, not for me. A long time later, I was at Target, in Cleveland, when I saw the *People* magazine with her wedding album. I know that in James Brolin, she found her soul mate. When I saw the picture of her mother, I cried. Because I *knew* this woman. She'd changed; I'd heard she'd had a stroke. Sometimes I think of calling.

STACY ("Scully"): I'm going to London to see friends and check out what the look-alike market has to offer; my agent interfaces with look-alikes over there. Do you want to know how I met my boyfriend? There was an English sci-fi magazine called *Dreamwatch*, and they have a pen pal section. I wrote in saying I was a Gillian Anderson look-alike and was seeking a pen pal from Great Britain. I got forty to fifty responses. Men were intrigued, especially after I sent my picture. I pretty much corresponded with all of them for awhile but I couldn't keep up with the mail. Now I only write to three or four, but my boyfriend's the only one I got involved with. We wrote each other—neither of us had computers at that point—and just really hit it off. He planned a trip to see me and we finally met last April ('98). He stayed at a hotel

Stacy ("Scully")

that first time. † I'd been doing look-alike work for around three years. Before that, I was a magician's assistant; I'd answered an ad in *Backstage West Dramalogue*. Most of the magic shows were on the night *The X-Files* was on, so I wasn't really familiar with the show. Then all of a sudden kids were coming up to me and saying, Are you Dana Scully? Finally, I watched; I didn't see the resemblance at first. Then, I heard Jenny Jones was looking for viewers who looked like look-alikes—I mean, who looked like celebrities. I sent in a photo and they asked me on. There was a Bill and Hillary, an Eddie Murphy, a Madonna, and a Fran Drescher. They asked me back two weeks later to do a parody called *The H-files*. It was all about women with bad hair. I was in a vignette with a lady telling her her hair looked alien. † I actually did work a few days on *The X-Files*. I thought I'd be perfect to be her stand-in/photo double. The show was moving down here and I knew that her stand-in had just had a baby. I went to Fox and auditioned and they expressed an interest in me doing her stand-in/photo-double work. But they never called back; I think they hired someone's girlfriend! I *did* work on the second episode of the season—"Drive"—as her stand-in, helping them light a complicated shot. Gillian was there but the way things were set up,

I didn't get a chance to meet her. If I'd known that was the only day I'd work—it was actually a night shoot—I would have tried to. † I went to the American Academy of Dramatic Arts, in Pasadena. I've wanted to act forever. I do lots of industrial and trade shows. I played Scully on an educational film warning of the perils of food-borne illnesses—they called it *The Eggs-File, starring Agents Mouldy and Scuzzy*. At the *X-Files* expo at Tustin Airbase, I went in costume, business suit and FBI badge, and I was *mobbed*. I'd brought a stack of pictures for fun, for autographs. It was weird—they *knew* I wasn't Gillian Anderson, but they backed me up against the *wall*. I had to leave the event and get more pictures because I ran out. I was really surprised, because on the other side of the auditorium were the real people—the Lone Gunman, the guy who plays X, Skinner, and one of the executive producers. But there they were, wanting my autograph. The people from *F/X* asked me to do a little promo for *The X-Files* reruns, but I don't think they ever ran it. † work at a clinical lab now. I'm a specimen processor. I wear a long white coat and latex gloves. We do testing for AIDS and different types of cancer.

I played Scully on an educational film warning of the perils of food-borne illnesses–they called it *The Eggs-File, starring Agents Mouldy and Scuzzy.*

MAURICE ("The Pope"): Next month, the pope is going to be seventy-nine—I'll be seventy-nine the following December. I kid around with people and tell them we were twins and got broken up at birth. † I was born in Winnipeg, Manitoba. I've been out here since I was two and a half. My folks migrated to Canada from Russia. We're Jews, and I still speak a little Yiddish. My oldest brother was bar mitzvahed, but he was the only one. † I retired in the late eighties. I used to sell food to restaurants, hotels, and country clubs; I got the orders and our trucks delivered: shrimp, lobster, scallops. I've been doing movie extra work for eleven years. People kept saying I looked just like the pope, so I went and had some pictures made. I improvised because I didn't have the robes; I had a black Members Only jacket. I got a lead from an agent who said someone was looking for a pope, for Comedy Central. They rented me the outfit and the high

Sean ("Whoopi")

hat that goes along with it. That was my first job. Later, I worked on *The Tracy Ullman Show*. She was supposed to be the Queen of England, interviewing celebrities. † I'm on my second marriage; my wife is too. We have five kids between us. Her son passed away last year—Hodgkin's. He did chemo for thirteen months and they said, "You're cured." Then, bam, he was gone. But that's life.

JOE ("Clint"): I've lived in the Joshua Tree area over twenty years. Five acres, about three hundred trees on the property. I ran a chain of karate studios but now I make my living with my face, plus I'm an agent for look-alikes. We shot a full-length feature on video called *Filthy Harry*, produced, directed, written, and paid for by yours truly. I cast fifteen to twenty lookalikes; did very well in Japan. We've got a few others—*Hang 'Em All* and *Magnum Farce*. Last night, we were over at the Renaissance Esmeralda Hotel. Two hours of mix and mingle: Marilyn, Indiana Jones, Cher, and myself. Other times we do mock Academy Award ceremonies for conventions. You know, hand out trophies for the most amount of carburetors sold or whatever. They might set up a western town and the convention people dress up and read from scripts and do a scene with the look-alikes. We video it and people take the tape home. It's a blast.

SEAN ("Whoopi"): I've been acting and doing comedy since I was sixteen. I've been doing the look-alike thing for almost four years now. People kept saying I looked like Whoopi but you know, when you're an actor, you want to be yourself. When they told me how much money I'd make, I thought, Well, I have to eat. So I put on the wig and the glasses and lower my voice a little. A few weeks ago, some people came in from Cleveland and this lady wanted to show them a good time. And she told them she knew Whoopi. I met them at Crustacean, that restaurant in Beverly Hills where the fish swim underneath your feet, I'd been

Kurt ("Harrison")

dying to go there anyway—and her friends really thought I *was* Whoopi. The whole restaurant did; they even brought the chef out to meet me. A grip from *Hollywood Squares* sent over dessert. As far as I know, she never did tell her friends who I was. I wouldn't tell because that's not what I'm being paid for. Why rain on their parade?

KURT ("Harrison"): The first time it happened, I was a sophomore in high school, in Santa Fe. *Star Wars* had just come out and a friend said, "You look like Harrison Ford." I didn't know who that was. After college, I moved to L.A. and *everyone* said, "You look like Harrison Ford." Okay—now what? A Madonna look-alike saw me in a club and came over—"If I can do Madonna, you can definitely do Harrison Ford." My first gig was a Diet Coke commercial, then I went to Japan for a show. They brought ten of us in from the States. I met what I'd say were the top 10 percent of look-alikes and they directed me who to work for, who not to—the agencies. I do corporate parties and meet-and-greets four to eight times a month. † I've never met him but I know he knows of me from the Diet Coke commercials. And because whenever I work, they have to get permission from Lucasfilm; I pretty much do Indiana Jones. I don't really hang out with the look-alikes. They're an elusive group. Though a Marilyn Monroe used to live here in Santa Monica and we'd have coffee. She was one of the best Marilyns out there.

STEWART ("Tom"): Ever since *Top Gun*, everyone told me I looked like Tom Cruise. I work with a lady who's a script doctor for Spielberg. I was doing her pool deck—I'm a general contractor—and she said, "You look just like Tom, but you've got blond hair and a better nose." I dye my hair for gigs, though I probably don't chase it hard as I could. It's fun being up there onstage; it's an adrenaline rush. I took a year off in '95 and went back to England to do some acting and modeling. I think that was the year Tom moved there, to Kensington. I was in a few plays and the reviewers always said, "...and the Tom Cruise look-alike, Stewart Rigby." Here's a funny thing: I was up at the Beverly Glen Plaza, at the deli. Do you know Tom Sizemore? Well, his wife was there with her personal assistant. I was having lunch outside with my partner—in our handyman shirts—and she came up and said I looked just like Tom Cruise. "I'm gonna tell my husband I've seen you up at the Plaza and you've dyed your hair blond and got an English accent for a new role." She said he was so gullible, he wouldn't even know. Sizemore had loaned Cruise some NFL tapes of games he'd missed and the wife said I should just walk in with some tapes and hand them back. But it never came to fruition.

VINCE ("Tom"): A few years ago, I got a call from a gentleman who lived in my apartment building who did JFK look-alike work. He said his agents needed a Tom Cruise look-alike; from then, things really started to roll. I was sent to New Orleans to do *Interview with the Vampire Lestat*. My uncle's a dentist and I had fangs made. They're flawless; I can eat with them. The party was for Microsoft. They'd rented a giant mansion. I had a very elaborate costume with the big hair—I looked great! Girls were literally touching my teeth.

Stewart ("Tom")

Inevitably, they'd say, *"Bite me."* And I bit them till it hurt! They were excited. I did that all night. It's funny, with the teeth. Because I met Willem Dafoe at Sundance, right after *Born on the Fourth of July*. He ran up to me and said, "Oh my God, I thought you were Tom—but your teeth are straighter." ■

Buster Keaton Looks in the Woods for His Love Who is a Real Cow

by

Rafael Alberti

Translated by Mark Strand

1, 2, 3, 4,

My shoes don't fit in these four tracks.
If my shoes don't fit in these four tracks,
whose tracks are they?
A shark's?
A new-born elephants? A duck's?
A flea's? A quail's?

(Yooo Hooo)

Georginaaaaaaaa!
Where are you?
I don't hear you, Georgina!
What will your father's mustache think of me?

(PaaaPaaaaa)

Georginaaaaaaaa!
Are you here or not?

Spruce, where is she?
Alder, where is she?
Pine, where is she?

Has Georgina come by here?

(Yooo Hooo, Yooo, Hooo)

She came by at one, munching grass.

Caw, caw,
the crow was leading her on with some mignonette.
Wooo wooo,
the owl with a dead mouse.

Excuse me, gentlemen, but it makes me want to cry!
(Booo hooo, booo hooo.)

Georgina!
Now you are short only one horn
of acquiring a postman's cap and a doctorate
in the truly useful profession of cyclist.

(Cri, cri, cri, cri.)

Even the crickets pity me
and the tick shares my sorrow.
Pity him in the tuxedo who looks for you and cries for you
in one rainstorm after another,
the soft-hearted one, the one in the derby,
who worries about you among the trees.

Georginaaaaaaaaaaaaaaaa!

(Moooooooooooo.)

Are you a sweet child or a real cow?
My heart always told me that you were a real cow.
Your father, that you were a sweet child.
My heart, that you were a real cow.
A sweet child.
A real cow.
A child.
A cow.
A child or a cow?
Or a child and a cow?
I never found out.
Goodbye, Georgina.
(Bang!)

In Praise of UNDERAPPRECIATED BOOKS AND WRITERS *and for this issue—MOVIES*

ON SAMUEL BECKETT'S *FILM*

By Barney Rosset

Around 1962, as a natural outgrowth of Grove Press (which I bought and began running in 1951), we started a separate film unit called Evergreen Theater to commission film scripts and produce them. The people involved in Evergreen Theater were me, Richard Seaver, Fred Jordan (all of us with Grove), and Alan Schneider—a seasoned director of Samuel Beckett's work in North America.

I had experience making films. In World War II, I went from the infantry to the Signal Corps's photographic units. After a short period as a student at the Army Film Unit in New York, where Frank Capra and John Huston taught, I was sent to China and put in charge of a motion-picture and still-photo unit. After the war I briefly studied at the University of Chicago, then returned to the camera world. In 1948, I produced my one feature film, *Strange Victory*. Directed and edited by Leo Hurwitz, *Strange Victory* was a semi-documentary about the continuing problems of racism in America after WWII. The film was not a commercial success, but it won best film honors at the Marienbad Film Festival around 1949. I left filmmaking behind after *Strange Victory*, but once Grove was well established and *Evergreen Review* had begun appearing, it was only natural for me to put film production on my hope list.

So we established Evergreen Theater, and made up a list of authors we thought would make great film writers. We asked eight authors to write scripts, six of whom were published by Grove. The two writers I had not previously published were a German, Günter Grass, and the Austrian, Ingeborg Bachman. I met Grass in torn-up Berlin and Bachman in not-torn-up Zurich, Switzerland. Both very graciously turned down my request for a film script.

Fred Jordan and I met with Jean Genet at the Ritz Hotel in London. Genet was then and later a Grove author, but that did not keep him from angrily (though with a wonderfully comic effect) dismissing our proposal. Using the room's TV set as a prop, Genet explained to us—or at least to himself—that the little people on the screen were not really there. He proved this by walking to the back of the set. Where were they? He wanted "real actors."

We had better luck with the other great Grove authors. Marguerite Duras and Alain Robbe-Grillet both wrote wonderful full-length scripts for us, but we were unable to produce either of the two for various reasons. For both scripts, the timing was wrong. Harold Pinter, Eugene Ionesco, and Samuel Beckett wrote the other three scripts. We intended their scripts to form a feature-length trilogy.

The Pinter script was later produced by the BBC. Ionesco's script could not be done at the time due to some very complex and very expensive special effects. Today, with computer animation and graphics technologies, those effects could be produced at a much-reduced cost—and maybe someone will do it. With Beckett's *Film* (a very Beckettian, though confusing, title) we were luckier than with all the other scripts. Jason Epstein, the great editor at Random House, introduced me to an executive from a TV production company. Neither Jason nor I can remember his name, though it will surely turn up somewhere. The man knew Beckett's work well and financed, as an Evergreen partner of some kind, the production of *Film*. Samuel Beckett came from Paris to New York for his one and only trip to the United States. He and Alan Schneider stayed with me and my wife in the Village in Manhattan during the film's making. In the end, there were no monetary receipts to show for these efforts, but we produced Beckett's film, and met with at least moderate success in the opinions of film critics.

The production staff was a talented one. I prevailed upon an old acquaintance with Sydney Myers, not only a fine director but also a master of film editing. Sydney became our editor. He and Sam quickly became friends. For cinematographer, I chose Boris Kauffman because of his work with Jean Vigo on two feature films, *Zero for Conduct* and *L'Atalante*. Though I did not know it then, Kauffman had become a famous cinematographer in this country—for his Oscar-winning work in *On the Waterfront* and many other big Hollywood films. Even stranger to me was the discovery that Boris's brother was Dziga Vertov, one of the great filmmakers during the Soviet Union's creative heyday.

Buster Keaton in *Film* (1964)

The first actor Beckett wanted for the only major role in *Film* was the Irish actor Jack McGowran. He was unavailable, as was Charlie Chaplin, and so was Zero Mostel, Alan's choice. Later, Mostel did a marvelous job with Burgess Meredith in a TV production of *Waiting for Godot* that Schneider directed. Finally, Alan suggested Buster Keaton. Sam liked the idea, so Alan flew out to Hollywood to sign Buster up. There he found Buster living in extremely modern circumstances. On arrival he had to wait in a separate room while Keaton finished up an imaginary poker game with, among others, the legendary (but long-dead) Hollywood mogul Irving Thalberg. Keaton took the job. During an interview, Beckett told Kevin Brownlow (a Keaton scholar) that "Buster Keaton was inaccessible. He had a poker mind as well as a poker face...He had great endurance, he was very tough, and, yes, reliable. And when you saw that face at the end—oh. At last."

As to what the film meant, what it was about, Beckett said:

> It's about a man trying to escape from perception of all kinds—from all perceivers, even divine perceivers. There is a picture which he pulls down. But he can't escape from self-perception. It is an idea from Bishop Berkeley, the Irish philosopher and idealist, 'To be is to be perceived'—*'Esse est percipi.'* The man who desires to cease to be must cease to be perceived. If being is being perceived, to cease being is to cease to be perceived.

How to distinguish between the modes of being perceived and self-perceiving became a technical problem that Beckett felt was never solved:

> ...the two perceptions—the extraneous perception and his own acute perception. The eye that follows that sees

> him and his own hazy, reluctant perception of various objects. Boris Kauffman devised a way of distinguishing between them. The extraneous perception was all right, but we didn't solve his own. He (Kauffman) tried to use a filter—his view being hazy and ill-defined. This worked at a certain distance, but for close-ups it was no good. Otherwise it was a good job.

Originally, *Film* was meant to run nearly thirty minutes. Eight of those minutes would be one very long shot in which a number of actors would make their only appearance. The shot was based on Orson Welles's *Citizen Kane*, wherein Welles and his genius cameraman, Gregg Toland, achieved "deep focus." Even when panning their camera, "deep focus" allowed objects from as close as a few feet to as far as several hundred to be seen with equal clarity. Toland's work was so important to Welles that he gave his cameraman equal billing to himself. Sad to say, our "deep focus" work in *Film* was unsuccessful. Despite the abundant expertise of our group, the extremely difficult shot was ruined by a stroboscopic effect that caused the images to jump around. Today it would probably be much easier to achieve the effects we wanted to capture. Technology is now on our side. Then, the problems proved too much for our group of very talented people.

We went on without that shot. Beckett solved the problem of this incipient disaster by removing the scene from the script. In his book, *Entrances*, Alan Schneider discusses working with Beckett:

> Sam was incredible. People always assume him to be unyielding, but when the chips are down, on specifics—here as well as in all his stage productions—he is completely understanding, flexible, and pragmatic. Far from blaming anything on the limitations and mistakes of those around him, he blamed his own material, himself.

Alan went on to say of *Film*:

> I was once told that the British director Peter Brook had seen it and said that half of it was a failure and the other half a success. I'm inclined to agree with him, although I'm not sure we'd both pick the same half. In fact, I change my mind about which half I like every time I see it.

We showed *Film* at the New York Film Festival and at many other international film festivals, garnering a number of awards along the way. Perhaps we spent too much money, we got almost no theatrical income, but at least today *Film* is available on videocassette, as is Schneider's and Mostel's fine TV production of *Waiting for Godot*. Today's audiences can form their own opinions.

BREAKFAST AT TIFFANY'S
by David Trinidad

In the 1960s, two novels had a profound effect on my impressionable teenage mind: *Valley of the Dolls* and *Breakfast at Tiffany's*. The author of the latter, Truman Capote, is considered a more literary writer than the author of the former, Jacqueline Susann, though there is nothing wrong with Susann's sentences: clean and tight, they snap together efficiently. Capote's sentences are also streamlined, only his manage to get under your skin: they vibrate like guitar strings, generating an emotional resonance Susann seldom achieves. It's fitting, I suppose, that my literary "parents" used respective appearances on Johnny Carson's *Tonight Show* to wage a brief but bitchy feud. As both had topped best-seller lists at the same time (Susann under "fiction" with *Valley*, Capote under "general" with *In Cold Blood*), their televised squabble was clearly a battle of metaphorical dick-size. Both were charismatic and witty personalities, both made the life of the writer look exciting. And their books, for better or worse, made a certain kind of life look attractive. *Valley* follows three pill-popping glamour gals through the back alleys of show business. *Breakfast* tells the story of Holly Golightly, a madcap Manhattan playgirl. Both books also feature charac-

ters who dream of becoming writers—something I, by that time, was also dreaming about. Ultimately, I related more to Capote's budding writer than to Susann's heterosexual, aspiring-novelist Adonis, Lyon Burke. The nameless narrator of *Breakfast at Tiffany's* is as anonymous as he is Capote-like: self-romanticizing, sharply observant, obviously gay. It was easy for me to step into his shoes.

I used to lie on top of the Naugahyde ottoman in our living room, legs and head draped over either end, blood rushing to my brain as I read whatever book lay on the floor below me. I first read *Breakfast at Tiffany's* this way. I remember having to hold the book with one hand because it wouldn't stay open on its own, it was so slim, and having to alternate hands every so often because this particular position cut off the circulation in my arms. The Signet mass-market paperback had cost me sixty cents—the equivalent of five comic books! It had a simple, seemingly unmemorable cover: title and author's name against a solid blue background. I didn't know, at the time, that the color was an approximation of "Tiffany blue," the shade of the store's gift boxes and shopping bags. (And I certainly couldn't have envisioned myself, decades later, aching with nostalgia for that blue cover, or how difficult it would be to relocate it. Relocating *Valley of the Dolls* was a snap: I spotted that pill-spattered Bantam bestseller in every used bookstore I walked into. But the Tiffany blue edition of *Breakfast* eluded me for years. Finally, thanks to the convenience of Bibliofind, I was able to track it down online.) The story flew by that first time I read it—faster than an episode of a favorite sitcom, as effervescent and sweet and fleeting as a can of cream soda. I burst into tears at the end, in part because the book was so suddenly over; in part because Holly throws her cat away; in part because the narrator loses his friend; but also because of something larger, something I didn't—and couldn't, at that point in my life experience—understand. It was my first taste of the Tiffany Blues, if you will. Despite its cartoonish characterizations and its sense of buoyant make-believe, Capote's novella is an exquisitely written and deeply moving ode to the impermanence of all of our earthly relationships.

Unfortunately, more people have seen the movie version of *Breakfast at Tiffany's* than have read the book, and that's a shame. The book's true charm, its subtle magic, gets lost in translation. Audrey Hepburn is wonderful to watch, though she, like almost all of the other actors, is miscast; she's too doll-like, changing from Givenchy outfit to Givenchy outfit, too finely chiseled and articulate, too composed. She misses Holly's innate wildness and terror—the way she's fueled by inner demons. The movie's real sin, however, is its heterosexualization of the narrator. Diminutive Paul Williams (just twenty years old when the film was made) would have been perfect for the part. Instead we get tall, manly, and bland George Peppard as Paul Varjak, boy toy to an older female "decorator"—a character invented for the film—played by a turbaned Patricia Neal. In the book, the narrator's namelessness aligns him with Holly's cat: though she calls him "Fred" (her brother's name) for awhile, he never *belongs* to her; he, too, is just some "poor slob without a name." In the movie, they can't seem to say "Paul Varjak" (an awful name) enough; we hear it again and again. Patricia Neal's character, on the other hand, is simply referred to as "2E"; so it is she who inherits that aura of unattachment. We won't talk about the party, or the ending, or Mickey Rooney in Oriental drag shrieking "Missa Gorightry!!!" Ironically, only the first few minutes of the movie come close to the magic of the book: a cab speeds up a deserted Fifth Avenue at dawn, and deposits Audrey Hepburn in front of Tiffany & Co., where—to the wistful strains of Henry Mancini's "Moon River"—she sips coffee and munches a croissant as she gazes into the store, comforted by "the quietness and the proud look of it." At that very moment we see: "Based on the Novel by Truman Capote."

We won't talk about the party, or the ending, or Mickey Rooney in Oriental drag shrieking "Missa Gorightry!!!" Ironically, only the first few minutes of the movie come close to the magic of the book

An Unfinished Piece for a Player Piano

By Chris Solomine

My Russian friends always smile when they hear the name "Anton Chekhov," even more so than when they hear "Tolstoy" or "Dostoevsky." A gleam comes to their eyes, a glazed look similar to the one my Italian-American father used to get when someone mentioned Joe DiMaggio. Lost in a nostalgic wave, they seem to be remembering some perfect instant in their imperfect past, like so many of Chekhov's characters themselves. But then the smile—one of pity, because try as they might to explain the depth of their connection, I remain an outsider and can never truly understand. It is culturally impossible, in much the same way that they fail to grasp my existential longing as I ponder the diamond at Yankee Stadium.

What my Russian friends mean is that the West cannot do their saintly writer justice, especially on film. The British are too stodgy and the Americans are too young historically. My friends invariably offer up the actor and director Nikita Mikhalkov's little-known film *An Unfinished Piece for a Player Piano*, made in 1977, as evidence of how Chekhov can be translated onto the screen.

That a Russian filmmaker should capture the soul and spirit of one of his own

Anton Pavlovich Chekhov

comes as no surprise, except when you consider that simply being part of a culture is no guarantee of success. (There have been less than stellar film versions of *A Streetcar Named Desire*, in which I don't know what the hell is going on.) *An Unfinished Piece* is not strictly a screen adaptation of a specific work. Although its opening credits read, "based on the stories of Anton Chekhov," it is more a unique creation combining pieces of the plays *Platonov*, *Uncle Vanya*, and *The Water Devil* with the imaginations of Mikhalkov and his collaborator A. Adabashyan. Perhaps a more apt credit would have been "inspired by," since Mikhalkov pays homage to the essence of Chekhov's work, a bold and risky task considering the pedestal on which the writer is held.

And having met Nikita Mikhalkov, nearly twenty years after he made *An Unfinished Piece*, but before I had seen it, I must admit that I was suspicious of this larger-than-life character's ability to sensitively interpret Chekhov. Not because I did not respect the other films of his I had seen—he is a wonderful filmmaker and actor—but one does not become a national treasure without having an ego, and after spending a New Year's Eve in his Russian dacha, I understood Mikhalkov was a man who knew his position in the world and liked it.

The country house was quite a Chekhovian location, complete with violins, gypsies, mounds of cabbage, and, of course, vodka. Vodka distilled in the village up the road and adorned with a private label. But Nikita's bottles did not bear the family crest or village name. Instead, emblazoned on a red background was a ten-inch, golden picture of the Academy Award he had recently won for his touching film *Burnt by the Sun*. And on the opposite side of the bottle, his picture accepting the statuette in the Dorothy Chandler Pavilion. The message received loudly and clearly by all his guests? You are in the presence of greatness. Consider yourself lucky.

I merely considered myself drunk and saw it as a joke, because I had been drinking unlabeled vodka for several hours already. Days later, however, when it came time to finally view *An Unfinished Piece*, I remembered the moment with trepidation. My God, I thought, the man probably tried to out-Chekhov Chekhov. But, as I watched I realized that was impossible. Instead, what I saw was one artist sewing the lustrous threads of another artist's work into a fresh tapestry. Paying tribute in a new medium, with much love.

All the favorite Chekhov characters are present in the film: the fading matriarch, the do-nothing idealist, the provincial doctor, and, at the center, the fallen schoolteacher, Misha Platonov. And as Chekhov was not afraid to display his characters' flaws, neither is Mikhalkov. He shines the cold light of truth on them and exposes their inner natures, without judgment, because being true to Chekhov means reveling in human weakness. Neither the author nor Mikhalkov flinch when confronted by this weakness, but take it on in the hope of examining the source. While Chekhov's and Mikhalkov's "heroes," in this case Platonov, usually have a past wound, the play or film is always about taking some step forward, no matter how tiny. And that is enough. Platonov explains his feelings of longing and remorse to his ex-lover Sofia with the lines, "One only thinks that all still lies ahead, that life is a long happy road which one can only half live now, and that all can be fixed up later. But this 'later' never comes," striking the core of Chekhov, at least as an outsider can grasp it. Accept the weariness of life, its untenable nature, then laugh a little and try to move on.

The way to move on for Nikita Mikhalkov, as for all Russians I know, is, of course, love. Love in the face of misery, of uncertainly, of loss. Love that is loud and unabashed, even if it is often tearful and stings the heart. As Platonov's wife, Sasha, reminds him as a counterpoint to his depression, "as long as we love, we will have a long and happy life"; and we finally see that the "later" can become the now, that living in the present provides a ray of sunlight to scare off the shadows of our remorse. It is this compassion for human frailty combined with an endless desire to overcome regret, I think, that makes my Russian friends wear their love for Chekhov on their sleeves. And thanks to Nikita Mikhalkov's film, now when someone says old Anton's name, my eyes glaze over and as a smile comes to my face I can smell the birch trees of the Russian forest and taste the cold, pure vodka in the back of my throat.

William Boyd's The New Confessions

By Kera Bolonik

Many years before James Cameron coronated himself "King of the World" at the 1998 Oscars, there was another filmmaker with a similar sense of grandiosity: John James Todd. Though far less accomplished, Todd would be the first to tell you that he is a genius, a man who would have been Orson Welles if only his lack of foresight hadn't gotten in the way. That, and if he hadn't been the invention of William Boyd, one of England's best contemporary fiction writers, who has somehow eluded the attention of the American reader.

The New Confessions is an autobiography of the most memorable, irrepressible, and under-appreciated hero you've never heard of. Born in 1899 in Edinburgh, Scotland, Todd narrates his story—in his words, "one man's life in the twentieth century"—as a septuagenarian in exile somewhere in the Mediterranean, opening with a confession that intentionally echoes the *Confessions* of Jean-Jacques Rousseau: "My first act on entering this world was to kill my mother. . . . The date of my birth was the date of her death, and thus began all my misfortunes." Never were truer words spoken from the mouth of John James Todd, whose life is comprised of a series of unfortunate entanglements with every major historical event the first half of the century has to offer.

Here is a man who enlists in the army during World War I to impress his mother's sister, only to end up on the Western Front. When he gets transferred to the War Office Cinema Committee to serve as its official cameraman, he accidentally winds up in occupied Belgium and gets captured by the Germans. It is during this dire time that Todd discovers Rousseau's *Confessions*, a book that forever changes him; in the philosopher he recognizes a kindred spirit. Todd vows to dedicate his life to bringing the astounding memoir to the silver screen.

After the war, Todd finally gets to enjoy some success, in London for his

For better or for worse,

John James Todd will

capture Rousseau's

life on celluloid

if it kills him.

two-reeler serial comedies and in the Weimar Republic for his cinematic adaptation of Rousseau's *La Nouvelle Heloise.* While his growing reputation as an artist enables him to work on *The Confessions: Part I,* Todd's blind ambition is the very thing that keeps him from becoming the renowned filmmaker he longs to be. By the time he finishes his silent magnum opus, talkies sound their first appearance in the cinema. But Todd's spirit never wanes: not when he is working as a war correspondent during World War II, making cowboy films in Hollywood, or ending up the eleventh member of the Hollywood Ten during the McCarthy era. For better or for worse, John James Todd will capture Rousseau's life on celluloid if it kills him.

Celebrated for his versatility and astonishing imagination, William Boyd has racked up Whitbred and Somerset Maugham Awards for *A Good Man in Africa,* the John Llewellyn Rhys Prize for *The Ice Cream War,* which also made the shortlist for the Booker Prize, the James Tait Black Memorial Prize for *Brazzaville Beach,* and the *Los Angeles Times* Prize for Fiction for *The Blue Afternoon. The New Confessions,* Boyd's fourth book, ranks right up there as one of his most extraordinary and wickedly humorous achievements, and yet, like the novel's hero, it has never received its due praise (though, admittedly, the book is far more deserving than the failed filmmaker). Thankfully, Vintage Books has just reissued *The New Confessions,* giving Boyd another opportunity to share this indelible life story with anyone who will listen. Hopefully, this time around John James Todd will finally win himself a rapt audience.

Xavier Villaurrutia's Nostalgia for Death

By Christopher Merrill

It is fitting that a Mexican poet wrote the first great poem about Los Angeles, not because the city is a magnet for economic migrants from Mexico but because it took an outsider to draw out its secret: that the City of Angels is at once a factory of illusion, an emblem of desire (and what is at the heart of desire but illusion?), and the last graveyard by the sea. Xavier Villaur-

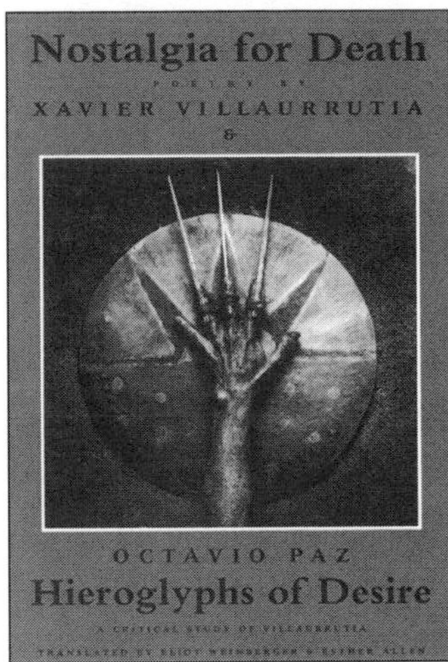

rutia (1904–1950) wrote just one book of poetry, *Nostalgia for Death*, which not only helped to inaugurate Spanish Modernism in the New World, inspiring, among others, a budding poet-essayist named Octavio Paz, but also ushered in a new poetics of desire. An elegant gay man, Villaurrutia was, in the words of his translator, Eliot Weinberger, "one of the great poets of desire: one whose beloved, finally, is not another man but Death itself, Death himself." And nowhere is this more apparent than in "L.A. Nocturne: The Angels," which is his hymn to "the enormous luminous scar" of desire, the last words of a film, the end of the American dream.

In this poem, Villaurrutia explores the intimate connections between sleep and poetry, hearing in that netherworld "a new throbbing, a new pulsebeat." The long free-verse lines course down the page like an underground river; thirsty creatures emerge, angels and men who "form unpredictable couples." It is as if Walt Whitman and García Lorca meet one night on an abandoned film set in Hollywood and let the poet drive them from the heart of the city to the sea and back again—"to set free their tongues of fire." Not until they fall asleep does Villaurrutia patiently record their astonishment and ecstasies.

"Villaurrutia's glory is secret, like his poetry," Paz writes in *Hieroglyphs of Desire*, a fascinating book-length study included in the Copper Canyon edition of *Nostalgia for Death*. "I don't regret this, and neither would he. He asked for nothing more than the fervent admiration of a few. In modern times poetry is not, nor can it be, more than an underground cult, a ceremony in the catacomb." Nevertheless this splendid volume deserves a wider readership, if only to confirm Villaurrutia's prophesy:

> I will be dust in the dust, oblivion's
>   oblivion,
> but someone in the wretchedness of
>   some empty night,
> without his knowledge, without my
>   knowing, someone still unborn
> will with my words speak the sorrows
>   of his night.

But then there is so much more to desire, isn't there?

L.A. Nocturne: The Angels

for Agustin J. Fink

by

Xavier Villaurrutia

Translated by Eliot Weinberger

You might say the streets flow sweetly through the night.
The lights are dim so the secret will be kept,
the secret known by the men who come and go,
for they're all in on the secret
and why break it up in a thousand pieces
when it's so sweet to hold it close,
and share it only with the one chosen person.

If, at a given moment, everyone would say
with one word what he is thinking
the six letters of DESIRE would form an enormous luminous scar,
a constellation more ancient, more dazzling than any other.
And that constellation would be like a burning sex
in the deep body of night,
like the Gemini, for the first time in their lives,
looking each other in the eyes and embracing forever.

Suddenly the river of the street is filled with thirsty creatures;
they walk, they pause, they move on.
They exchange glances, they dare to smile,
they form unpredictable couples . . .

There are nooks and benches in the shadows,
riverbanks of dense indefinable shapes,
sudden empty spaces of blinding light
and doors that open at the slightest touch.

For a moment, the river of the street is deserted.
Then it seems to replenish itself,
eager to start again.
It is a paralyzed, mute, gasping moment,
like a heart between two spasms.

But a new throbbing, a new pulsebeat
launches new thirsty creatures on the river of the street.
They cross, crisscross, fly up.
They glide along the ground.
They swim standing up, so miraculously
no one would ever say they're not really walking.

They are angels.
They have come down to earth
on invisible ladders.
They come from the sea that is the mirror of the sky
on ships of smoke and shadow,
they come to fuse and be confused with men,
to surrender their foreheads to the thighs of women,
to let other hands anxiously touch their bodies
and let other bodies search for their bodies till they're found,
like the closing lips of a single mouth,
they come to exhaust their mouths, so long inactive,
to set free their tongues of fire,
to sing the songs, to swear, to say all the bad words
in which men have concentrated the ancient mysteries
of flesh, blood and desire.

They have assumed names that are divinely simple.
They call themselves *Dick* or *John*, *Marvin* or *Louis*.
Only by their beauty are they distinguishable from men.
They walk, they pause, they move on.
They exchange glances, they dare to smile.
They form unpredictable couples.

They smile maliciously going up in the elevators of hotels,
where leisurely vertical flight is still practiced.
There are celestial marks on their naked bodies:
blue signs, blue stars and letters.
They let themselves fall into beds, they sink into pillows
that make them think they're still in the clouds.
But they close their eyes to surrender to the pleasures of their
mysterious incarnation,
and when they sleep, they dream not of angels but of men.

THE WICKER MAN

By Steven Katz

The best horror movies are always, like found footage, sui generis: one-of-a-kind, never-before-seen, disorienting. Sequels are never scary. Neither are big-budget Hollywood frightfests whose production values insulate the viewer from the chill experience of the uncanny, as well as from the sneaking suspicion that what you're seeing is taboo. Because, like snuff films and Hitler's home movies, what you are seeing is real. The scariest movies are documentaries.

The Wicker Man (1973), British TV director Robin Hardy's sole feature, begins as a documentary: thanking a certain Lord Summerisle (played in the movie by *Dracula* veteran Christopher Lee) for his cooperation in the production of the film. Summerisle is the ruler of a mysterious island located somewhere between Scotland and the North Pole, which, because it lies on the Gulf Stream, is endowed with a tropical climate (all hogwash, the invention of the film's screenwriter, Anthony Shaffer, who also wrote *Sleuth*). It also falls under the jurisdiction of the priggish West Highland's constable Neil Howie (*Breaker Morant*'s Edward Woodward) so that when Howie receives an anonymous letter hinting that a Summerisle girl may have been the victim of foul play, he's forced to investigate.

Police investigations have become a staple of spooky movies lately, but the thing that makes this one so singular is that it evolves into a kind of oddball journey into the dark heart of Howie's stiff-necked Christianity. Summerisle, it turns out, is peopled with pagans who have turned their backs on Christian values and embraced that mishmash of witchcraft, nature worship, and free love that optimistic hippie chicks call "wicca." Borrowing freely from the Bible and *The Golden Bough* the film chronicles the temptation of Sergeant Howie against a mythological backdrop of seasonal rebirth. In the 1970s, this may very well have been seen as an examination of the Establishment's resistance to the lures of the counterculture. But as Howie and countless flower children learned to their regret, the gods you worship by screwing your brains out in the furze demand steep sacrifices. The film ends with their bloody appeasement—unless you believe Howie's final rant about pagan doom and Christian rebirth, as I do—in an epic May Day ritual of stomach-turning strangeness.

To be honest, this is a movie you'll either love or hate. The characters are flat, the writing and the direction lack tension, the hymns and rites are risible, and finally it isn't all that scary. A decision having been made that a pagan community is, outwardly, not dissimilar from a Christian one, a lot of the movie is of the shifty-sod-in-a-rural-English-pub variety beloved of 1960s English television.

Still, there are scenes of extraordinary weirdness: the apothecary popping the frog into the little girl's mouth to cure her sore throat, or the innkeeper's daughter (Britt Ekland, voice-dubbed and butt-doubled) de-virginizing a seventeen-year-old boy (a scene omitted from the eighty-seven-minute U.S. version, as is an important prologue examining Howie's devoutness; better to see the 101-minute U.K. version). And of course there's the wicker man of the title (if you've read Caesar's history of the Gallic Wars, you'll know what the Druids used them for): an image that both the directors of *The Blair Witch Project* and the organizers of the annual Burning Man performance festival have claimed as an inspiration.

At its worst, *The Wicker Man* feels like a stale episode of *The Avengers*. Yet at its best, it has some of the power of, say, *A Midsummer Night's Dream*, where the saccharine imagery of the English fairy tale becomes haunted.

Betty MacDonald's *The Egg and I*

By Mark Caldwell

The Egg and I is one of those phrases that shows up on the edge of the American cultural radar, but only fuzzily. Almost everyone's heard the title, but almost nobody under sixty can track it back to its origin, the 1945 bestseller by Betty MacDonald (1908-58), a Seattle writer who is now nearly—and undeservedly—forgotten. Her first and best known (though not necessarily her best) book, it's an account of four years on a godforsaken chicken farm in the Olympic mountains. MacDonald described it as "a sort of rebuttal to all the recent successful I-love-life books by female good sports whose husbands had forced them to live in the country without lights or running water." Its huge success led, in 1947, to a so-so Fred MacMurray and Claudette Colbert movie (two of its supporting characters, played by Marjorie Main and Percy Kil-

MacDonald, though very much an original, recalls Raymond Chandler in her blend of noir, slapstick, verbal resourcefulness, hard-edged lyricism, and a distinctive, almost violent mordancy.

bride, later appeared in Universal's low-rent, high-profit Ma and Pa Kettle series). But the pedestrian predictability both of the movie *Egg* and its even broader pre-*Green Acres* spinoffs is a far cry from MacDonald—whose work, mercilessly observed and subversively funny, recalls the zestful anarchy of thirties screwball rather than the comfy, white-knuckled harmlessness characteristic of so much post-World War II comedy. Indeed, read today, her writing still feels fresh and completely undated—eerily postmodern in its dark-tinged edginess and its cheerful assault on all smug convention.

MacDonald's later books, though not so well remembered as *The Egg and I*, are at least as remarkable. *The Plague and I* (1948) describes a harrowing year in a Dickensian Pacific Northwest tuberculosis sanatorium in the early thirties. All things considered, *Anybody Can Do Anything* (1950) is probably her strongest book, chronicling her life as a divorced woman in Seattle during the Depression, scrounging for jobs and a normal social life while trying to bring up two toddlers. (It contains perhaps her best single piece—an unforgettable riff on Depression Christmases, "Let Nothing You Dismay," which involves a desperate truck-company ad campaign, a female stalker in a fur coat, and a series of obscene letters.) Her last volume, *Onions in the Stew* (1954), evokes her life on Puget Sound's Vashon Island from the closing years of World War II through the early fifties.

MacDonald, though very much an original, recalls Raymond Chandler in her blend of noir, slapstick, verbal resourcefulness, hard-edged lyricism, and a distinctive, almost violent mordancy. To that she adds a knack for acid-etched character portraits, and a rare ability to convey emotion without sentimentality. In genre, I suppose she belongs among the great 30s and 40s American humorists like Thurber, Benchley, Parker, Perelman. But next to her work, theirs sometimes comes off as brittle and self-conscious in its urbanity. MacDonald's books are, by contrast, wholly authentic, animated by her implacable eye for the nasty disguised as the cornball, and by a shrewd seriousness about real problems—death, disease, poverty, the power of human bungling to turn life into a serious ethical morass.

I'm not sure why MacDonald vanished from the American literary map—probably her premature death from ovarian cancer in 1958 and her identification with the Pacific Northwest, which in the fifties isolated her from the New York-based writers and critics who might have kept her reputation alive after her death, *à la* Gore Vidal's resuscitation of Dawn Powell. MacDonald has always had a following of sorts. She wrote a classic children's series, the Mrs. Piggle-Wiggle stories, and they've sold steadily since their first appearance. Her adult works, though much less visible, occasionally surface in academic reading bibliographies, and after years of unavailability are all now back in print in the United States. You can even visit the Betty MacDonald Farm—the Vashon Island house where she wrote in the forties and fifties, and which has been turned into a bed-and-breakfast and a place of pilgrimage.

But she'd be better served by gaining the prominence she deserves in anthologies and American Lit reading lists. And readers would be served better yet if they could find her there.

FAMOUS MONSTERS OF FILMLAND

By Ron Carlson

The first inklings of self, of who I might actually be separate from my fine mother and father and my fine classmates and friends, stirred for me in 1959, when my father finished the basement in our first house on the west side of Salt Lake City, and I began sleeping down there in my room. He also finished the "den," which was the room in which we had a television, and where on Friday nights when I was ten and then eleven, I could watch Shock Theater, the late-night series of horror movies hosted by Roderick and

I ordered a necklace from Captain Company for my wife. It was a little Lucite coffin filled with dirt from the site of Dracula's castle in Transylvania.

his able assistant, Igor. I see now that in the fifth grade I was essentially a bachelor with cable. I started a Monster Club, and weekly we'd sleep over at the home of one of its members: Darryl Perry, Johnny Eugster, Brent Griffith, and me. It was in that group that I saw my first copy of a magazine that spoke directly to my secret heart: *Famous Monsters of Filmland.* A pulp magazine edited by the worst punster in the Western world, Forrest J. Ackerman (known as Forry or The Ackermonster), the journal carried thrilling black-and-white photos from the classic horror films: *Frankenstein*, every sequel; *Dracula*, every sequel; *The Wolf Man*, every sequel; *King Kong*; *Son of Kong*; *Mighty Joe Young*; *The Invisible Man*; *The Mummy*; et cetera, every sequel and every combination. The photographs that dominated every page were accompanied by broad synopses of the films, pun-ctuated by Ackerman's corny wordplay. Some of the text was black and white pages and some was white on black pages. In the back of every magazine was all the good monster stuff you could order from Captain Company: fake blood, masks, scary and not-so-scary this and thats. The magazine carried no outside advertising.

Spurred by this publication and by the films we were seeing Friday nights and at the matinees: *Tarzan* (and all the sequels), *It Came from Beneath the Sea, 20 Million Miles to Earth*, and so on, I started writing short skits, which the benevolent Mrs. Thornton would let our club perform in her classroom. When I think of her interrupting geography to tell the class, "Now we're going to watch another of Ronnie's little stories," I am reminded again of why I have become a tolerant and encouraging teacher. The skits were generally about Tarzan meeting Dracula, or Frankenstein and the Invisible Man fleeing the Blob. We used the whole classroom, including the nifty coat closets.

After I'd been married a few years and could really judge how appropriate it would be, I ordered a necklace from Captain Company for my wife. It was a little Lucite coffin filled with dirt from the site of Dracula's castle in Transylvania; the thing came with a certificate of authenticity. Twenty-five years later, she still has it.

While I was writing my first novel, I took the opportunity to go to New York and interview the new publisher of *Famous Monsters of Filmland*. This was 1975, and the piece was probably my first national publication when it appeared in the *Village Voice* that fall.

It was a good article, tracking Jim Warren's career as publisher, and it included bits on each of the sister magazines: *Creepy*, *Eerie*, and *Vampirella*. I also toured the aisles of Captain Company and saw the fake blood, masks, and the rest. The article ended: "...and I took the elevator to the street and hailed a cab, still burning with that ardor, that torchfire, that sympathy for the monster we all know as youth." I mean, this was writing.

The week it appeared Elaine and I had to be in New York, so we took the train in one night, which was a big deal. We're from Utah, you know, and those years it was one big deal after another. At the corner of Grand Central, under the extended roof, a newsdealer had his magazines arranged in stacks, and I saw the *Village Voice* with my article in it. It was easy that glowing night to imagine the magazine on every corner of the island uptown and down, and this is true: I spoke to the man. I told him I had an article in that issue. He came forward in his apron, his smile emerging, as if to welcome me into the world of this mysterious city and the many writers who worked here.

"You do?" he said. I said, yes, I did. And what he said next may as well have been: welcome to the world of writers. He said, "Well, listen, why don't you buy the whole fucking stack?"

We didn't, but we bought one, and Elaine took this writer's arm and we walked over toward Fifth.

Famous Monsters of Filmland was lost, but after a hiatus of several years it is being published again. The editor is Ray Ferry, and he's not afraid of puns, but how the film synopses (of *The Mummy*, *The Invisible Man*, et cetera) are not riddled with them. Some of the text is black on white pages and some is white on black pages. Captain Company ads fill the back. The Web address is: www.famousmonsters.com.

Famous Monsters of Filmland

was lost, but after a hiatus of several years it is being published again. The editor is Ray Ferry, and he's not afraid of puns.

Sympathy for the Devil

Scripts written, locations scouted, money squandered: is the ghost of Stalin working overtime to prevent the 1930s Russian novel *The Master and Margarita* from coming to the screen?

By Mia Taylor

"'And what will come of it?' you ask. I don't know. In all probability you will put it away in the writing desk or the cupboard where the corpses of my plays lie, and from time to time you will remember. However, we cannot know our future."

—MIKHAIL BULGAKOV, IN A LETTER TO HIS WIFE

What do Federico Fellini, Roman Polanski, and Ray Manzarek have in common? They have all tried and failed to bring *The Master and Margarita*, one of the greatest Russian novels of the twentieth century, to the screen.

First published in 1967, twenty-seven years after the death of its author, Mikhail Bulgakov, *The Master and Margarita* filled a void in Eastern Europe and Russia, where it was instantly and passionately embraced. In Russia there is a joke that seven out of ten people today will tell you it's their favorite book. Travel agencies offer walking tours of *The Master and Margarita*'s Moscow, and the walls of the building Bulgakov lived in are scrawled with loving graffiti tributes to the novelist and his immortal characters. Phrases from the book have entered the common vernacular.

Joseph Stalin

THE CAST:

Mikhail Bulgakov: (1891–1940) Russian novelist, author of *The Master and Margarita.*

András Hamori: Hungarian-born producer of *Crash, The Sweet Hereafter, Sunshine.*

Michael Lang: Founder and promoter of the Woodstock rock festival, film producer.

Menno Meyjes: Dutch-born screenwriter of *Empire of the Sun, The Color Purple,* and the upcoming film *Lindbergh,* all for Steven Spielberg.

Roman Polanski: Polish-born director of *Rosemary's Baby, Chinatown,* and *The Ninth Gate.* In the early eighties, wrote an adaptation of *The Master and Margarita* with John Brownjohn (*The Ninth Gate*) for Warner Brothers.

Ray Manzarek: Keyboard player for the Doors. Attended UCLA film school before forming the Doors. Recently directed his first feature, *Love Her Madly,* a thriller shot on digital media.

Peter Medak: Hungarian-born director of *The Ruling Class* and *The Krays.*

Ellendea Proffer: Owner/founder Ardis books, Bulgakov biographer and translator.

Mikhail Bulgakov, 1926

To readers in the West, even those unfamiliar with the political subtext, it is a magical, fantastic tale, a bold retelling of Faust and the Bible. With its vivid, feverish, and hallucinatory descriptions—from a huge talking black cat stalking the Moscow streets on its hind legs and bloodcurdling beheadings to the climactic grand demonic ball attended by history's greatest villains—what filmmaker could resist the temptation to make it his own?

It's a stifling spring evening in a Moscow park when the devil, in the guise of a mysterious foreigner named Professor Woland, materializes before two writers debating the existence of Jesus Christ. Woland asserts that Jesus did indeed exist and evokes an eerily vivid picture of Christ's first meeting with Pontius Pilate in Jerusalem. He then prophesies the death of one writer by decapitation, which occurs moments later. Soon Woland and his retinue, including the impudent talking cat, and a seven-foot-tall "choirmaster" wearing a cracked pince-nez, are living in the dead writer's apartment and wreaking havoc throughout Moscow, preying on the greed, pettiness, unbelief, and cowardice of the Muscovites, driving some victims to seek incarceration in the local mental institution. One longtime resident of the institution is the Master, a writer crushed by persecution in reaction to his life's work, a book on Pontius Pilate, a book that bears an uncanny resemblance to the devil's narrative. He tells another inmate the story of his love for his Margarita, whose devotion to him and his art could not save him. Margarita has searched for him in vain since his disappearance. When the devil asks Margarita to act as hostess for his annual ball, her love is so boundless that she is willing to forfeit her soul for the mere chance of saving the Master. Margarita is queen of the ball, the perfect hostess, spending one long night, naked, greeting a seemingly endless procession of ghoulish guests disgorged from hell. In gratitude, Woland reunites her with the Master. The Master himself must first complete his novel, and suffer the fate of Pilate himself, before being granted eternal peace with his Margarita.

Rights have been bought, scripts written, rights lapsed, money squandered, locations scouted. Obscure adaptations have even been made, ones that seem impossible to track down. But something seems inevitably to bedevil these efforts. Thirty-three years after the book's publication, the definitive film has yet to be made.

Among the idealistic youth who read the book in the late sixties and early seventies were some who grew up to be filmmakers, and some of those were cultural icons of their own generations, like Fellini, Polanski, and Manzarek

Among the idealistic youth who read the book in the late sixties and early seventies were some who grew up to be filmmakers, and some of those were cultural icons of their own generations, like Fellini, Polanski, and Manzarek (Though Manzerek earned his renown as the keyboard player for The Doors, not as a filmmaker). What is it that captivates them? What drives them to cling so tenaciously

Kremlin Tower and Gate

to an apparently cursed project? What hubris pushes them to attempt the adaptation of such a complex and elusive work? What has prevented their efforts from reaching fruition? Has the time passed for this film? Is it too late? And what would Bulgakov, the master satirist and also a brilliant adapter, make of the movie people and what they want to do to his book?

Mikhail Bulgakov was no stranger to heartbreak and crushing disappointment. He lived through one of his country's darkest eras, and his courage and tragic history became part of the novel's myth. Like Pasternak, Mandelstam, Babel, and Akhmatova, he wrote in the shadow of Stalinism and indeed developed a perverse kind of relationship with the general secretary himself. Compared to many of his contemporaries, he was lucky. He was not imprisoned, exiled or executed, but he was silenced.

Paradoxically, through sheer will, tenacity, and faith, he was able to overcome poverty, illness, oppression, and constant fear, and maintain the playfulness, buoyancy, and dazzling imagination of his writing. Bulgakov, his voice stifled, his works "corpses," a prisoner in his own country, toiled in secret for eleven years on his masterpiece, knowing he would never see it published.

Starkly modern and fresh even now, in 1967 *The Master and Margarita* was a radical work, both politically and artistically. A dangerous book, it said the unsayable. It expressed thrilling, forbidden ideas and emotions, satirizing Soviet ideology, glorifying individual love and portraying a living Jesus when collective love and atheism were creeds, rejecting socialist realism and unapologetically embracing the supernatural, the irrational, the divine.

In the West where it was published simultaneously by the YMCA Press in Paris, it became a cult classic. The Vintage imprint consistently sells ten thousand copies a year.

To make a film is never simple. The development process can seem like a labyrinth without exit, financing has to be fought for tooth and nail, egos clash, and scripts are carted to the recycler by the truckload daily, but even by these standards, the unmade film of *The Master and Margarita* has a particularly snarled history. Some filmmakers have come tantalizingly close to their goal, even reaching the first day of principal photography, only to have the prize cruelly ripped from their grasp.

As Woland says to the Master, "Your novel has some surprises in store for you."

Andras Hamori: "I went to a Russian high school in Budapest in the late sixties. We had a very rebellious Russian teacher who instead of Gorky and Kataev taught us Russian from *The Master and Margarita.* It was a subversive cultural icon of the late sixties. It broke taboos. When I left Hungary for good in '81, I smuggled out *The Master and Margarita* as a cultural asset. I guess the first reason I thought of making it into a movie was I believed this was a hidden masterpiece of the twentieth century, unknown in the West."

Michael Lang: "Someone gave me the book about fifteen or sixteen years ago. I always thought it would be an amazing film."

Menno Meyjes: "It was a much talked about novel in the late seventies. One reason was the Stones song "Sympathy for the Devil." That's sort of how it entered the cultural stream. Abel Ferrara (director of *Bad Lieutenant*, *King of New York*, and *The Funeral*) and I were in the very early stages of our careers. We had both read this book, were fascinated by it, and decided to give it a shot."

Roman Polanski: "In Poland it's a cult book. We were much more sensitive to all that Soviet absurdity and surrealism. I was looking for material in the late eighties, and I thought of *The Master and Margarita.* The desire to make a movie comes from what you would like to see, and at that time, that was what I wanted to see on the screen. I have a very good relationship with Warner Brothers. When I mentioned the book, the development department got very excited. They knew and loved it. They said yes, definitely, let's do that."

Ray Manzarek: "I first read the book ten or fifteen years ago. I didn't necessarily think, I've got to make this into a movie. I thought, how incredibly cinematic this book is. Then I got together with the screenwriter Rick Valentine,

BULGAKOV BEGAN WORK ON *THE MASTER AND MARGARITA* IN THE SPRING OF 1929, AND ALTHOUGH HE LATER BURNED THE FIRST MANUSCRIPT, HE CONTINUED WORK ON THE NOVEL INTERMITTENTLY UP UNTIL THE END OF HIS LIFE.

who said he was working on a script, and I said, "Impossible! I love it, man, but it's impossible!" Then I read his script—a work of genius! I said, 'Okay, man, let's see if we can sell this baby, let's get it up on the screen.'"

Peter Medak: "I read it in the late sixties and thought it was amazing, but I never thought it could actually make a film. It's very difficult to translate into filmic terms, and there were so many special effects needed. I completely forgot about it until Ray Manzarek got hold of me."

Bulgakov's first career was as a physician, but after serving in the civil war as a doctor to the White army, he erased his past and reinvented himself as a writer. His first success was as a playwright, but not without cost. From the very beginning, he was plagued by censorship, and denounced from the pulpit of political correctness.

In May 1926, Bulgakov's apartment was searched by the OGPU (precursor to the NKVD and KGB), and his diaries and the manuscript of the novel Heart of a Dog *were confiscated. After repeated protests, they were returned to him. He burned the diaries, and never again kept another. Ironically, it was the OGPU that preserved the diaries for posterity, as they had made copies.*

By 1929, all of Bulgakov's works had been banned. He compared his situation to "being buried alive."

Bulgakov began work on The Master and Margarita *in the spring of 1929, and although he later burned the first manuscript, he continued work on the novel intermittently up until the end of his life.*

Hamori: "I guess this project has been circling me for the last twenty years. I went to Moscow because I really liked the Russian director, Elem Klimov, the director of *Come and See*, who in the late eighties had backing from Columbia Pictures and David Putnam for his *Master and Margarita* project.

I thought it should be a Russian director. Plus, economically, it sounded like a great deal, because it was still the cheap ruble Soviet Union. Even if the special effects cost a lot, the location shoot was inexpensive. So I went to Moscow and got drunk with Klimov. He wanted about seven to eight million, but he didn't have a script. He said we have to make a deal without a script, without a cast, without anything. So we never made a deal. Maybe I should have done it, because at that time you could have gotten someone like a Daniel Day Lewis to work with Klimov, because it was romantic to work with a Soviet director, especially on a novel like this. But I really didn't like Klimov. I felt his reasons were more mercantile than artistic.

Then I heard that Roman Polanski wanted to make it. Roman is one of my idols. His script came the closest, but it wasn't entirely there.

One day I was sitting in my office on Sunset Boulevard, and Ray Manzarek came in. He had heard from Peter Medak that I'm crazy about *The Master and Margarita*. He said he owned a script of it, and would I like to read it. I said great, and he put the script on my desk and left. A half an hour later my secretary came and said, this man is outside waiting for you, and I said, which man, and she said, well, the man who was here earlier. I went out, and Manzarek was sitting on the terrace. He said, have you read it yet? And I said, no. He said, well, then, I'll just wait. I eventually read the first twenty pages and it

Stalin

sounded so amateur that I never followed up. And then he hated me.

Since then, I've read that it's going into production with this director, or that producer, but none of it ever happened. Later I heard that this guy in New York, Michael Lang, owned the rights. His partner, Ira Deutschman actually brought it to me, when I was running Alliance Pictures. They said they have Polanski attached, so I called Roman, and he said, I used to want to do it, but I don't know anymore. So the whole thing disappeared, but never completely."

Josef Stalin himself, at key junctures, intervened in Bulgakov's affairs and decided his fate. A word from Stalin got his plays banned. A phone call revived his career. But it also left him waiting the rest of his life for the other shoe to drop.

In 1929, Bulgakov, in despair, took the enormous risk of addressing a frank letter to Stalin himself.

"At the end of this tenth year my strength is broken. Since I no longer have the strength to survive, since I am persecuted and know that it is impossible that I shall ever be published or staged within the USSR again . . . EXPEL ME FROM THE USSR TOGETHER WITH MY WIFE."

July 29, 1929—letter to Stalin, Kalinin, Svidersky, and Gorky

He received no reply to this letter, and in May 1930, tried again.

"It is not only my past works that have perished, but also my present and my future works. And I personally, with my own hands, threw into the stove a draft of a novel about the devil . . . All my things are past rescuing.

"Not being allowed to write is tantamount to being buried alive." If they would not allow him to leave the country, he requested some kind of job to keep himself alive.

"This letter did receive a reply, in the form of a phone call from the General Secretary himself, one that would haunt Bulgakov for the rest of his life."

The novel's film rights have been in constant question. In most cases, a limited option, a percentage of the final purchase price, is paid to the owner of the copyright. The purchaser must make the film before his option expires. If the film is made, the remainder of the purchase price is paid to the owner of the copyright. If the film is not made, the film rights then revert to the owner, who is then free to option them to another party.

Ellendea Proffer: Owner/founder Ardis books, Bulgakov biographer and translator: "We get inquiries about film rights as often as once a month, and it's not that easy to find us since we moved from Ann Arbor."

Lang: "It was assumed to be in public domain, but I was never comfortable with that, and I was doing a project at the Kremlin, where I met Bulgakov's grandson. I made a deal with him for the rights. You need a translation to prepare the screenplay from, so we bought the rights to the Ardis translation, which is the best I've read."

When Russia joined the Berne convention on international copyright in 1993, it officially restored the rights to Bulgakov's heirs. He left all his copyrights to his "Margarita," his third wife, Yelena Sergeevna Bulgakova. They had no children together, but Yelena had two sons with her first husband, Evgeny Shilovsky, and it is to these descendants that the copyrights reverted.

The grandchildrens' Paris attorney, Andrè Schmidt, maintains that since only a censored version was published in the Soviet Union in 1967, and the full text only in Paris the same year, the book has been covered by the Berne convention since its original publication, France being a member. It is the Shilovskys' contention that the copyright has always belonged to them.

Further complicating matters, according to Ellendea Proffer, is that under the Uruguay Round convention of '93, if a translation was completed before that time it doesn't fall under Uruguay and therefore is not subject to the family. There are documents proving the Ardis translation was completed by '93.

Proffer: "There are three major translations, Mirra Ginsburg's (Grove Press, 1967) which is incomplete, as it works from the censored version, Michael Glenny's (Harper & Row, 1967) which is not reliable, and our Ardis edition, published in 1995, (Diana Burgin and Katherine O'Connor, with annotations and afterword by Ellendea Proffer)."

A filmmaker has to attach himself to one of these translations. They've all been attached at various times.

Manzarek: "We have a private translation. I have a Russian friend who translated the whole damn novel. We based the script on his translation."

Bulgakov was awoken from a nap. When he was told the General Secretary wished to speak with him, he assumed at first that someone was playing a prank. But it was indeed Stalin on the other end. Stalin first asked Bulgakov if he really wished to go abroad. Bulgakov's entire future rested in his answer. He said, "I have thought a great deal recently about the question of whether a Russian writer can live outside his homeland. And it seems to me he can't."

Stalin then promised him a position at the Moscow Arts Theatre.

Finally, Stalin said that he would like to meet with Bulgakov at some point and have a conversation. Bulgakov was excited at the prospect, and waited years for the invitation, which never came.

May 30, 1931, Bulgakov once again wrote to Stalin.

"I want to tell you, Iosif Vissarionovich, that my dream as a writer would be to be summoned to see you in person . . . because your conversation with me over the telephone in April 1930 left a deep mark in my memory."

There was no reply. Later that year, he wrote to his friend, the writer Vikenty Vereseyav.

"I suffer from one tormenting unhappiness. And that is that my conversation with the General Secretary never took place. What

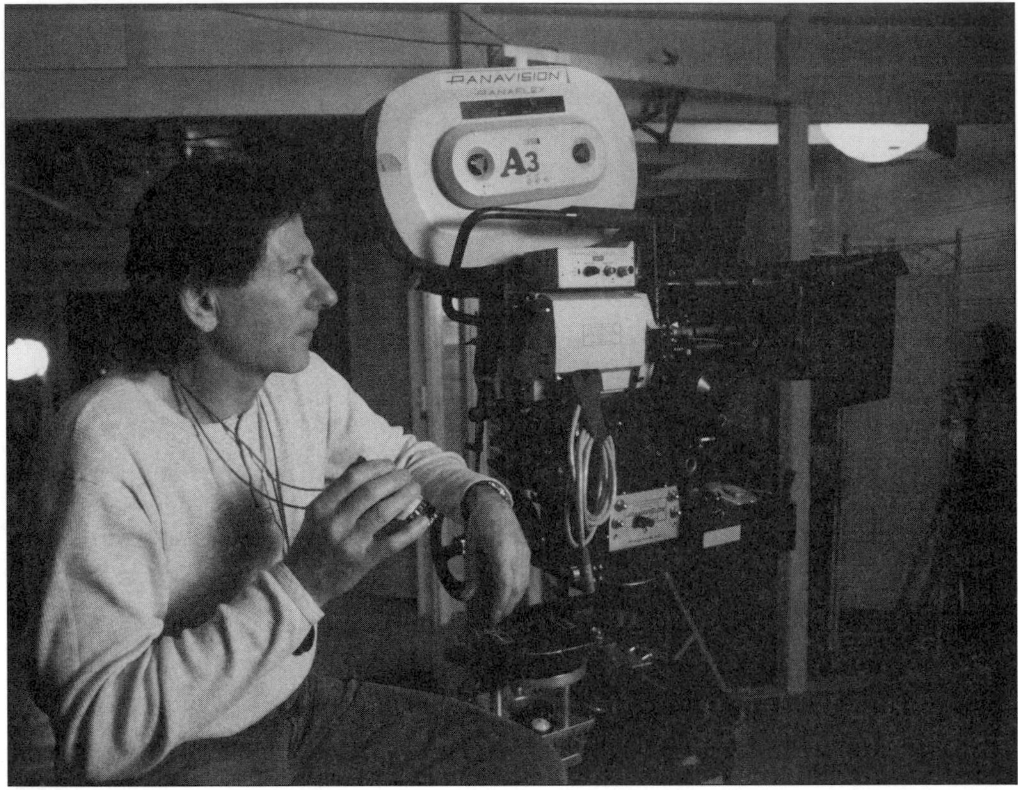

Roman Polanski

that means for me: horror, and the darkness of the grave. I have a frantic desire to see other countries, if only briefly. I get out of bed with this thought every morning and I go to sleep with it.

"For a year I have been racking my brains, trying to work out what happened. After all, I wasn't hallucinating, was I, when I heard his words? After all, he did utter the phrase 'Perhaps you really do need to go abroad . . .' ?"

"Hope flared up in this writer's heart: only one step remained—that I should see him and discover my fate.

"But then a thick veil descended."

July 1, 1939—letter to writer Vikenty Veresayev.

Proffer: "This needs to be a film. All the elements are there . . . it is cinematic at its core, really visual. But there is the question of what genre this is. It is a love story, it's a mystery, it's supernatural, it has horror, and it's told in a defamiliarizing way. It has Jesus before the mythmaking. Sometimes the adaptations go too grotesque. An unerring blend is necessary. The supernatural must push against something. If the devil comes to a supernatural

Moscow, that's not funny. There is the horror and comedy of Soviet Russia, not just any period, but Russia during the Terror. It's about the 'suffering questions'. If there's a God, why is there evil?

Friends in Moscow told me that Fellini wanted to make the film. *The Master and Margarita* came out in Italy in 68-69. He wanted to do it when he was in his surrealistic mode. But first he had to do another film. It was always on his back-burner. He would have had marvelous stage design, but back then you wouldn't have had the right special effects."

Polanski: "Special effects back then were not digital. They were done in a way that was quite expensive. The final result today would be much more effective, because you can digitally morph the cat into a man and vice versa. This would be just beautiful."

Polanski, in his adaptation with John Brownjohn, while mercilessly paring away the plot of Satan in Moscow, is faithful to Bulgakov's serious and electrifying retelling of the story of Pontius Pilate and the man Bulgakov calls Yeshua Ha-Notsri.

Polanski: "Passing from those three different plots, one to the other, in such a smooth way is very cinematic. It works beautifully in the literature, but I daresay would work even better on the screen.

"The greatest moment in the movie is right at the beginning when Woland (the devil) starts telling the story of Jesus Christ in such a manner that it becomes extremely human and moving."

The greatest moment in the movie is right at the beginning when Woland (the devil) starts telling the story of Jesus Christ in such a manner that it becomes extremely human and moving. The story of Pontius Pilate is non-pareil."

In Polanski and Brownjohn's script, the Master and Margarita are no longer adulterous lovers, but neighbors, with Margarita as a young music teacher.

"I did that to simplify, to get the emotions that bind those two people, so their separation would affect the viewer. You have to compensate for what is non-existent as a scene or scenes in the book. You have to develop the relationship where it doesn't exist.

"I THINK IT APPEALS TO ALL ARTISTS, THE IDEA THAT AT LEAST IN HEAVEN THEY UNDERSTAND YOUR WORK, AND NOT ONLY THAT, THEY INTERVENE ON YOUR BEHALF, AND SLAY ALL YOUR CRITICS."

A film script requires a rigid, economical construction. Already the way it is written, would be a film on the long side. And I feel sometimes scenes that seem evident don't change much in the overall piece. I don't think that Satan's ball, which is so prominent in the book, matters really for what Bulgakov is trying to tell. Sometimes the most popular pieces can be removed without hurting much. How much would Hamlet suffer without 'To be or not to be'? In fact it would not change a thing."

Michael Lang: "Polanski and I met in Paris and spent an afternoon together. Polanski is a very engaging guy, with strong ideas about the films he makes. I thought leaving out the ball was a mistake. It's such a great scene. He said Hamlet would have been Hamlet without 'To be or not to be,' and I said, but what do people remember?"

Polanski: "I thought of doing part of it in Poland and the rest in France, with some shots in Moscow. I went location scouting in Moscow, but there is nothing left from that period, with the exception of the Kremlin, and even the Kremlin changed a little bit. I felt it could have been done much better in a place like Krakow with some construction."

Meyjes: "Abel and I did a very traditional version. It begins: New York has never looked so much like Moscow. You have these somber buildings, there's drift snow in the street. A woman in a fur coat walks through the night, enters a small church, and puts a charred manuscript on the altar, prays, and leaves. The pages of the manuscript rustle on the altar, and the movie begins.

I always think of Margarita as an haute bourgeois. There has to be something very straight about her in the beginning. I think we had her as the wife of the Belgian cultural attaché.

Where the book works the best, is where it is jaunty and not too out-of-worldly. Like when Likhodeyev, the theatre director, wakes up with this horrendous hangover to find the devil and his retinue in his apartment, the cat drinking vodka and spearing mushrooms with a fork, and having this very playful conversation, before they kick him to Yalta.

Then you can have things like the Escher-like apartment that grows and grows, and it really works. And Woland is particularly compelling, a wonderfully realized character. He is a specifically Russian devil, not the Satan we're familiar with in the western world. He is a kind of louche angel with his own agenda, but who obviously answers to a higher court.

The Master is kind of a whiner, always wringing his hands. He's passive and Margarita takes care of everything. But in the end, the Master prevails. I think it appeals to all artists, the idea that at least in heaven they understand your work, and not only that, they intervene on your behalf, and slay all your critics."

Lang: "We're approaching it around the relationship between the Master and Margarita. Neither of them appear till way late in the book. We've brought that to the beginning, and made it the vehicle that takes you through the story. Moving it to present day New York is not the way to go. Too many people have fond feelings about the story, and it would be a big mistake to change it that much."

Hamori: "I would start the film with the Master and Margarita's story. It's probably the most beautiful love story of the twentieth Century. That is what makes it contemporary. People think, oh, nobody cares about 1930s Moscow. It's so remote. But you could have a love story that's 2000 years old and people want to see it.

That's the frame, not Pontius Pilate. You can then incorporate 1930s Moscow and the supernatural, and Pontius Pilate, and Jesus and so on."

Although faithful to the setting and period of the novel, Manzarek and Valentine's script takes perhaps the greatest liberties with the story. It also emphasizes the love story, and goes a step further in transforming the Master into a character named Mikhail, a version of Bulgakov himself. They have reverted the defamiliarized story of Yeshua Ha-Notsri and Pontius Pilate to the New Testament version of Jesus of Nazareth.

Manzarek: "It was as though Bulgakov was over Valentine's shoulder, saying, you can cut all of that. Go ahead, you can cut that too—no that's the essential, the Master, Margarita, the love affair. We need Jesus and Pontius Pilate, okay, but we don't need the betrayal of Jesus for a movie. Judas is not a character who enters into our equation. It's basically the biblical story of Jesus and Pontius Pilate, and the Master and Margarita, the things that go on with the Master and his novel, and Margarita with professor Woland, the magic show, and of course the devil's ball. All those highlights.

Bulgakov is the writer. He is the master. When Rick did it, I thought, what a great idea man, yes! The author himself of the book, of *The Master and Margarita*, is the Master, is the writer. Perfect.

We have two possible endings. One is, the book is then published in 1967. They've had the devil's ball in Moscow, and they're off to somewhere else. Now, where is professor Woland going to go with his little troupe? And he says, 'I know! Los Angeles, the Summer of Love' and the Cat goes 'Whoah! Rock and Roll! Los Angeles!' Cut to: a bookstore in Venice Beach, bunch of hippies milling around. One hippie pulls *The Master and Margarita* off the bookshelf and says 'Hey, this looks groovy'. It ends with "Sympathy for the Devil," cause you hear 'Please allow me to introduce myself' and here they come, down the Venice Boardwalk, up to no good once again.

The second ending is actually the one I prefer. I like the hippie ending, but I think even better is the straight love story of the Master and Margarita, Margarita sacrificing everything for the Master, their love carrying them ultimately into the light.

Although Bulgakov himself would have liked the summer of love. He'd say, "Perfect, man! You had what in 1967, you called it the Summer of Love?' He would love the irony.

They say, what would the author think? The author would say, fine, entertain! I've written an extremely entertaining novel. You're going to put it on the screen, make it entertaining. Bulgakov himself would be more than happy."

Manzarek: "I talked to Mick Jagger about the possibility of him playing Professor Woland. Jerry Hall said to me, 'Don't make the movie until he's finished with the tour. It's his favorite book! The part is his! He is professor Woland.'

"We were talking to Julie Delpy, who wanted to play the role of Margarita. She's at William Morris, so we thought, gosh, let's see who else they have and package it over there. Bruce Willis would be very off the wall as Professor Woland. Peter Medak was going to direct. Peter wanted to do it. He would have been great."

Medak: "We were thinking about Uma Thurman. She loved the book. I remember sending the script to her. I never heard back."

Lang: "We've been talking to directors the last year or so. It's important to have someone who is familiar with the novel, who understands it. We talked to Polanski, and Milos Forman who also loves the story, but didn't have the time to work on the screenplay. He would have been perfect. We're in discussion right now with a director who I think would work out really well. I can't discuss him yet, because we're in the works."

Hamori: "I would cast Kate Moss as Natasha, the maid."

Bulgakov was a hypochondriac, preoccupied with his health but also the premonition that he would die young, as his father had. As a doctor he was acutely sensitive to physical symptoms.

He began to fall prey to phobias, agoraphobia, and a fear of being alone. By the end of his life, he who deemed himself a prisoner, and risked his life for the chance to see other countries, was afraid to leave his apartment.

"I began to suffer from ... the filthiest thing I have ever experienced in my life, a fear of solitude, or to be more precise a fear of being left on my own. It's so repellent that I would prefer to have a leg cut off!"

1934 July 11—to V. Veresayev

Proffer: "Imagine the kind of fear he had to block in order to create."

"A demon has taken hold of me. I suffocate in these little rooms, I have begun to scribble down all over again page after page of that novel I destroyed three years ago. Why? I don't know."

In the summer of 1935, Bulgakov finished the first complete draft of The Master and Margarita. *He gave occasional readings of it to a very select group of trusted friends. It is only within these circles that the existence of the novel was known until its publication in 1967. He never allowed the pages to leave his apartment.*

1937 saw one of the darkest years of Stalin's Terror, with the murder of Sergei Kirov and subsequent widespread arrests, trials and executions.

By 1937, feeling he was nearing the end of his life, Bulgakov started to concentrate on The Master and Margarita, *revising the 1936 draft from the beginning.*

"Having become convinced over the last few years of the fact that not a single line of mine will ever be printed or staged, I am trying to develop an attitude of indifference towards this fact...

"All the same, however much you might try to throttle yourself, it's difficult to stop seizing your pen. I am tormented by an obscure desire to settle my final accounts in literature.

"At the moment I am engaged in a job that is entirely senseless from the point of view of everyday life—I am doing a final revision of my novel."

March 11, 1939—letter to V. Veresayev

Proffer: "The grinding process of developing a movie is not unlike what Bulgakov went through mounting a play for the Moscow Arts Theatre, the drawn out process of rewrites, the revisions, the story meetings, disappointments ..."

Meyjes: "We set it in New York. Right there, you run into a huge amount of problems... so many things were untranslatable. It's very specific to a time and place: the Soviet Union and the petrified world after the NEP (New Economic Policy). What is the equivalent of the institutionalized atheism, which is the wall that the rubber ball bounces off of in the book? Here, you have a society that has

IN A WAY, THE NOVEL'S BIBLICAL PLOT LINE IS MORE IMMEDIATE THAN THE MOSCOW ONE, SINCE IT'S SOMETHING THEY ARE GIVEN BY TRANSMISSION FROM GENERATION TO GENERATION.

declared itself atheist and the devil comes to town. That's joke number one.

But then, you can't honestly start comparing, say, the Writers' Guild, (although some of us do, at times,) to the one described in the book. The only thing we felt that still played was this hunger for real estate. There's also the specter of Stalin, hovering. You can have your differences with America, but it certainly doesn't compare to the Soviet Union in the thirties."

Lang: "We met with Ray Manzarek a couple of years ago. His script didn't quite seem right. Polanski's was better, although I had problems with that as well."

Medak: "About seven years ago, Manzarek said he's got the whole thing set up and ready to go. All I have to do is say yes. And then I read the script and it was not good. It proved a very difficult piece to pull off, which doesn't mean that it shouldn't be made.

"Also I knew Roman was thinking of doing it. I know him as a friend, and I love his work, so if he was really going to do it, I wouldn't have seriously gotten involved, because it's an unwritten etiquette for directors who like each other."

Polanski: "It was quite expensive and complex, and I suspect Terry Semel, the head of Warner Brothers, did not read the book himself. He knew only what was reported to him. And when it came time for him to give the so-called green light, he must have read the script for the first time, because we had long talks, and he didn't believe the picture had commercial potential to justify the expense. Finally, it was dragging for long time, and I said, okay, let's forget it. I tried to set it up with some other companies, which I think was a mistake, because once the word goes around that the studio dropped the project, even if you asked them to, the word is out, and I could not put it together.

"My problem is I suspect it's no longer relevant. Today, I am flabbergasted when I talk to young people in Poland about things that ended only a decade ago, and they know nothing about it!

Grant you, in Poland, we didn't have seventy years of Soviet rule, but we had thirty or thirty-five, and previous generations were so much affected, I would say destroyed by it, that those youngsters should at least know that it was not always the way it is now. Now it is just a normal country, you go from Poland to Germany to Belgium, it seems the same. So if they don't know how it was in their own country, let alone Russia . . . and to youngsters in America it's pure abstraction. You would have to spend more time on motivating, making people understand why things are this way.

"In the eighties, newspapers were carrying articles about Russia—about changes, about Stalinism, about Marxism, about lack of freedom. There was still a cold war going on. Now it's history. It's another plot set in some virtually biblical time. In a way, the novel's biblical plot line is more immediate than the Moscow one, since it's something they are given by transmission from generation to generation. But Moscow? Stalin? They hardly know who Stalin was."

Manzarek: "Making it depends on bringing the right players together. It's very tough. It's a big budget film and it's not exactly the kind of thing studios want to see."

Lang: "I think it could reach a very broad audience. One of the problems it's had over the years is that studios have always looked at it as an art house film and it's too big to do as a low budget art movie. That's why it hasn't been made yet, other than the fact that nobody ever bothered to get the rights. It is a substantial budget. We have a lot of interest, much of it from overseas. We haven't gone to tie those ends up until the director is selected."

Meyjes: "I'm hell-bent on trying again, I've got it figured out this time"

Hamori: "I still would want to make it if I find the right director and the right script. Sometimes this takes ten years to put together. The only film director today who I would be very intrigued to see what he thinks, is Emir Kusturica."

Polanski: "I'm still very much attracted to this book, because it presents to me, as a director, the possibility of doing very exciting things in those two parts we talked of. One is the biblical stuff, and the other is special effects. These are very tempting. The old Moscow reality is very difficult to show, very difficult to understand."

Manzarek: "There's an Everest and it's called *The Master and Margarita.* It's a race and we'll see who the winner is. It'll be interesting, because on a psychic level, which is the script that deserves to be made? And which is the script that'll be the most faithful to the essence of Bulgakov? Of course, I think that is Ray Manzarek and Rick Valentine's script. I think I intrinsically understand what that man was getting at: the fun, the darkness, the joy, the cleverness, the whole thing."

Proffer: "All that's needed is the will. In my dealings with people who do movies, I've met some who've had success, but even they seem defeated. When it works, it's a sort of miracle, so they guard themselves against disappointments. To make this you need a lot of hope, confidence, verve. I think he's up there saying, it's about time, and I hope it's a good movie, but he was also the supreme realist, so I'm sure he won't be surprised if it isn't."

Bulgakov's final play, Batum, was about Stalin, written in honor of his sixtieth birthday. Bulgakov's contemporaries were perplexed at his accepting this commission. Some saw him as finally capitulating to the regime he had defied throughout his career, but for a writer who insisted on telling the truth, the assignment was a dangerous one.

In August 1939, on their way to Batum to do research, the Bulgakovs were abruptly called home. Stalin had spoken. He would not permit the play to be staged. Bulgakov feared this was the end, but the knock on the door never came. However, this latest disaster was a crushing blow to his health from which he never recovered

In September of 1939 Bulgakov began to go blind. He diagnosed the symptoms in himself of the nephritis that had killed his father.

In February of 1940, his condition dramatically worsened. Blind and with agonizing pain throughout his body, he continued to dictate changes to Yelena, adding the epilogue to the novel after the manuscript was bound. He believed that one should continue to work up until the last moment of consciousness.

Until two weeks before his death, he continued to dictate to Yelena, who sat on a pillow on the floor by his bed, copying out his revisions in a notebook. She wrote in her diary that she told him four days before he died,

"I promise you faithfully that I shall make a fair copy of the novel and deliver it to them. You shall be published!" He listened fairly lucidly and attentively and then said, "so that they know . . . so that they know."

On March 10, 1940 he died, as his father had, from nephrosclerosis, at the age of forty-eight, holding Yelena's hand.

The following day there was a telephone call from Stalin's office. "Is it true Comrade Bulgakov is dead?" they asked.

After keeping the manuscript hidden for twenty-seven years, Yelena was able to have it published in 1967, three years before her own death.

Proffer: "Bulgakov had some kind of hope, he had a belief in his future. It must have been so hard to write for generations you won't see."

As Woland says to the Master, "Your novel has some surprises in store for you." ☗

THE WALK OF SHAME

A Few Words From Inside the System

Long before Sammy Glick had been shot through my life like a bullet I had had Hollywood on my mind. I had wanted to go for all the usual reasons: I was anxious to investigate the persistent rumors that the "streets paved with gold" which the early Spanish explorers had hunted in vain, had suddenly appeared in the vicinity of Hollywood and Vine. I was half convinced that Southern California was really the modern Garden of Eden its press agents claimed it to be. And like all the other writers outside of Hollywood I had seen enough of its product to convince myself that I could do no worse.

—Budd Schulberg, *What Makes Sammy Run?*

As an adjective, the word "Hollywood" has long been pejorative and suggestive of something referred to as "the System." The System not only strangles talent but poisons the soul, a fact supported by rich webs of lore.

—Joan Didion, "I Can't Get That Monster Out of My Mind"

You either love Hollywood or you hate it. It's a question of age. It's a question of generation. It's practically a question of physiology. . . . You either love it or it fills you with horror from the moment you land, from your first step onto its streets.

—Blaise Cendras, *Hollywood, Mecca of the Movies*

The mere mention of Hollywood induces a condition in me like breakbone fever. It was a hideous and untenable place when I dwelt there, populated with few exceptions by Yahoos.

—S. J. Perelman in the *Paris Review*

At this point, Chandler admitted that he was frustrated by the Hollywood system telling a friend that once you find out how films are really made you'll be astonished that any of them can be good. Making a fine motion picture is achieved with immense difficulty: It's like painting *The Laughing Cavalier* in Macy's basement with [the janitor] mixing your colors.

—William F. Nolan, "Marlow's Mean Streets"

No single man with a serious literary reputation has made good there.

—F. Scott Fitzgerald, in a letter to Harold Ober

In earlier periods, American writers made a living on newspapers and magazines; in the 40s and 50s, they went into the academies. But in the late 20s and 30s they went to Hollywood ... Hollywood destroyed them, but it did wonders for the movies.

—Pauline Kael, "Raising Kane"

Sometimes I think if I do one more treatment of a screenplay, I'll lose whatever power I have as a writer.

—William Faulkner, quoted in David Minter, *William Faulkner: His Life and Work*

The Day of the Locust is Hollywood without glamour, without the slightest softening of the actual absurdity and cruelty implicit in a town—actually an industry—so geared to "success" that it automatically rides over anyone who falls under its wheels.

—Alfred Kazin, introduction to Nathanael West's *Day of the Locust*

If you have an idea for a script, don't put it down in writing and, as tempting as mailboxes can be, don't mail it to Hollywood, and above all don't give yourself any illusions, because even if your idea is brilliant, it's not worth the postage: It will be sent back to you without having been read.

—Blaise Cendras, *Hollywood, Mecca of the Movies*

It's hard not to sign a pact with the devil. People do it every day, especially in Hollywood.

—Anonymous author, sixties pulp novel *Swivel Hips*

From the earliest days of the motion picture industry (always in Hollywood referred to as "the Industry"), the screenwriter has been regarded at best as an anomalous necessity, at worst a curse to be borne .... It was as if the screenwriter lacked the kind of soul in which an idea might boil and ultimately send a thrill through the world, but could contribute what Mr. DeMille dismissed as a technical detail—the plot.

—John Gregory Dunne, *Monster*

I saw that the novel, which at my maturity was the strongest and supplest medium for conveying thought and emotion from one human being to another, was becoming subordinated to a mechanical and communal art that, whether in the hands of Hollywood merchants or Russian idealists, was capable of reflecting only the tritest thought, the most obvious emotion. There was a rankling indignity, that to me became almost an obsession, in seeing the power of the written word subordinated to another power, a more glittering, a grosser power.

—F. Scott Fitzgerald, "Pasting It Together"

These nonwriters think they can do what they want to a carefully constructed script and it won't turn into a piece of crap. They're wrong. But nobody tells them that.

—A. I. Bezzerides in Lee Server's "Thieves' Market," an interview with Bezzerides

Like all good Hollywood novelists, West saw the place as a symbol of whatever is most extravagant, spoiled, and uncontrolled in American life.

—Alfred Kazin, introduction to Nathanael West's *Day of the Locust*

They came in with big ideas, rebellion, divorce, revenge, honor. They offered atmosphere: It's sort of a red mood, it's kind of a gritty future, it's funny. Each idea represented a million adjustments to reconcile the difference between the writer's movie of his dreams, which would be the really immortal movie, that tour through the brilliant connections of his freely associating but always focused mind, and the studio's version of that dream, toward the production of which the writer conceded the banal necessity to tell a story.

—Michael Tolkin, *The Player*

It was like a game of pitch and catch; the producer pitches ideas, the writers catch them; passed balls are not allowed. Pitching is the important part of the creative process; writing is simply taking dictation, and the writer a highly paid stenographer.

—John Gregory Dunne, *Monster*

It looked like a quiet afternoon. Brimmer asked him why the producers didn't back the Anti-Nazi League.

"Because of you people," said Stahr. "It's your way of getting at the writers. In the long view you're wasting your time. Writers are children—even in normal times they can't keep their minds on their work."

"They're the farmers in this business," said Brimmer pleasantly. "They grow the grain but they're not in at the feast. Their feeling toward the producer is like the farmers' resentment of the city fellow."

F. Scott Fitzgerald, *The Last Tycoon*

A novel that has been accepted for publication, and has been edited for publication—and is in all other respects ready for publication—does not "fall through." That is one of the principal reasons I prefer my day job as a novelist to my occasional job as a screenwriter. I can count on the fingers of one hand the number of truly good novels I have read in manuscript that have not been published, but good screenplays don't get made into movies all the time.

—John Irving, *My Movie Business*

It's very easy for these executives—businessmen running an art—to begin to fancy that they are creative artists themselves, because they are indeed very much like the "artists" who work for them, because the "artists" who work for them are, or have become, businessmen. Those who aren't businessmen are the Hollywood unreliables—the ones whom, it is always explained to you, the studies can't hire, because they're crazy.

—Pauline Kael, "Raising Kane"

Although he had little success in his first attempts to make a living in the "story factory," he (Nathanael West) eventually reconciled himself to the artificiality and sensationalism required of him.

—Alfred Kazin, introduction to Nathanael West's *Day of the Locust*

When I feel like being a director, I write a novel.

—John Irving, *My Movie Business*

Even in his relatively short time as a wage earner in Hollywood, he had seen the system so corrupt novelists of great promise that their new books, if they wrote them at all, were little better than potboilers, scarcely recognizable as the work of the same authors. There were even writers who became so habituated to turning out pages only when the first check was in their hot, greedy hands that they could never again write on speculation. "Whores," Bill said of them.

—Meta Carpenter Wilde and Orin Borsten, *A Loving Gentleman*

If my books had been any worse, I should not have been invited to Hollywood, and if they had been any better, I should not have come.

—Raymond Chandler, in a letter to Charles W. Norton

Prevailing Industry wisdom is that the more writers there are on a script, the better that script will be.

—John Gregory Dunne, *Monster*

"What are you writing?"

"Heaven help me, I am writing about a Boy Scout—The Boy Scout."

"Is it Stahr's idea?"

"I don't know—he told me to look into it. He may have ten writers working ahead of me or behind me, a system which he so thoughtfully invented."

—F. Scott Fitzgerald, *The Last Tycoon*

They had been so smart, so gifted, and yet they hadn't been able to beat Hollywood's contempt for the writer . . . They lived in the city where Thalberg was enshrined. Thalberg, the saint of M-G-M, had rationalized Mayer's system of putting teams of writers simultaneously and in relays on the same project. It had been lunatic before, but Thalberg made it seem mature and responsible to fit writers into an assembly-line method.

—Pauline Kael, "Raising Kane"

Even with a million-dollar payoff, one should never bet against writers being replaced; a fresh face is comforting to a studio, and management takes a perverse pride in high story costs.

—John Gregory Dunne, *Monster*

Some tried to condense their ideas to twenty-five words, in and out, as they'd learned in some screenwriting class taught by someone who'd made a science of yesterday's formula. They'd talk about the "arc of the story." They'd use little code words and phrases like paradigm and first-act bump. They were exact. "At minute twenty-three she finds out . . ." What does she find out? That this movie won't get made.

—Michael Tolkin, *The Player*

If I had learned anything at all from Hollywood, it was that nothing was to be counted on until it happened. I had seen too many actors replaced at the last moment, too many writers with empty hands on the day that contracts were to be signed for movie rights to their books.

—Meta Carpenter Wilde and Orin Borsten, *A Loving Gentleman*

Jack Warner thought you had to create from nine to five. He'd be at the window when you got in later and you'd get a note or some such thing. He thought you could create at a certain time and then stop. But it doesn't work like that. You're creative at home, when you're driving in your car, it could be any time. But he could never understand it.

—A. I. Bezzerides in Lee Server's "Thieves' Market"

There was the story of the new producer who had gone down the line one day and then reported excitedly to the head office.

"Who are those men?"

"They're supposed to be writers."

"I thought so. Well, I watched them for ten minutes and there were two of them that didn't write a line."

—F. Scott Fitzgerald, *The Last Tycoon*

It is frivolous stuff, and how rare, how precious is frivolity! How few writers can prostitute all their powers! They are always implying "I am capable of higher things."

—E. M. Forster, "Ronald Firbank"

Until the screenwriter does his job, nobody else has a job. In other words, he is the asshole who keeps everyone else from going to work.

—John Gregory Dunne, *Monster*

"But how are you going to get rid of the illiterate mockies that run it? They've got a stranglehold on the industry. Maybe they're intellectual stumblebums, but they're damn good businessmen. Or at least they know how to go into receivership and come up with a gold watch in their teeth."

—Nathanael West, *Day of the Locust*

So an offer is made you by those with the power to make it. It is not quite what you want but it is the only one made.

You have a choice: take it and your work breathes life. Refuse it—and your work gathers dust in your files to rot and die.

—Anonymous author, *Swivel Hips*

He took the best terms he could get. Collie would give him four thousand dollars for writing the script, two thousand tonight, two thousand when it was done. If the script was not sold, it would belong to Munshin; if it was sold, Collie would take two thirds of the sale price. Subsidiary rights would belong to Collie, but he would make certain Eitel got a percentage. It was a simple arrangement, Eitel would do the work and Collie would get the money.

—Norman Mailer, *The Deer Park*

Hollywood money isn't money. It's congealed snow, melts in your hand, and there you are.

—Dorothy Parker, in Malcolm Cowley's *Writers at Work, First Series*

And there is something about the movie business that is even worse than not being paid—it is the presumption on the part of the people putting up the money that they have an unassailable right to interfere with what happens in the screenplay and with the outcome of the film. (Please don't forget that people put up money to publish books, too.) Publishers, among them even the toughest editors, ask writers to make changes; they don't tell you that you have to make the changes, or simply make them for you.

—John Irving, *My Movie Business*

In Hollywood, the author is considered an ass——. They've paid him for the rights, all he has to do is keep quiet.

—Blaise Cendras, *Hollywood, Mecca of the Movies*

Faulkner lived at my house. He was fond of me, considered himself a member of the family. He was making $300 a week and he was starving on it. He was sending the money home. That was one of the reasons why he stayed with me. He'd been drunk so often that no producer would hire him anymore. But Warner Bros. hired him, and Warner boasted that he had the best writer in the world for "peanuts."

—A. I. Bezzerides in Lee Server's "Thieves' Market"

But no matter how it's gilded, it's still a pact with the devil in which you sell your soul for a mess of pottage.

—Anonymous author, *Swivel Hips*

I said, "Scott, what do you think this picture is really about?"

"It's about two movie stars," Rudin said.

—John Gregory Dunne, *Monster*

We're not writers, we're hacks... My God, I wrote once. I wrote a book—a darn good book. I was a promising novelist... And now I'm writing dialogue for a horse.

—James Cagney, in *Boy Meets Girl*

I think I have had about all of Hollywood I can stand. I feel bad, depressed, dreadful sense of wasting time, I imagine most of the symptoms of some kind of blow-up or collapse.

—William Faulkner, quoted in David Minter, *William Faulkner: His Life and Work*

They've accepted the idea of being third-class citizens, the Industry's pain in the ass. Our position is that maybe someday we could forget the old joke about the Polish starlet, you know, she thought she could get ahead by fucking the writer.

—Frank Pierson, former Writer's Guild of America President

I love Hollywood and I believe in its future and its fortune, not because Hollywood is the universal capital of a new industry in which the roar of money is annually calculated in billions of dollars, but because this city, still in its infancy, is situated, like all cities of art that have played a role in the history of civilization, upon seven hills.

—Blaise Cendras, *Hollywood, Mecca of the Movies*

It is hard to laugh at the need for beauty and romance, no matter how tasteless, even horrible, the results of that are. But it is easy to sigh.

—Nathanael West, *Day of the Locust*

The words "Kiss Kiss Bang Bang," which I saw on an Italian movie poster, are perhaps the briefest statement imaginable of the basic appeal of movies.

—Pauline Kael, *Kiss, Kiss, Bang, Bang*

Oh, the film was a contemptuous art to be sure, a fifteenth-century Italian art where to do one's work, one had to know how to flatter princes and lick the toes of the condottieri, and play one's plots and intrigues, and say one's little dangerous thing, and somehow delude them all, exaggerate one's compromises and hide one's statement until if one were good enough, one could get away with it, and five centuries later, safe in a museum, the tourists would go by and say obediently, "What a great artist! What a fine man he must have been! Look at the mean faces of those aristocrats!"

—Norman Mailer, *The Deer Park*

All Hollywood corrupts; and absolute Hollywood corrupts absolutely.

—Edmund Wilson

It was an unreal world, this Hollywood. But within it there was also the attainment of greatness, of creativity, and I was glad to be part of it, no matter how filled with shame a great deal of it was.

—Anonymous author, *Swivel Hips*

The trouble with Hollywood is that too many people who won't leave are ashamed to be there. But when a moving picture is right, it socks the eye and the ear and the solar plexus all at once and that is a hell of a temptation for any writer .... Hollywood may be full of phonies, mediocrities, dictators and good men who have lost their way, but there is something that draws you there that you should not be ashamed of.

—Budd Schulberg, *What Makes Sammy Run*

To the Film Industry in Crisis

by

Frank O'Hara

Not you, lean quarterlies and swarthy periodicals
with your studious incursions toward the pomposity of ants,
nor you, experimental theater in which Emotive Fruition
is wedding Poetic Insight perpetually, nor you,
promenading Grand opera, obvious as an ear (though you
are close to my heart), but you, Motion Picture Industry,
it's you I love!

In time of crisis, we must all decide again and again whom we love.
And give credit where it's due: not to my starched nurse, who taught me
how to be bad and not bad rather than good (and has lately availed
herself of this information), not to the Catholic Church
which is at best an oversolemn introduction to cosmic entertainment,
not to the American legion, which hates everybody, but to you,
glorious Silver Screen, tragic Technicolor, amorous Cinemascope,
stretching Vistavision and startling Stereophonic sound, with all
your heavenly dimensions and reverberations and iconoclasms! To
Richard Barthelmess as the "tol'able" boy barefoot and in pants,
Jeanette MacDonald of the flaming hair and lips and long, long, neck,
Sue Carroll as she sits for eternity on the damaged fender of a car
and smiles, Ginger Rogers with her pageboy bob like a sausage
on her shuffling shoulders, peach-melba-voiced Fred Astaire of the feet,
Eric von Stroheim, the seducer of mountain-climbers' gasping spouses,
the Tarzans, each and every one of you (I cannot bring myself to prefer
Johnny Weissmuller to Lex Barker, I cannot!), Mae West in a furry sled,
her bordello radiance and bland remarks, Rudolph Valentino of the moon,

its crushing passions, and moonlike, too, the gentle Norma Shearer,
Miriam Hopkins dropping her champagne glass off Joel McCrea's yacht
and crying into the dappled sea, Clark Gable rescuing Gene Tierney
from Russia and Allan Jones rescuing Kitty Carlisle from Harpo Marx,
Cornel Wilde coughing blood on the piano keys while Merle Oberon berates,
Marilyn Monroe in her little spike heels reeling through Niagara Falls,
Joseph Cotton puzzling and Orson Welles puzzled and Dolores del Rio
eating orchids for lunch and breaking mirrors, Gloria Swanson reclining,
and Jean Harlow reclining and wiggling, and Alice Faye reclining
and wiggling and singing, Myrna Loy being calm and wise, William Powell
in his stunning urbanity, Elizabeth Taylor blossoming, yes, to you

and to all you others, the great, the near-great, the featured, the extras
who pass quickly and return in dreams saying your one or two lines,
my love!
Long may you illumine space with your marvelous appearances, delays
and enunciations, and may the money of the world glitteringly cover you
as you rest after a long day under the kleig lights with your faces
in packs for our edification, the way the clouds come often at night
but the heavens operate on the star system. It is a divine precedent
you perpetuate! Roll on, reels of celluloid, as the great earth rolls on!

[A continuity shot from *Ex-Lady,* 1933]

[A continuity shot from *Larceny Lane (Blonde Crazy)*, 1931]

DEFENDING

The Searchers

THE WRITER BEGS MOVIEGOERS TO TAKE A CLOSER LOOK AT THIS WESTERN DISMISSED AS DATED AND RACIST

1. BENNINGTON

What's weird in retrospect is how I seem to have willed the circumstances into being, how much I seemed to know before I knew anything at all. There shouldn't have been anything at stake for me, seeing *The Searchers* that first time. Yet there was. Going to a Film Society screening was ordinarily a social act, but I made sure to go alone that night. I smoked a joint alone too, my usual preparation then for a Significant Moment. And I chose my heavy black-rimmed glasses, the ones I wore when I wanted to appear nerdishly remote and intense, as though to decorate my outer self with a confession of inner reality. The evening of that first viewing of *The Searchers* I readied myself like a man who suspects his first date might become an elopement.

John Wayne with director John Ford

BY JONATHAN LETHEM

Oh, I wasn't a man. I was nineteen, a freshman at Bennington, a famously expensive college in Vermont. I'd never been to private school, and the distance between my experience and those of the other students, most of whom had never set foot inside a public school like those I'd attended in Brooklyn, was impossible to overstate. On the surface I probably came off like an exuberant chameleon. I plied my new friends with stories of inner-city danger when I wanted to play the exotic, aped their precocious cynicism when I didn't. Beneath that surface I was weathering a brutally sudden confrontation with the reality of class. My bohemian-artisan upbringing — my parents could safely be called hippies—had masked the facts of my own exclusion from real privilege, more adeptly than is possible anymore. It was 1982.

Soon the weight of these confusions crushed my sense of belonging, and I dropped out. But my initial response was to cloak my abreaction in a hectic show of confidence: I was the first freshman ever to run the Film Society. The role freed me to move easily through the complex social layers at Bennington, impressing people with a brightness that hadn't affixed to any real target. Plus I was able to hire myself as a projectionist, one of the least degrading work-study jobs, then pad the hours, since I was my own manager.

So when I walked into Tishman Hall, Bennington's small, freestanding movie theater, I was entering my own little domain on a campus that really wasn't mine at all. That had everything to do with the episode that night. The wooden seat-rows in Tishman were full—deep in the Vermont woods, any movie was diversion enough for a Tuesday night—but I doubt any of my closest friends were there. I don't remember. I do remember glancing up at the booth to see that this night's projectionist was my least competent. The lights dimmed, the babble hushed, and the movie began.

A cowboy ballad in harmony plays over the titles. You're thrust into a melodrama in blazing Technicolor, which has faded to a color like worrisome salmon. A homestead on the open range—no, not the range. This family has settled on the desolate edge of Monument Valley, under the shadow of those baked and broken monoliths rendered trite by Jeep commercials. You think: they might as well try to farm on the moon. The relationships between the characters are uneasy, hard to parse, despite broad performances, corny lines. At the center of the screen is this guy, a sort of baked and broken monolith himself, an actor you might feel you were supposed to know. John Wayne.

I'd seen part of *Rooster Cogburn* on television. The only feature western I'd seen was *Blazing Saddles*, but I'd passingly absorbed the conventions from *F Troop*, from *Gunsmoke*, from a *Mad* magazine parody of *3:10 to Yuma*. Similarly, I'd caught a sense of John Wayne's iconographic meaning from the parodies and rejections that littered seventies culture. I knew him by his opposite: something of Wayne's force is encoded in Dustin Hoffman, Elliott Gould, Alan Alda. And the voice—in high school I'd sung along with a hit song called "Rappin' Duke" which mimicked his bullying drawl: "So you think you're bad, with your rap—well I'll tell ya, pilgrim, I started the crap..."

As for movies—or "film"—was a perverse muddle, another result of my parents' milieu. I'd seen dozens by Godard, Truffaut, and Bergman, never one by Howard Hawks or John Ford. My parents had taken me to *The Harder They Come*, not *The Wizard of Oz*. In my scattershot reading I'd sensed something missing in my knowledge, something pretty central, a body of Hollywood texts the European directors revered like a bible. But I'd never seen an American film older than

Wayne's character, Ethan, is tormented and tormenting. His fury is righteous and ugly at once, resentment brandished as a fetish. It isolates him in every scene.

2001: *A Space Odyssey*. Somewhere in my reading I'd also gleaned that *The Searchers* was terribly important, though not how, or why, or to whom.

Wayne's character, Ethan, is tormented and tormenting. His fury is righteous and ugly at once, resentment brandished as a fetish. It isolates him in every scene. It isolates him from you, watching, even as his charisma wrenches you closer, into an alliance, a response that's, well, almost sexual. You try to fit him to your concept of hero, but though he's riding off now, chasing a band of murderous Indians, it doesn't work. No parody prepared you for this. Wasn't Wayne supposed to be a joke? Weren't westerns supposed to be simple? The film on the screen is lush, portentous. You're worried for it.

Now Wayne and the other riders falter. The Indians, it seems, have circled back, to raid the farmhouse the riders have left behind. The family, the whole cast the film introduced, they're the ones in danger. The riders race back in a panic. They've failed. The farmhouse is a smoldering cinder, the family dead. The woman Wayne seemed to care for, raped and murdered. Her daughter, Wayne's niece, kidnapped. The sky darkens. The score is a dirge, no ballad now. Wayne squints, sets his jaw: the girl would be better dead than in the hands of the savages. John Wayne's a fucking monster! So are the Indians!

Now you're worried in a different way.

That's when the audience in Tishman began laughing and catcalling. Some had been laughing from the start, of course, at the conventions of 1950s Hollywood film. Now, as the drama deepened and the stakes became clear, the whole audience joined them. It was the path of least resistance. The pressure of the film, its brazen ambiguity, was too much. It was easier to view it as a racist antique, a naive and turgid artifact dredged out of our parents' bankrupt fifties culture.

Benefit of the doubt: what cue, what hint of context was there to suggest to this audience why it should risk following where this film was going? These were jaded twenty-year-old sophisticates, whose idea of a film to ponder was something sultry and pretentious—*Liquid Sky*, *The Draughtsman's Contract*. If an older film stood a chance it would be in black and white, ideally starring Humphrey Bogart, whose cynical urbanity wouldn't appall a young crowd nursing its fragile sense of cool. The open, colorful manner of *The Searchers* didn't stand a chance. A white actor wearing dark makeup to play the main Indian character didn't stand a chance. John Wayne, above all, didn't stand a chance. The laughter drowned out the movie.

I was confused by the film, further confused by the laughter. *The Searchers* was overripe, impossible—it begged for rejection. But the film was beginning to reach me, speak to me in its hellish voice, though I didn't understand what it was saying. And I clung to my shreds of received wisdom: this was the film that meant so much to—who was it? Scorsese? Bogdanovich? There had to be something there. The laughter, I decided, was fatuous, easy. A retreat. Sitting there, trying to watch through the hoots and howls, I boiled.

Then the film broke. The crowd groaned knowingly. This wasn't uncommon. The lights in the booth came up, illuminating the auditorium, as my projectionist frantically rethreaded the projector. It was then I began daring myself to speak, began cobbling together and rehearsing words to express my anger at the audience's refusal to give *The Searchers* a chance. A print brittle enough to break once in Tishman's rusty projectors was likely to do it again, and by the time the film was up and running I'd made a bargain with myself: if there was another break I'd rise and defend the film.

My silent vow scared the shit out of me. I sat trembling, hating the crowd, hating myself for caring, and praying the film wouldn't break again. *The Searchers* was supposed to be the center of this experience, but with one thing and another it was reeling away from me.

It did break again. I did stand and speak. What I recall least about that night are the words which actually came out of my mouth, but you can bet they were incoherent. I'd love to claim I said something about how presentational strategies that look natural to us in contemporary films would look just as silly to an audience in the future as those in *The Searchers* did to us now, how it was our responsibility to look past those accidents of style to the essence of an art. I'd love to think I said something about an American tendency to underestimate the past, that I called for judgment withheld in favor of the possibility that *The Searchers* had been put together by artists with something to say, artists with a self-consciousness, possibly even a sense of irony, of their own.

Of course, I didn't. I was nineteen. I called them idiots and told them to shut up. What I didn't do, couldn't do, was defend *The Searchers* itself. I hadn't seen

John Wayne starred in many Westerns that were less controversial than *The Searchers*, including *Red River*, *Rio Bravo* and *Rio Lobo*, all directed by Howard hawks, pictured above with Wayne.

more than a third of the film, after all, and what I had seen I hadn't understood. My schoolmates might be wrong to condescend to this film, but I couldn't tell them why. Years later I'd come to see that part of what I was defending, by instinct, was the fact that the film had the lousy taste to be a western in the first place. The aspiring novelist who'd soon make his first clumsy attempts to work out his surrealist impulses in the despised medium of science fiction felt kinship with John Ford, a director who persistently cast his moral sagas in the despised form of the genre western. The indignation I felt was partly on my own behalf, indignation I couldn't express because I was ashamed of it. So *The Searchers* and I began our relationship with a grudge in common, but at that moment, under the astonished eyes of my schoolmates, I was only sure I'd made some irrevocable commitment, laid my cards on the table. I didn't know which cards, or what table.

I sat. The film started again. The audience was quieter, mostly because it had thinned. In the face of this unpromising night, this ludicrous film they'd now been informed they weren't supposed to laugh at, and who knew how many breakages to come, half the audience opted for the campus cafe, for an early corner on a booth and pitcher of beer. Face burning, I settled in for my hard-won film, determined now to see its greatness. But the worst was to come. For it was then that *The Searchers* betrayed me. Fifteen minutes after my speech came a scene of such giddy misogyny, such willful racism, it seemed indefensible by design.

During a comic mix-up at an Indian barter session, Wayne's sidekick has accidentally acquired an Indian wife. The sidekick and Wayne tolerate her presence, barely, until nightfall. Then they bed down by the fire and the chubby Indian girl slides in beside the sidekick, drawing exaggerated and unfunny derision from Wayne. The sidekick, enraged, kicks the girl out of his bedroll, so hard she cascades down a hill. There she ends in the dust, weeping, her ludicrous dream of marriage in ruins. Wayne hoots with pleasure, his eyes maniacal. The scene is odious. The chance that Wayne might be some kind of hero, that the filmmakers might redeem him, or themselves, has been pissed away.

The crowd bellowed, shrieked. There were more defections. Those who stayed were ruthless, their suspicions confirmed, surpassed. *The Searchers* had slapped me down. I had to sit it out, of course, though now I was suspicious of the film, of the audience, of myself. My watching brain did worse than withdraw. It became autistic. After the turmoil of the first half, I followed the rest as a plot schematic, unable to risk any identification or strong response. *The Searchers* was only a camp opportunity after all. I was a fool.

2. SAN FRANCISCO

D. was a junkie, though not at first. When we met, D. was one of the most dauntingly clever, well-read, and pop-culturally savvy people I'd known. He'd written for a legendary L.A. fanzine, was friends with a famous underground cartoonist and a famous punk singer. I was honored to be collected into this company. D. was also a sweet and devoted friend. Just a bit of a drinker, with a weakness for speed, then overly fond of Ecstacy. I'd indulged with him at times—we went to see the first Batman movie together on mushrooms—but I could never keep up with him, never go the lengths.

When D. got involved with heroin he began pilfering from and lying to his friends, as though working by rote through some shopworn guidebook to junkie behavior. I avoided him, not systematically, but in guilt at his decline and my complicity. The pleasures in knowing D. had slowly evaporated anyway, mercurial charm replaced by boozy maunderings, devoted attentiveness by passive-aggressive gambits. Besides, I had to protect my stuff, my pawnable books and records. Our friendship became a room we'd both abandoned.

Then D. came to share a large apartment in San Francisco with three roommates, one of whom was my girlfriend. There I'd edge past him in the corridor and kitchen, exchange pleasantries, try not to get caught alone. His Method-actorish comings and goings for "cigarettes," his jittery, sweaty jags, all were made awfully plain there. The three roommates and I were a microscope D. was under, and we took too much satisfaction from watching our sample squirm, nodding and rolling our eyes at one another to excuse our collective failure, the fact that we'd let someone rare and fragile plummet into depravity on our watch. It was a terrible place, and we were all locked into a terrible stasis.

One day I rented a videotape of *The Searchers* and brought it to the apartment. This was seven years after the screening at Bennington. I hadn't seen the film since, though I'd prepared plenty, read about it anywhere I could, gathered evidence of its greatness. I needed to justify being stirred that first time, to prove that the force of that moment was more than a neurotic projection, that it resided in the film intrinsically. In the process, of course, I'd repeated my mistake: this second viewing was already overburdened. (In

Armed with cribbed defenses of various aspects of the film, I was ready to lecture my girlfriend as we watched: see, Wayne's the villain of the piece until the end; see, it's a film about racism, obsession, America.

fact, I was about to begin a novel I'd predetermined should be influenced by *The Searchers*.) Armed with cribbed defenses of various aspects of the film, I was ready to lecture my girlfriend as we watched: see, Wayne's the villain of the piece until the end; see, it's a film about racism, obsession, America. John Ford was made an honorary member of the tribe, you know—he actually spoke Navajo. She: Gosh! So went the fantasies. I was plotting to remake my scene in Tishman Hall, only this time the audience would be completely under my guiding hand. We would enter the temple of *The Searchers* together. Her awe would confirm and justify my own.

D. paced into the living room about ten minutes into the running of the video, and my heart sank. I hadn't known he was home. When he joined us I hastily, despairingly, sketched the start of the film's plot to bring him up to speed. D. couldn't keep still, but between mysterious time-outs behind his bedroom door he gave the film what he could of his slipshod attention. I went back to watching as hard as I could, hell-bent on preserving the sacredness of the moment, feeding my girlfriend just as many interpretations as I thought she'd bear. We both pretended D. wasn't listening.

D. was smart enough to detect my near-hysterical reverence, and it irritated him. The veneer of civility between us was thin by then. Seizing an advantage, he began picking at the film.

"Come on, Jonathan. It's a Hollywood western."

I wanted to reply that any film became generic if you reduced it to a series of disconnected scenes by flitting in and out of the room. Instead I bit my tongue.

"You're giving it too much credit."

What *The Searchers* requires is focus, patience, commitment, I thought. Things you're now incapable of giving.

"You don't really think John Ford was conscious."

A thousand times more conscious than you, I thought. My heart was beating fast.

Then he burst out laughing. We'd come to the first battle scene, where Indians forgo a chance to ambush Wayne and his party from behind, only to be slaughtered in a face-off across a riverbank. For D. the scene was gross and malicious, calculated to make the Comanche look like tactical morons. The film had become contemptible to him, and he let me know. He'd missed the contextualizing moments that render the scene ambiguous—the other characters' dismay at Wayne's murderous fury, the shots Wayne takes at the departing braves as they carry off their dead. Nor would he happen to be in the room for the scene half an hour later when Wayne is elaborately censured for shooting an opponent in the back.

I began a defense and immediately contradicted myself, first insisting that the Indians weren't important as real presences, only as emblems of Wayne's psychic torment. The film, I tried to suggest, was a psychological epic, a diagnosis of racism through character and archetype. The Indians served as Wayne's unheeded mirror. Then, unable to leave my research on the shelf, I cited Ford's renowned accuracy. Maybe he knew a few things about Comanche battle ethics...

D. scoffed. For him it was impossible to honor Indians by showing them mowed down in a senseless slaughter—never mind that senseless slaughter was historical fact. He paced away, leaving me in a kind of hot daze, mouth dry, eyes locked on the screen, still grasping at my dream of a sanctified viewing of *The Searchers*, not seeing that it had already slipped away, that I'd again failed to defend the film, this time with an audience of just two.

D. returned, and now his trembling effort to appear casual had as much to do with the freight between us as with any junkie symptom. Rightly—he knew me well enough to sense what was coming.

"How can you expect to understand anything when you're too fucking distracted to give it more than a passing glance?"

"Relax, Jonathan. I only said I thought the movie wasn't very good . . ."

I'd couldn't stop. "How do you decide so easily that you're superior to a work of art? Ever worry that cheap irony won't carry you through every situation?"

"I've got eyes. It's a fifties western."

"That's what's so pathetic about people our age—" I silenced myself before I'd widened his crimes to cover our whole generation. Still, the damage was done. D. stalked off. I wouldn't speak with him for five years from that day. Under the astonished eyes of my girlfriend I'd burst the bubble of silence in the apartment. Anger stemmed for years had risen and found a conduit. In D.'s underestimation of the film's makers I saw his underestimation of his friends, we who weren't fooled by his dissembling but indulged him, maintaining guilty silence as though we were fooled. D. had been an ambitious and generous soul when I first met him, and a champion of artistic greatness. In his sniping at *The Searchers*—at the film itself and my galactic openness to it—I saw the slow-motion embittering of that soul condensed to one sour-grapes snapshot.

What may have astonished my girlfriend more, and shames me in retrospect, forever, is the Nietzschean chilliness of my actions. As in a priest-and-doctor-in-lifeboat puzzle, two things cried for saving and I could save just one. Seeing a friend spiral into desolation, I reserved my protective sympathy instead for a work of art, for John Ford and John Wayne, remote, dead, and indifferent though they might be. Again my cards were on the table. Greatness above all.

But that was in retrospect. At the time my concern was for my relationship with *The Searchers*. How ill-fated, how aggrieved, it had become. What was it with this film? Would I ever get to watch it without yelling at someone?

3. BERKELEY

I snuck into the Pacific Film Archive on the heels of a crowd of perhaps sixty students, then sat with them in the theater, waiting—for what I didn't know. The screening room there is a lot like Bennington's Tishman, an austere, whisper-absorbing little hall, only built into a large museum in the center of a city instead of standing free in the Vermont woods. It was two years since my argument with D., and I was two years into the first draft of my quasi-western. A grad-student friend, apprised of my need to refurbish my mind's eye with a constant stream of imagery, had tipped me off to the existence of an undergraduate course on the western, mentioning that the professor who taught it had once written about *The Searchers*. So I was there that afternoon to see a screening and lecture, without any clue what was on the syllabus.

The lights dimmed. The Warner Bros. logo, a strum of acoustic guitar, the familiar credit sequence—today's movie was *The Searchers*. Sure, why not? Sitting there anonymous amid the murmuring, notebook-rustling students, I stifled a laugh. I'd been watching the movie regularly on video, in private trysts. This would be the first time in the company of others since my early disasters.

Other films can live in the tunnel-vision light of video, but *The Searchers* aches for air. Not only the air of a screen big enough so Wayne and his rage can loom like those distant towers of rock, but for the air of a crowd. The film is a ragged slice of American something, and it wants to be met by another slice—to be projected, ideally, on a canyon wall, for an audience of millions. The Cal freshmen at the Pacific Film Archive that afternoon were just forty or fifty shapeless little minds, there half willingly, dreaming of dates or Frisbees, yet they somehow gave the film the air it needed.

What I caught was an old boot of pride lodged at the bottom of a stagnant lake of academic ennui, that reflexive self-censorship of real enthusiasms.

Or maybe after five or six watchings I was ready to respond to every frame of *The Searchers*, to meet it completely. Maybe there was something freeing about my place there as an official ghost, voiceless. As the lights came up I wept, discreetly, steadily.

I stayed while the professor spoke. In his lecture he gestured at the film's deep ambiguities without ever reaching, apparently with nothing to prove. He might have seemed a bit perfunctory, enclosed in a bubble of weariness, but if I noticed I blamed the bubble on the students. They were slightly interested, slightly more vague and restless. The vibrant ridicule of the Bennington students had been replaced here by automatic, spaced-out respect—sure it's an important film: it's assigned, isn't it? In the professor I grokked a fellow obsessive. But I mistook him for an unfulfilled obsessive, instead of the vanquished one he turned out to be.

The next day I tried not to be self-conscious waiting in the English Department corridor behind a couple of his students. When my turn came I apologized for sneaking into his class, described the book I was writing, praised his lecture, then fished—he'd written about *The Searchers* somewhere, yes?

What I caught was an old boot of pride lodged at the bottom of a stagnant lake of academic ennui, that reflexive self-censorship of real enthusiasms. I dragged the boot up to the surface, if only for a second. "My article's about the iconography of Monument Valley," he said, with unguarded brightness. "I only published an excerpt. The long version's much more—I'm still working on it, actually."

"I'd love to see it." I scribbled my address.

"Yes, yes . . ." But he was already slipping back into those opaque depths. He'd noticed that he ought to be bewildered to have me in his office, that he didn't really need a wild-eyed autodidact tugging his obsessions into the light. By then I was familiar with how so many grad students, hunkered down inside their terrifying careers, spoke of teaching loads, job postings, anything but the original passions at the cramped secret center of their work. Now I saw it was the same for the professor. Or worse. Armies of yawning undergraduates had killed that part of him. Long or short, published or unfinished, I never saw any version of that essay.

4. DEFENDING THE SEARCHERS

I surrounded *The Searchers*, ambushed it at every pass, told it to reach for the sky. In my pursuit I watched hundreds of other westerns, studying the tradition, looking for glimpses. I studied Ford, learned his language, first in good films, then rotten ones. I watched Scorsese's *Taxi Driver*, Paul Schrader's *Hardcore*, those unofficial remakes, wanting to triangulate my obsession or feel the pulse of someone else's. I read the source novel, the shooting script, biographies of John Wayne—what made him ready to play the part? Did he understand or was he Ford's tool? I mowed through scholarship, hoping to assemble a framework that would free me to understand all I felt. And I wrote my novel; like a child with dollhouse figures I manipulated my own versions of the characters and crises that had overpowered me, trying to decant *The Searchers*, unmake it, consume it. I watched the film and thought about it and talked about it too much, and when I eventually became a bore, *The Searchers* shot me in the back and walked away.

I diminished the film, I think. By overestimating it, then claiming myself as its defender, I'd invented another, more pretentious way of underestimating it. My need to control its reception had more to do with my need to control my own guilt and regret than with anything the film really needed from me, from anyone. If the case for *The Searchers* could be made airtight, then my dropping out of Bennington was justified, my cruelty to D. excused. My own isolating intensity pined for some tidy story of struggle and triumph. But there might not actually be anything to struggle with, no triumph to capture, nobody to rescue. Wasn't it possible that John Wayne should have left Natalie Wood in the tepee—that she was happier there? Weren't he and I a couple of asses?

For years I'd chastised the crowd at Tishman in my fantasies, my words ever more blistering, my argument ever more seamless. Now I concocted a balm for the burning ears of my imaginary schoolmates: I can forgive your resistance to this film. *The Searchers* is a thing I seem doomed to spend a lifetime trying to fathom, and how often do you have a lifetime to spend? Then I'd add, Can you forgive me my absurd responsiveness?

Oh, I've perfected my defense of the film. It hinges on the notion that in certain of the greatest films of the studio era a major star can be placed under examination as a set of neurotic symptoms, a condition, a disaster embodied—and yet simultaneously operate as a creature of free will and moral relevance, a character whose choices matter. For loads of reasons it's easier for a contemporary viewer to grant that notion to other stars in other films—James Stewart in *Vertigo*, say. If the notion is refused, *The Searchers* becomes unwatchable, an explosion in a vacuum.

Grant it and the rest falls into place. The weird stuff, the racist stuff, the hysterical stuff—it all serves to split Wayne away from the other characters and from the viewer's sympathies, and to foreground his lonely rage, and the nest that rage builds in racism. It's very, ah, Brechtian. I could chart the way even the most distractingly unfunny pratfall contributes to the thesis, I swear. In my fantasies I do. Imagine a laser disc of *The Searchers* featuring a hidden audio track—the Lethem Defense Edition—with my filibuster of articulations covering every frame.

Snore. Who'd listen to the hidden track? *The Searchers'* detractors are casual snipers, not dedicated enemies—like D., or the audience at Tishman, they take a potshot and wander off, their interest evaporated. Those who care as much as I do cherish their own interpretations. They don't need mine. I know this because as a minor consolation I've collected those people. There's the rock critic who'd screen *The Searchers* in his living room. The biographer who searched Monument Valley to find the charred remains of the cabin that burns in the film's first reel, chunks of which he hoards at home in L.A. Others . . . the novelist, the bookseller . . . with fellow cultists the title itself is enough, passed like a talisman.

A new friend remarks he's surprised to read in an interview that I consider *The Searchers* an influence.

"Have you seen it?" I ask, falsely casual.

"Long time ago. I just remember how racist it was."

"*The Searchers* is racist the way *Huckleberry Finn* is racist," I say, of course. But it's cant, and stale in my mouth. He'll see it again and understand, or he won't. *The Searchers* is my private club, and if you don't join you'll never even know you've been rejected. I'm like the Cal professor—caring has worn me out. *The Searchers* is too vast to be digested in my novel, too willful to be bounded in my theories. I watch or I don't, doesn't matter: *The Searchers* strides on, maddened, obsessed, through ruined landscapes incapable of containing it: John Ford's oeuvre, and John Wayne's, the "Studio-Era Film," and my own defeated imagination—everywhere shrugging off categories, refusing the petitions of embarrassment and taste, defying explanation or defense as only great art or great abomination ever could. ☗

Alex
COX

INTERVIEWED BY LOU MATHEWS

AFTER BEING KICKED OFF *Fear and Loathing in Las Vegas*, THE DIRECTOR LEARNS TO WORK OUTSIDE THE SYSTEM

In January 1990, Gene Siskel and Roger Ebert did what journalists do at the turn of the calendar and picked their best films of the decade. Siskel had a small surprise on his list, *Sid and Nancy*, at number nine. He talked of the film's daring and originality and credited the director, Stephen Frears. This was something of a surprise to the actual director, Alex Cox, but in keeping with Cox' s Hollywood luck.

Cox had preceded *Sid and Nancy* with the enduring punk anti-classic, *Repo Man* (1984), which Universal Pictures creative accounting department finally put in the black in 1999. He followed with a spaghetti/punk homage to Sergio Leone, *Straight to Hell*, which its distributor Island Pictures dubbed Straight to Video, and dumped. The budget was $1 million and the cast—Joe Strummer, Courtney Love, Elvis Costello, Jim Jarmusch, The Pogues, Kathy Burke, Grace Jones, Dennis Hopper and Miguel Sandoval—"could never be reassembled"—is hard to match for a low-budget film. Tim Robbins and John Cusack, cast in cameo parts, were thrown off the picture when, with upcoming parts requiring full heads of hair, they wouldn't shave their heads to play marines. It remains a midnight hit in Japan where the twinned elements of coffee addiction and sexual tension apparently resonate. In 1987 Cox directed his first genuine studio film, *Walker*, the story of the American soldier of fortune William Walker, who conquered Nicaragua and ruled it from 1855 to 1857, when Nicaragua looked like the most logical canal route. The movie, starring Ed Harris as Walker, was shot in Nicaragua, defying the Reagan-era embargo, on a budget of $7 million. It was abandoned by both its producer, Ed Pressman (who was concentrating on his winner, Oliver Stone's *Wall Street*), and Universal after disastrous early screenings. The parallels that Cox saw between nineteenth century U.S. expansionist arrogance and 1980s U.S. support of the Contras, didn't play with the politically unmotivated. The creak of expensive leather, as irritated mid-level executives fled the studio premiere and reception was deafening. After *Walker*, Cox dropped off American radar—and did some of his best work.

From 1987 to 1994, Cox made most of his living hosting a popular BBC television series, *Moviedrome*, which introduced a new generation of filmic youth to him as a film historian and enthusiast.

In 1991, in Mexico, Cox directed his first feature in five years, the remarkable *El Patrullero* (*Highway Patrolman*), from an excellent script by *Walker* co-producer Lorenzo O'Brien. It was released with English subtitles in 1994, and won a number of festival prizes including the Grand Prize at the Santa Barbara Film Festival. Reviews were great. Kevin Thomas of the *Los Angeles Times* said, "*Highway Patrolman* is maverick director Alex Cox's finest film to date . . . (It) opens just the way one would expect of Cox—with a darkly satirical take on the subject, an idealistic young Mexican's training at the National Highway Patrol Academy in Mexico City. . . While it rightly skewers American hypocrisy and complicity in Mexican drug trafficking, Highway Patrolman abounds in the virtues of traditional filmmaking." Indeed, there is an epic quality, moral as well as visual, to the hero's odyssey that recalls the westerns of John Ford and such John Huston films as *Treasure of the Sierra Madre*. F. X. Feeney of the *L.A. Weekly* was equally moved: "Cox's calm, feline gaze never judges or reproaches, never telegraphs to us what we're supposed to feel about what we're looking at. *Highway Patrolman* is an astonishing, mature piece of work. It's like a Bresson film with a rock & roll pulse." Neither reviews nor festival prizes helped. The movie sank like a stone because it received no real distribution, advertising, or promotion and also because it was, unreconstructedly, a Mexican movie and didn't jibe with the public perception of Cox.

Between 1996 and the present, Cox has maintained a remarkably busy low-budget workload and even blipped again on Hollywood radar screens. In 1996, BBC 4 paid for Cox's adaptation of a Borges' short story "Death and the Compass" with Peter Boyle, Christopher Eccleston, and Miguel Sandoval, which was later expanded to feature length and four-walled in L.A. and London. In 1998, Dutch television financed a millenial fea-

NO POSTAGE
NECESSARY
IF MAILED
IN THE
UNITED STATES

BUSINESS REPLY MAIL
FIRST-CLASS MAIL PERMIT NO 99027 Escondido CA

POSTAGE WILL BE PAID BY ADDRESSEE

TIN HOUSE
MAGAZINE

P O Box 469049
Escondido CA 92046-9049

ENJOY HOME DELIVERY OF TIN HOUSE! USE THE CARDS TO SUBSCRIBE TODAY.

NO POSTAGE
NECESSARY
IF MAILED
IN THE
UNITED STATES

BUSINESS REPLY MAIL
FIRST-CLASS MAIL PERMIT NO 99027 Escondido CA

POSTAGE WILL BE PAID BY ADDRESSEE

TIN HOUSE
MAGAZINE

P O Box 469049
Escondido CA 92046-9049

SUBSCRIBE AND SAVE OVER 50% WITH THIS CHARTER OFFER

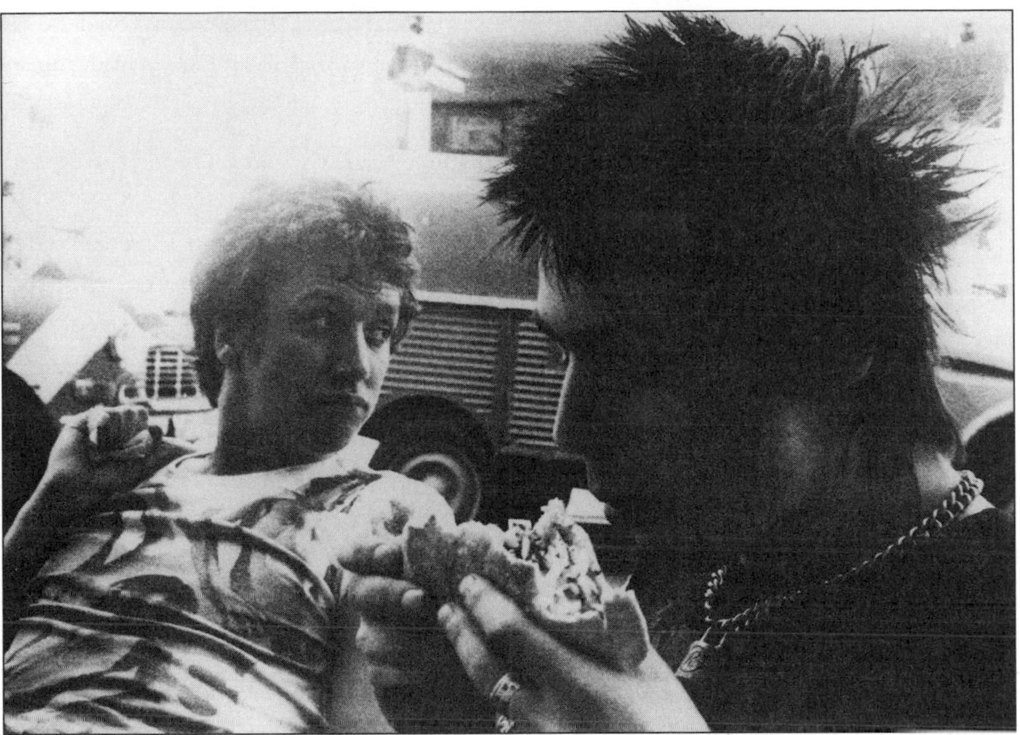

The real Sid Vicious (right), who was portrayed by Gary Oldman in Alex Cox's *Sid and Nancy*

ture, *Three Businessmen*, a strange tale of three businessmen looking for dinner, which starts in Liverpool, segues to Amsterdam, then Singapore, and ends in Tokyo. In 1999, Cox directed an affecting documentary for BBC 4, *Kurosawa, the Last Emperor*, featuring interviews with Akira Kurosawa's long-time collaborators, as well as well as with fans such as Paul Verhoeven, John Woo, Bernardo Bertolucci, and Francis Ford Coppola. This year he directed *Emmanuelle—A Hard Look*, about the celebrated softcore porn series, also for BBC 4. Over the last five years he has also enjoyed an acting career in Mexican movies, often playing evil gringos, most recently in *Herod's Lot*, Luis Estrada's groundbreaking movie about corruption in Mexico's PRI party, which was initially suppressed by the PRI-influenced Incine (The Mexican National Film Production Company) and which may have had some effect on the presidential elections in Mexico.

During the same productive five-year span, Cox has dipped his toes back in Hollywood waters twice, as a hired director, and had them gnawed off. The 1996 movie *The Winner*, was an intriguing project based on the play *A Darker Purpose,*

COX WAS HIRED TO WRITE AND DIRECT HUNTER THOMPSON'S *FEAR AND LOATHING IN LAS VEGAS.* FOLLOWING AN INSANE MEETING WITH THOMPSON, THE PROJECT WAS TAKEN AWAY FROM HIM AND HANDED TO TERRY GILLIAM.

by Wendy Riss, with an intriguing cast that included Rebecca De Mornay, Vincent D'onofrio, Delroy Lindo, and Billy Bob Thornton. The producers reedited Cox's version to suit executive producer De Mornay and Cox disowned the film. In 1999, through a convoluted series of machinations, Cox was hired to write and direct Hunter Thompson's *Fear and Loathing in Las Vegas*. Following an insane meeting with Thompson, the project was taken away from him and handed to Terry Gilliam,—though Cox and co-writer Tod Raines received screenplay credit after Writers Guild arbitration.

This interview was conducted by E-mail, three different salvos and replies.

Lou Mathews: I expected you'd be in England. What the hell are you doing in Oregon?

Alex Cox: My partner, Tod Davies, and I have a place in the woods with large dogs. If we are away too long the older dog (more conscious of mortality) begins to chew obsessively at a patch of fur.

LM: So you live in Oregon.

AC: And sometimes in Mexico, and Liverpool.

LM: What's all this about a studio in Liverpool?

AC: Tod and I have been collaborating with an editing and training facility in Liverpool for the last couple of years. They are Media Station; we are Exterminating Angel. By the end of 2000 we hope to have pooled our resources and be setting up shop in Toxteth, Liverpool. The idea is to have a production and postproduction facility since there is a lot of TV and feature work up there but as yet no full-time facility for local producers or visiting productions. But it isn't a studio in the sense of soundstages and camera equipment. We rent that stuff. And there is already studio overcapacity in the vicinity of London.

LM: Why hasn't *Waldo's Hawaiian Holiday*, the sequel to *Repo Man*, been made?

AC: It is a sad tale. Peter McCarthy, one of the original producers of *Repo Man*, pursued the film diligently for about five years. Right from the beginning we had calls from Emilio Estevez, wanting to be in it, to play the lead. Peter and Michael Nesmith and Jonathan Wacks and I discussed it and thought, Well, why not? Let's keep the old team together . . . So we offered Emilio the part and for years Peter tried to raise money for the picture, which with Emilio attached was pretty difficult. But Peter managed it. We put the crew together, were six weeks from the start date, and Emilio dropped out. No explanation. Picture put on hold. By then it was way past due in studio terms.

And maybe it is past due. *Waldo's Hawaiian Holiday* was the story of a young man, a punk rocker from 1984, who went for a drive in a flying car, and came back fifteen years later, in 1999. Only as far as his mind and body were concerned, he'd only been gone fifteen minutes. It was the brain-dead nineties versus the thrashing, still-conscious corpse of the eighties. We'd have to do something completely different with it if we made it now.

LM: Is it my imagination or does Paul Verhoeven essentially apologize for not remaining pure in your documentary, *Kurosawa, the Last Emperor*?

AC: I think the director of *The Fourth Man* is much too sophisticated to expect anyone to remain pure, no matter what they do. Maybe celibate monks and nuns or members of sex cults or nudists are pure, but the odds are against it. Can you imagine what goes on in their minds? Who would want to?

Whatever you wish to do involves getting it done. The idea may be pure, or perfect, whatever those words mean. But the process of doing it will entail compromise, and doing things with which not everyone is happy. Stevenson's Rocket—the world's first passenger railway locomotive—ran over and killed the MP for Liverpool on its maiden voyage. Riding a bicycle, building public transport networks, directing *Starship Troopers*: these things are not congruent with purity.

Paul Verhoeven has nothing to apologize for. He has chosen his path and is making the most of it. What he does say is that he much prefers the great films of Kurosawa to the Los Angeles diet of "special effects, special effects, special effects."

LM: What do you think about the Dogma '95 rules for filmmaking?

AC: I am against rules. There should be as few as possible. If I have any, they only apply to me. I find the idea of making a simpler, nonrepetitive cinema admirable. Remember all the great films of Fassbinder! But he worked in a way that was both authoritarian and highly permissive. The Dogma rules are inconsistent. No artificial lighting is allowed, yet artificial and reactionary editing styles are permitted. If there is to be no lighting, there should be no editing. All sequences should take place unmanipulated, in the moment, in a single take. You also have to wonder about rules whose proponents don't observe them. The rules of Dogma say there can be no director credited, yet their followers take a traditional director's credit. It doesn't make sense logically or aesthetically, though I suppose it is a good publicity stunt. And there is nothing wrong with that.

LM: What are "artificial and reactionary editing styles"?

AC: Predictable editing styles which imitate the close-up-close-up intercutting of almost all television drama, whether soap opera or cops. This is now the language of (almost all) feature film. You can predict the cuts with the snap of a finger. Snap! Close up of Mel Gibson! Snap! Close-up of Sharon Stone. And so on and so forth.

If you want examples of the opposite, consider *Slacker* (where every scene is a moving master), or the recent films of Arturo Ripstein (*Profundo Carmesi*, for example), or—best of all—*I Am Cuba*, which has some of the most complicated and admirable long takes of all time.

LM: Do you feel that the new DV [Digital Video] technology will change the game, as Mike Figgis insists that it will, and undermine studio control?

AC: I think Mini DV is great for television since it is of broadcast quality. When DV is transferred to 35mm film it looks like video transferred to 35mm. It is in the interests of the big distributors and the studios (normally one and the same) to shoot films on video and to send out videotapes (digital or otherwise) because they are much cheaper than 35mm prints. But the visual quality is not the same.

There is also the annoyance of competing video standards—there are at least three, PAL, NTSC and SECAM, plus scads of studio-driven "DVD zones." All of this makes for confusion and difficulty in seeing films. 35mm, 16mm are universal standards. If you have a projector, you can show a print anywhere in the world. If the bulb is right and the environs dark, it will look great—even on a wall. 35mm is a worldwide standard, like the HTML language of the Internet.

LM: After hanging out on a number of movie sets, I've come to the semblance of a conclusion that art or craft may be involved in the directorial process, but organizational skills are as important. It's more like a military campaign than any ethereal process. Comment? Would you have made a good general?

AC: When we were in Nicaragua a commandante called Valdivia from Granada told me that after watching the film being made, a movie on location did seem like a military campaign. Especially all that behind-the-scenes stuff—transport, logistics, food. If I had been a general I would have got fired (or whatever they do in the military) and ended up in exile somewhere, counting the spoons. Probably poisoned by my own side.

"If I had been a general I would have got fired (or whatever they do in the military) and ended up in exile somewhere, counting the spoons. Probably poisoned by my own side."

LM: Was Vincente Fox the suspected angel behind the distribution of *Herod's Law*? What effect do you think Fox will have, if he wins (editor's note: he won), on artistic freedom in Mexico?

AC: You mean, did Fox put up the money for the distribution? I don't know . . . Certainly anything is possible, and the more free-trade and pro-American the politician, the more money he has to throw around. Fox is the ex-head of Coca-Cola in Mexico. He understands marketing. But the PAN is also the party of the reactionary hierarchy of the Catholic church. It is unlikely they would support *Herod's Law*, given its portrayal of a completely corrupt, money-obsessed priest and its rampant sexuality.

What effect do the US Government and the Catholic Church and Coca-Cola usually have on artistic freedom? Fox will be a disaster for Mexico. The country's independence will continue to leach away; more and more people will become poor; a tiny handful of billionaires will get even richer and salt their money away in Monaco and Miami; repression will increase. Just the same as if the PRI get reelected, only faster. It is the free-trade, IMF/World Bank pattern, endlessly repeated everywhere in Latin America, except for Cuba.

In this context artistic freedom at a street level may increase, but there will be no state support for anything rivaling Hollywood or the American hegemony; the more it flourishes, the more it is likely to be discouraged.

LM: Will you direct more movies in Mexico?

AC: If I'm lucky! Exterminating Angel is trying to make the bio-pic of Luis Buñuel. We'll see.

LM: Can you imagine making another studio film?

AC: It's hard to imagine.

LM: Any recent films you admire?

AC: I thought *Galaxy Quest* was funny. And I enjoyed a Russian film called *The Iron Heel Of Oligarchy*, which I saw at the Rotterdam Festival last year.

LM: Do you have a top-ten list?

AC: Of what? Films? I made the following list for my Japanese producer friend Katsumi Ishikuma, a.k.a. Stonebear, (not in order) about five years ago:

1. *2001*
2. *Citizen Kane*
3. *Wages of Fear*
4. *Toby Dammit* (Fellini's episode of *Histoires Fantastiques*)
5. *The Mattei Affair*
6. *Throne of Blood*
7. *King Kong*
8. *The Wild Bunch*
9. *Exterminating Angel*
10. *For A Few Dollars More*

It still seems like a pretty good list, though I'm tempted to scratch the Leone and put another Spaghetti Western—*Quien Sabe*? Or *Big Silence*—there instead. Or replace *Throne of Blood* with *Seven Samuri* or *Ikiru* or even *Madadayo*, Kurosawa's very last film . . . Or put *Treasure of Sierra Madre* somewhere? Only ten films is hard.

LM: You've adapted two screenplays from prose works, Borges' *Death and the Compass* and Hunter Thompson's *Fear and Loathing in Las Vegas*. Is it a far different task than an original screenplay? Is it more difficult? Is it easier if the author is dead?

AC: Most of the scripts I've written have come from some sort of biographic material—*Repo Man, Sid and Nancy*, and *El Patrullero* all come from lengthy interviews—while the source material of *Walker* is all to be found in books. There isn't a lot of difference, except that in the case of a book or story there is already a structure. But then the structure may not be appropriate for a film.

In the case of *Fear and Loathing*, the structure of the script was entirely by Tod: she had taught the book to undergraduates at UCLA and pondered long and hard the various adjustments necessary for it to work as a film. She dumped all the self-conscious nonsense about "The American Dream Diner." The climactic sequence in the hardware barn (a passing fancy early in the book) was hers.

LM: In *Repo Man* there is a harrowing moment or two when Zander Schloss cheerily sings the jingle, "Feelin' 7Up. I'm feelin' 7Up. . ." I don't think the influence of corporate advertising has ever been better defined. But back then, there was still some sense that advertising lied, that's what advertising did. Does it seem to you that it's swallowed whole now?

AC: Unfortunately, yes. That is the difference between the late seventies and the later nineties, if you like. I taught a production class at UCLA in 1998 and most of my students were completely corporate-controlled. For example, they thought it was okay for Apple Computers to appropriate all those images of dead cultural heroes and use them as advertising "because they're in a war with Microsoft and they're the underdog." They were rooting for one of the protagonists in a profits battle between two mega-rich corporations.

That was how far things had sunk. However, these students were all in their twenties and early thirties. I suspect their younger siblings are a lot more radical. And their children may yet reject all this fatuous corporate propaganda in the same way as they reject hamburgers.

LM: Is the audience educable or will *Star Wars* always win?

AC: The audience is already educated, or at least a substantial portion of it. Listen to one of those vocal black audiences in

"THE PURPOSE OF MAKING FILMS IS TO ENCOURAGE REVOLUTION. IF THAT FAILS YOUR FALLBACK POSITONS ARE THAT YOU HAVE MADE ART OR MONEY."

the U.S. Most of the time the people are way ahead of the film. They're shouting at it, answering it back.

The problem isn't with the audience. It's with the handful of huge "entertainment" corporations which keep consolidating, which decide what gets made, what people see. It's their game.

LM: A quote from James Whale, in the movie *Gods and Monsters*: "Making Movies is the most wonderful thing in the world. Working with friends . . . entertaining people . . ." Does that adequately describe the addiction?

AC: It sounds like crap to me. The purpose of making films is to encourage revolution. If that fails, your fallback positions are that you have made art or money.

Henry Miller in Lotos Land

To paint is to love again

On Henry Miller's first evening in Hollywood in the summer of 1941, he arrived at the home of a millionaire in a "handsome black Packard," having accepted a dinner invitation from a complete stranger. He did not know his host's name, nor did he ever find it out. He would later write of the soirée, "The first thing which struck me, on being introduced all around, was that I was in the presence of wealthy people, people who were bored to death and who were all, including the octogenarians, already three sheets to the wind." The dinner party went downhill from there, but Miller was nonetheless initially enthralled by the town in which "everyone thought he was a marvel."

BY *Victoria Price*

Hollywood was forty-nine-year-old Henry Miller's last stop on the cross-country automobile journey that would lead to his quirky travelogue, *The Air-Conditioned Nightmare*. A New Yorker by birth, Miller had moved to Paris in 1930. There he finally escaped the surreal series of love affairs, failed marriages, and degrading jobs that had been his dismal life and dead-end career to become a writer with one of the most distinctive voices in the English language. The three semi-autobiographical novels he penned in Paris in the 1930s'—*Tropic of Cancer*, *Tropic of Capricorn*, and *The Black Spring*—were acclaimed by such literary lights as T. S. Eliot, Ezra Pound, William Carlos Williams, and Aldous Huxley for their raw sexuality, unflinching honesty, and chaotically spirited language. He was hailed as the twentieth-century Walt Whitman, an uncompromising genius both of the written word and of the libido. Miller not only found his voice and his calling in Paris, he found a home. He came to be regarded as the living incarnation of the Left Bank bohemian lifestyle. He knew every nook and cranny of the City of Lights, and he embraced Paris just as it embraced him. But when war clouds began to loom ever more ominously over the Continent in the late 1930s, the Brooklynite decided to return to safety across the Atlantic.Safe though Miller might have been in New York, he was also poor and virtually unknown. The books that had made Miller a literary sensation in Europe had been censored in the United States by virtue of the Comstock Act, which forbade the circulation of obscene literature. Indeed, in his home country, if Miller was known at all, it was as an author of "dirty books." The only way to get a copy of the *Tropics* or *Black Spring* was to smuggle them in from Europe or to purchase them from an underground press. Not surprisingly, Miller's American agent was unable to drum up any buyers for his latest work, *The Colossus of Maroussi*, a lyrical book about Greece. But when the restless writer decided to travel across America and record his impressions of the homeland to which he had finally returned, Doubleday decided there was enough interest in this literary prodigal son to offer him a five-hundred-dollar advance.

Miller promptly purchased a 1932 Buick and headed west in the fall of 1940. For the next nine months, he wandered around the country, staying with friends and fellow authors and recording his adventures. The result, *The Air-Conditioned Nightmare*, is a disjointed, cranky view of an America that Miller regarded as oppressive, warped, and cruel. "Nowhere have I encountered such a dull, monotonous fabric of life as here in America. What have we to offer the world beside the superabundant loot which we recklessly plunder from the earth under the maniacal delusion that this is a sane activity? The land of opportunity has become the land of senseless sweat and struggle." Miller completed his petulantly disillusioned opus in Hollywood, where he arrived on May 12, 1941. Moving from hotel to hotel, Miller hoped to find his way in California by contacting his many admirers in the film community. Having spent most of his twenties and thirties borrowing money from both friends and strangers, he saw this as merely a more elevated round of panhandling. Erotica had always been popular in the film community, and Miller's books were an underground sensation. At least two bookstores, the Hollywood Book Shop and the Satyr Book Shop, did heavy trade in pornography, and many of the top actors and directors were known to have extensive collections of international erotica of all kinds. But unlike during his early days in New York, Miller now regarded himself as a legitimate writer, so he tried to devote most of his time to his newest literary efforts. He sold selections from *The Air-Conditioned Nightmare* to magazines, and finally even found a publisher for *The Colossus of Maroussi*. Thus, when Hollywood came calling that summer, offering the infamous author a screenwriting job, Miller turned it down. He had just enough money to stay on the West Coast until October before returning home to New York for the winter. Back on the East Coast, however, all Miller could talk about was the "desert colony" of artists and writers he had met in California. It wasn't long before he began planning his return to the place he called "Lotos Land." During the early 1940s, Hollywood had become a destination for many great European writers, artists, and musicians fleeing Hitler. From Thomas Mann and Bertolt Brecht to Igor Stravinsky and Sergey Rachmaninoff, Hollywood provided work for many of the world's great talents during this international time of turmoil. Similarly, American writers as diverse as William Faulkner, Dorothy Parker, and Lillian Hellman all found their way to Los Angeles, lured by the big bucks offered by the movie studios. In this heady atmosphere, Miller hoped he had found another Left Bank, where artists, writers, and musicians could nurture their talents among like-minded men and women. But unlike the Left Bank, the motion picture industry had the potential to make them all rich. Truly, Miller reasoned, Hollywood must be his Lotos Land. After just seven months on the East Coast, Miller was so restless that he began making plans for his return to the West. But it wasn't until he received an offer of a free room from another writer, Gilbert Nieman, that Miller boarded the train for California. His ambition was clear: get a job as a screenwriter and make a ton of money. Like so many ambitious and creative hustlers before him, Miller saw Hollywood as Mecca of the get-rich-quick scheme. But in fact what Miller would find in Hollywood was his soul. Upon his return to Los Angeles in the summer of 1942, Miller took up lodging in a small apartment in the Beverly Glen house of Gilbert and Margaret Nieman. As the main thoroughfare running through Holmby Hills—the opulent but understated enclave that has been home to Hollywood's movie stars since the 1920s—Beverly Glen eventually winds into a narrow canyon filled with sycamore trees and small cottages. Close to UCLA and Westwood, the movie studios and Hollywood, during the 1940s the canyon area was popular with students and professors, artists and writers, and lower-end studio employees. In this somewhat bohemian neighborhood, the Niemans lived in The Green House, which Miller described as "a snug, cozy place, more like an aquarium than a guest house." Miller immediately felt right at home.But if Henry Miller had high hopes for his time in Hollywood, they were quickly shattered by what he discovered about the reality of Hollywood filmmaking. Far from the collective creative process he had envisioned, Miller soon realized that making movies was largely a technical endeavor, and that the job of the writer was to crank out low-minded scripts that the studios hoped would rake in big profits. The 1940s was the culmination of the golden age of cinema, an era in which the studios were run by megalomaniac tycoons who controlled not only every aspect of the movies they made, but also the lives of the men and women who worked for them. Hollywood was a company town, and Miller was anything but a company man. In his one stint in corporate America during the 1920s, Miller spent five years as the highly corrupt employment manager for Western Union in New York City. He used his position to seduce women, pocket kickbacks, and shake down messengers for their tips. Still, Miller had fans in Hollywood's high places and, after settling in at the Green House, he landed an agent quickly. But for all his big plans, when it came right down to it, the hard-boiled writer wasn't sure he could do the work that his agent described as "just plain shit wrapped in cellophane." Miller wasn't the first writer to feel that way. William Faulkner worked on more than fifteen screenplays over the course of his contentious twenty-year relationship with the film industry. Continually drawn back to Hollywood by the money, Faulkner admitted that he "whored himself" to Hollywood as a script doctor. Although his movie work paid him so well that he was able to buy a large Mississippi estate and even his own airplane, he would later write of Hollywood, "I don't like the climate, the people, their way of life."After a few months in Hollywood, Henry Miller felt much the same. He was disillusioned by Hollywood; moreover, he was poorer than he had ever been. But it was these adversities that would provide the impetus for a major life change. As he would come to see it,"Who knows what is good for man in this life? Poverty is one of the misfortunes people seem to dread even more than sickness . . . But is it so dreadful? For me this seemingly bleak period was a most instructive one, because not being able to write for money I had to turn to something else to keep going. It could have been shining shoes; it happened to be watercolors." Henry Miller had always loved art. He first began painting after seeing some Turner prints in a Brooklyn department-store window. There was only one minor drawback: he couldn't draw. But his best friend, Emil Schnellock, could, and Miller became his disciple. It wasn't long before he realized that what he lacked in draftsmanship, he made up for in color and composition sense. He discovered watercolors in 1928, shortly before leaving for Europe, a time during which, as he later wrote, "My writing was getting me nowhere fast, my domestic life was a shambles, and my ability to panhandle had become nil. When I found what the left hand can do—'the left hand is the dreamer'—I became active as an ant. I painted morning, noon, and night, and if I ran out of paint, I used crayons, pencil, or hunks of coal." Painting became Miller's release and he returned to it almost fifteen years later, at a time when nothing else worked.Miller would later claim that he "could have had a good-paying job in the film industry. It wasn't that I despised the handsome salary that was simply couldn't pretend to kill time, which was part of the bargain." Whether a handsome salary had really been offered on this second sojourn in Tinseltown, we will never know, but we do know that Miller had recognized a fundamental truth about himself. He could never write for others. And so, much as he had begun writing as a form of panhandling in New York, churning out short pieces and sending them to potential patrons, Miller painted watercolors and began sending them to friends and, eventually, even to strangers. It started at an art shop in Westwood run by a man with the unlikely name of Attilio Bowinkel. Miller went in one day to buy two tubes of paint, asking for the cheapest brand that the proprietor had. When Mr. Bowinkel had filled the order, he politely asked if that was all his customer needed. Whereupon Miller quite frankly told him that it was all he could afford. Intrigued by Miller's honesty, Bowinkel engaged him in conversation, at the end of which he said, "Choose what you like . . . paper, paints, brushes, whatever you need. It's a gift." A few days later, Bowinkel came up to the Green House to see his new friend's work, and when he left he took a few paintings with him. When Miller next passed the shop, he was surprised to see them framed in the window. He was even more surprised when they were sold to MGM producer Arthur Freed, a collector of modern European paintings. Taking heart from Bowinkel's sale of his paintings, Miller next sent out a letter to the actor Vincent Price, a noted art connoisseur, who had recently opened a gallery in Beverly Hills. With his connections to the Hollywood glamour set, the European expatriate crowd, and the New York art world, Price was known for bringing adventurous new work by both American and European artists to the West Coast. Frequent gallery guests ran the gamut from Tallulah Bankhead, Katherine Hepburn, and Greta Garbo to Igor Stravinsky, Thomas Mann, and Aldous Huxley. When Price opened Miller's missive, he found a loose, primitive, and very vibrant watercolor that had clearly been influenced by Henri Matisse and Marc Chagall. The letter stated that, if he liked the piece, he had only to send a tube of vermilion paint and a pair of socks in return. When he reached the bottom of the letter and read the signature, Price was thrilled. As a young man in the 1930s, he had traveled to Europe and eagerly smuggled back Miller's books to the United States. And,

With his connections to the Hollywood glamour set, the European expatriate crowd, and the New York art world, Price was known for bringing adventurous new work by both American and European artists to the West Coast.

"Catering to my clients in my own sweet way was quite different, it seemed to me, from accepting a handsome advance of a commercial publisher and getting tied up in knots struggling to produce the pap which they expect . . . I earned just enough to keep my head above water.

as a man with an adventurous eye for art, he immediately liked Miller's bold style. Soon a regular socks-and-paint-for-art exchange was flourishing between Price and Miller.

Price collected twenty or so Miller watercolors, and began showing them both to his clients and to other dealers. In December 1943, Price interested the Contemporary Art Gallery on Hollywood Boulevard in having a Miller show. As Margaret Nieman recalled, "It was just a wonderful time for him to experiment and to explore with watercolors. Henry always gave the paintings away except when Vincent Price got interested. Then it got to be more fun, and he sold a few."

By the end of 1943, Miller had developed a happy routine with his painting. As he described it, "Catering to my clients in my own sweet way was quite different, it seemed to me, from accepting a handsome advance of a commercial publisher and getting tied up in knots struggling to produce the pap which they expect . . . I earned just enough to keep my head above water. It was like writing songs and getting paid to whistle them. They went fast, my little jobs. Some must have been absolutely frightful, no question about it. Even Vincent Price, generous and indulgent as he was then, balked at some I offered him. On the whole you might say that a happy atmosphere prevailed."

The happy atmosphere included many new friends who supported Miller in his work. Margaret and Gilbert Nieman kept a roof over Miller's head and food on his plate. Artists such as Man Ray and Fernand Léger supported Miller's increasing dedication to his watercolors. Actors such as Geraldine Fitzgerald, Hollywood moguls like Arthur Freed, and wealthy women such as Melpomene Niarchos, wife of the shipping magnate, were patrons and frequent visitors to the Green House. Even the L.A. police chief once drove up in a limousine to introduce the director of a famous art museum. Soon Miller was selling his brightly colored paintings, with subjects ranging from clowns and fantastical creatures to nudes and landscapes, for what seemed to him an incredible sum of fifty dollars each.

In 1944, Miller produced a limited-edition, oversize book called *The Angel Is My Watermark*, which included an original watercolor, photographs of the artist at work, and an "Open Letter" in which Miller requested supplies and clothes in exchange for his work. He even provided his measurements and noted that he "loved corduroys." Miller was working at a fevered pace, but he was not writing. The ardent, personal voice he had discovered in Paris remained lost in America. But he was painting, and in painting, he soon realized, he had found his passion. In *The Angel Is My Watermark*, he wrote of the solace he managed to discover in art, even with the world at war: When you put your mind to such a simple, innocent thing as the making of a watercolor you lose some of the anguish which derives from being a member of a world gone mad. Whether you paint flowers, stars, horses, or angels, you acquire respect and admiration for all the elements that go to make up our universe. You don't think of flowers as friends and stars enemies, of horses as Communists and angels Fascists. You accept them for what they are and you praise God that they are what they are. At the end of the 1944, Miller left Hollywood for Big Sur, on the central coast of California. There he would make his home for twenty-one years, finally write the books that would bring him an American audience, and even succeed in getting *Tropic of Cancer* published in the United States. When he finally returned to Southern California in 1965, it was as a rich, successful, and celebrated author, who lived among movie stars such as Ava Gardner and Gloria Swanson, in a colonial-style house in the opulent community of Pacific Palisades. But just as he had done two decades earlier, he spent his days painting watercolors for his friends. Thinking back on his first stay in Hollywood, Miller often reminisced about the Green House, "where I made so many watercolors, sold them for a song or for an umbrella I had no use for, but where I also made and found friends I never knew existed." The fame and fortune Miller had envisioned for himself in Lotos Land never came to pass during that first sojourn in Southern California. But his time in Hollywood did prove idyllic, for it was there that he began to paint, and, as he put it, "to paint is to love again, and to love is to live life to the fullest." By making watercolors, "turning them out like a madman," Miller began "wriggling out of the straightjacket" of writing for others instead of for himself. And the love he found in painting led him to the joyous new voice with which he wrote as "the sage of Big Sur." Far from the angry, avant-garde writer he had been in the 1930s, in the second half of his life Miller was known as a mild-mannered man with the spiritual air of a guru, a genius writer, a passionate painter. By painting as an amateur in the truest sense of the word—one who loves what he does—Miller finally became the person he had always dreamed of becoming. As he put it in Big Sur and the Oranges of Hieronymous Bosch, "Whoever uses the spirit that is in him creatively is an artist. To make living itself an art, that is the goal."

To the end of his life, my father, the actor Vincent Price, spoke with wonder about his first encounter with Henry Miller and their ensuing friendship. In the early 1940s, my dad was a rising star at Twentieth Century-Fox who desperately missed the intellectual and creative stimulation of the New York art world. Educated at Yale and the Courtauld Institute in London, he was a well-respected art historian and collector. So, to stave off boredom in the company town that was Hollywood in those days, he and his friend, and fellow actor George Macready, started the Little Gallery in Beverly Hills.

During the war years, the Little Gallery was the place to see and be seen, as well as to enjoy the work of a wide range of new and established modern artists. My dad knew everyone in Hollywood, from Thomas Mann to Tallulah Bankhead. But when he received a letter one day from a man named Henry Miller, containing a vivid watercolor, he was tickled with the idea of meeting the celebrated author of "those dirty books, the real thing, an American legend."

The friendship that ensued involved the exchange of dozens of Miller's watercolors, and my father did much to launch Miller's career as a painter. Their close relationship was relatively short-lived, however, as Miller, known for his short-fused temper, one day took offense at something my father could never remember having done. After Miller's temper calmed, the two men remained on good terms, but were never again close. But to the end of his days, my dad treasured his interactions with Miller. And he particularly treasured his watercolors. He never sold them, but instead gave them away to close friends and family members. He gave me three. The first is a very primitive painting of a man in a house, dedicated to my father. It has never been reproduced, and now hangs in the Vincent Price Gallery at East Los Angeles College. The other two can be seen in the retrospective book on Miller's artwork. Ice Creatures is a fluid, watery world filled with ghostlike figures. It, too, hangs at my father's gallery. The last, Agape, is a colorful triptych of three nude women that I absolutely adore. It hangs in my home, where I enjoy it every day. It always serves to remind me of Miller's credo: "Paint as you like, and die happy."

DIANE ARBUS:
TWO TREATMENTS

Diane Arbus

Tamara Jenkins, the director and screenwriter of *Slums of Beverly Hills*, is currently writing a screenplay about the life of maverick photographer Diane Arbus. For source material, Jenkins is adapting Patricia Bosworth's 1994 biography of Arbus. The following is a section from the biography and the corresponding scene in Jenkins's script. For this scene, in which Arbus photographs Jacqueline Susann and her husband, Irving Mansfield, Bosworth interviewed Mansfield. Jenkins started with one page in the biography, then went back to Bosworth's original notes from her interview with Mansfield in order to create the drama of the scene.

AN EXCERPT FROM

DIANE ARBUS: A BIOGRAPHY

BY

PATRICIA BOSWORTH

DIANE THEN FLEW TO CALIFORNIA AND PHOTOGRAPHED Jacqueline Susann with her husband, Irving Mansfield, for *Harper's Magazine*.

Susann was currently promoting her novel *The Love Machine*, which was high on the best-seller list, and between interviews (some six a day) she was ensconced in a Beverly Hills hotel suite overlooking banks of geraniums and a smoggy sky. When Diane arrived, Susann began patting her jet-black Korean hair fall and adjusting her bubble glasses until Diane asked her to take them off.

"This Diane Arbus character was bossy," Irving Mansfield remembers. "She made us move all over the place. Then she wanted us to pose in our bathing suits next to the TV set. I didn't get it, so I said no to the idea, but Jackie, who was always cooperative with the press, said of course. And when we were in our suits and Arbus asked Jackie to plunk down in my lap, Jackie said yes to that, too. Particularly after Arbus assured us this shot would be for her portfolio—*not for publication.** Her exact words. We held the pose for what seemed like hours—until my kneecaps went numb. The flashbulbs kept blinding us, she kept assuring us we looked terrific. Arbus looked tense. She told us as soon as she finished shooting she was taking the next plane back to New York; she'd flown out specifically to photograph us and she seemed a little angry about it."

* The resulting portrait of the Mansfields appeared in the October 1969 issue of *Harper's* and Diane sold the picture to other publications. "It was seen all over the world," Mansfield claims. "We thought it was undignified."

A SCRIPT IN PROGRESS

DIANE ARBUS

by

Tamara Jenkins

BEVERLY HILLS HOTEL—HALLWAY—DAY—1969

Down at the far end of the hall, a woman heads toward us. Short black hair sprouts from her head. Dark shadows circle her eyes. This is DIANE ARBUS (46).

Loaded down with a collection of cameras and flash units that hang from her neck, she hustles down the long corridor checking room numbers. A huge equipment bag is slung over one shoulder and a tripod leans up against the other one like a rifle.

Despite her age, she appears girlish. In her sleeveless frock and bare legs, Diane resembles a dark, latter-day Alice after a serious fall down the Rabbit Hole.

A MALE VOICE
Diane Arbus?
(a beat)
She was a ballbuster.

CUT TO:

INT. LOS ANGELES HOME—DAY (1980)

The voice belongs to Irving Mansfield (70s). He's a wealthy man who has spent many years in the sun. He sits in his living room talking to an off-screen female interviewer. He adds an ice cube to his drink and speaks directly into the camera

IRVING:
You saw the picture she took of us?

Off screen and off microphone we can barely hear the Interviewer.

INTERVIEWER (OS):
Of course. What year was it taken?

IRVING:

1969. It was a nutty time. The new book had just knocked *Portnoy's Complaint* right off the best-seller list.

CUT TO:

INT. BEVERLY HILLS HOTEL SUITE—1969

JACQUELINE SUSANN (48) sits at a dainty desk talking on the phone. Copies of her book *The Love Machine* are neatly piled up beside her. She autographs one. Exquisite penmanship.

IRVING (VO):

Jackie was doing a ton of press. There were lots of photographers around in those days.

Jackie lifts her enormous false eyelashes, strikes a smile, and stares straight at us for what feels like an uncomfortably long time.

Lights flash over her face.

REVERSE ANGLE REVEALS—A PHOTO SESSION IN PROGRESS

A GROUP OF NEWSPAPER PHOTOGRAPHERS—
all men—call out to their subject. "Over here Jackie." "How does it feel to be back on the best-seller list?" "Give a smile." "C'mon Jackie."

Jackie gives them their photo op. In one hand she holds up a copy of *The Love Machine*. In the other a copy of *Portnoy's Complaint*. She strikes a theatrical wink and holds the pose for the photographers.

SHUTTERS SNAP and FLASH UNITS erupt into a chorus of popping white light.

INT. BEVERLY HILLS HOTEL—HALLWAY—DAY

Back with Diane. She hurries down the hall checking room numbers. She refers to a wrinkled-up piece of paper she holds in her hand.

Her ballet slippers are soundless against the plush carpet. We only hear Diane's BREATH and the JIGGLING and CLINKING of her photographic equipment gently hitting up against each other.

IRVING (VO)
This Diane Arbus character was bossy. I mean—it's not like I have a problem with strong women—I was married to Jackie Susann, but this one was something else.

Diane arrives at Suite 489. She takes a moment to fluff her hair with her hand and then knocks. SOUND OF A SMALL YELPING DOG.

The door swings open to reveal a YOUNGER IRVING MANSFIELD. A small poodle races out of the suite into the hall.

DIANE
Irving Mansfield?

YOUNG IRVING
Yes.

DIANE
Diane Arbus from *Harper's*. I'm here to take your picture.

Diane reaches for a handshake. Irving is sizing her up. He looks down at her bony dirty feet plunged into a pair of ballet slippers.

YOUNG IRVING
You alone?

DIANE
Yes. Do you think I can use your toilet?
I came straight from the airport—

Diane's mouth opens to a pleading smile revealing a crooked collection of small gray teeth. Irving continues to stare. She quickly seals her lips shut, a reflex she has developed in order to hide her teeth in mixed company. Hold on Diane.

IRVING (VO)
She didn't look like a photographer. Dirty feet. Terrible teeth.
She could have been a drug addict.

YOUNG IRVING

Can I see some accreditation.

Diane burrows her hand deep into an overstuffed equipment bag looking for her press cards—

The poodle still YELPS and races around the hallway.

DIANE

Weren't you expecting me?

YOUNG IRVING

Yes, it's just our security precaution.

Diane mumbles something to herself.

BACK TO:

INT. IRVING'S INTERVIEW—DAY

IRVING

(defending himself)

I asked to see her credentials like I did with everybody. You don't just let strangers walk into your hotel room, do you. The look on that girl's face. You'd think I asked her something indecent.

CUT TO:

HOTEL HALLWAY—SUITE 489

Diane dumps the entire contents of her bag onto the hallway floor, folds herself onto her knees and sifts through the entrails: Dozens of rolls of film. Light meters. Extra flash units, notes, tampons, paperbacks, and prescription pill bottles.
The POODLE is YELPING and circling around Diane.

YOUNG IRVING stands above her apologetically.

YOUNG IRVING

I'm sorry to put you through this—I'm sure our publicity girl would have mentioned it to your editor. It's been a policy of ours—

Ceaseless YELPING.

JACQUELINE (OS)
(calling from an inner room) Irv, she needs to go out—

YOUNG IRVING
(calling OS) She just went.

JACQUELINE (OS)
Did she do her business?

Irving's chutzpah is momentarily diminished.

YOUNG IRVING
(calling out)
I'm talking to the girl who's here to take our picture—

DIANE
Irving—

YELP. YELP.

YOUNG IRVING
Yeah?

DIANE
Could you move your foot?

YOUNG IRVING
What?

Diane taps his Italian loafer with her finger.

DIANE
Your foot. You're standing on something.

YOUNG IRVING
(lifting his foot) I'm sorry.

From under Irving's Gucci loafer, Diane finally produces the press pass. She holds it up to Irving's face. The *Harper's* magazine logo is printed on the top and right below it is an ID picture of a weary Arbus.

DIANE

Now can I use your toilet?

CUT TO:

INT. STUDY—A LITTLE LATER

Camera tracks across a collection of...

...framed family photos on a mantel. Diane glances at them. Pictures of Jacqueline and Irving at various functions with various celebrities. Diane reaches for one small frame that stands behind all the others. Diane studies it.

CLOSE ON THE PHOTO—It's a picture of Jacqueline and Irving standing with a visibly retarded young boy on the lawn outside of an institutional building. The boy beams proudly with a crooked grin.

CLOSE ON DIANE—She is transfixed by the boy's defenseless face. She delicately runs her finger over the photo.

Diane turns it over and slips the velvet backing off the frame. On the back of the photo in elegant penmanship it reads, "Gary Mansfield on his 13th birthday at Gracewood."

Out of nowhere.

YOUNG IRVING (OS)

The photographer likes to look.

Diane looks up. Irving stands nearby. Diane swallows hard.

DIANE

I didn't know you had a son.

YOUNG IRVING

Well, now you do.

Irving holds out his hand. Diane hands him the framed picture. Irving looks at the photo and then puts it back on the mantel in its rightful place behind all the other pictures.

CUT TO:

INT. BEDROOM OF HOTEL SUITE—A LITTLE LATER

The doors of an enormous closet are rolled open. It's packed with designer clothes perfectly hung from wooden hangers.

Diane sits on the side of the bed loading film into her camera. She watches as Jaqueline, wrapped in a terry-cloth robe, pops a cigarette in her mouth and browses through her wardrobe . . .

JACQUELINE

Whatever we decide on, I want to make sure that we can see the ankhs in the picture.

Irving arrives in the doorway with the dog on a leash.

DIANE

Angst?

Jackie bursts into a fit of laughter. Irving joins her.

JACQUELINE

Not angst, sweetheart. Ankhs.

Jacqueline holds up a piece of jewelry that hangs from her neck. It's a large gold cross with a loop on the top.

JACQUELINE (CONT'D)

A-n-k-h. It's an ancient Egyptian symbol.

Diane leans in to examine the pendant and finds herself staring into the hollow of Jackie's blouse. There, Diane is quietly startled to discover a bit of scar tissue poking out from Jackie's bra. This is clearly the result of a mastectomy. Diane takes the pendant between her fingers.

DIANE

It's beautiful. What does it mean?

JACQUELINE

(hushed reverence)

Life.

Diane releases the ankh and looks up. For a brief suspended moment Diane and Jackie stare into each other's eyes. Then . . .

YOUNG IRVING
Yeah. We found a terrific jeweler in New York.
(showing off his ankh cuff links)
He can turn anything into an ankh.

JACQUELINE
It plays a major role in the plot of the book. So anyway we can tie it into the publicity material—

DIANE
Oh. Okay. Well, I was thinking about the two of you in matching suits.

JACQUELINE
We're aiming for something a little younger, hipper.

YOUNG IRVING
Business suits seem a little stiff, don't they?

DIANE
Not business suits. Bathing suits.

Jacqueline and Irving are stone-cold silent . . .

IRVING'S INTERVIEW—

IRVING
She wanted us to pose in our bathing suits next to the TV set. I didn't see the point, so I said no, but Jackie liked the idea.

CUT TO:

INT. HOTEL SUITE BEDROOM—A LITTLE LATER

Jackie, now dressed in an expensive black one-piece bathing suit, screams with laughter.

JACQUELINE
Irv, don't be a prude!

YOUNG IRVING, uncomfortable in only his bathing suit briefs and ankh medallion, reluctantly shuffles into sight from the adjoining bathroom.

IRVING

It's not about prude. You're a writer for Christ's sake. You ever see Norman Mailer posing in his bathing suit?

JACQUELINE

(rubbing suntan grease between her hands)

No, thank god.

Diane is pulling the wall of curtains closed.

DIANE

Norman Mailer doesn't have Jackie Susann's legs.

JACQUELINE

(delighted)

Touché!

Diane, seizing on the levity, starts directing her subjects. She hunches over her Rolleiflex camera trying to frame up the shot.

DIANE

Irving, let me see you seated here.

Irving passes in front of Diane.

Jacqueline and Irving are off-screen. We do not see them pose. Instead, we stay on Arbus. We watch her work.

DIANE

Now, Jackie, ah . . . how 'bout you on Irving's lap.

YOUNG IRVING (OS)

(to Diane)

C'mon—

JACQUELINE (OS)

Oh Irv. Have some fun...

(to Diane)

We're going for sexy, not vulgar, right?

DIANE
Right.

JACQUELINE (OS)
How's this?

DIANE
Swing your legs over there.

JACQUELINE (OS)
Like that?

Jackie is laughing. Giggling.

DIANE
Yeah. Jackie, chin. Yeah.

YOUNG IRVING (OS)
I don't feel right about this.

DIANE
(staring down into the ground glass)
Really? I think this is ... It's so right. It's ... terrific.
Irving, look at me.

A surprise attack. Arbus clicks the shutter. A WHITE FLASH POPS.

YOUNG IRVING
Wait a minute. I said ...

DIANE
Jackie, look right at me.

ANOTHER FLASH POPS. WHITES OUT THE SCREEN.

IRVING (VO)
I think she flew right back to New York that same night.

CUT TO:

INT. BEVERLY HILLS HOTEL—HALLWAY—DAY—LATER

Diane steps out of the hotel suite. Irving appears behind her. He calls after her ...

IRVING
Don't forget the work print.

DIANE
I promise.

She hustles down the long corridor. The little dog YELPS and chases after her. A small smile of satisfaction creeps across Diane's face.

IRVING (VO)
They ran that picture.

BACK TO:

IRVING'S INTERVIEW—DAY

INTERVIEWER (OS)
But you saw it in advance—

IRVING
No. She never sent us any work print. She just went ahead and did it. Look, all we knew was *Harper's*. Nice magazine. Good circulation. We didn't know from Diane Arbus. Later we find out—this is the lady famous for photographing freaks. Fuckin' freak photographer. What can I tell you?
(beat)
We didn't care much for the picture.

INT. DARK ROOM—NIGHT

Diane works under the red glow of the darkroom light.

The photo of Jacqueline and Irving emerges in a batch of developing solution.

Black-and-white portrait. Jackie sits perched on Irving's lap. Matching bathing suits. Matching deep tans. And matching ankh pennants dangle from their necks. They stare straight out at us. They glisten from suntan oil. A wall of curtains behind them.

IRVING (VO)
Felt it was undignified. She must have made a lot of money on it though. That photo was seen all over the world....

[A Continuity Shot from *Goodbye Again,* 1933]

[A continuity shot from *Three On A Match*, 1932]

5 FIVE QUESTIONS

The EDITORS OF *TIN HOUSE* ASKED SOME OF THEIR FAVORITE FILM AND FICTION PEOPLE THE FOLLOWING FIVE QUESTIONS ABOUT WHICH BOOKS AND MOVIES THEY LOVE AND HATE.

1) What is your favorite film adaptation of a book? 2) What is your least favorite film adaptation of a book? 3) What film has had the most influence on you personally and/or professionally? 4) What book has had the most influence on you personally and/or professionally? 5) What book would you most like to adapt for the big screen?

Michael Tolkin

(novelist and screenwriter, *The Player*; also writer and director, *The Rapture* and *The New Age*)

1) *The Wizard of Oz*. It's an unsatisfying book, forced into continuous and if not unread then unfinished print by the film, but independent of the film a curiosity. The book doesn't compare to *Alice in Wonderland* or *Wind in the Willows*, the allegories weigh too heavily. The film is a work of precise genius. The power of the fantasy, not just for whatever lies over the rainbow, but for fellowship and courage, with such great music and color, coming out of a book that's almost unreadable, makes this the great emerald example of an adaptation. I like *Double Indemnity*, but they fudged the ending. See answer to number 2.

2) Hitchcock's Patricia Highsmith has never been well served by film, if helping a writer get more readers is the payment of a debt. The adaptations of her books take a brilliant setup and then always cheat on an understanding of emotion, morality, and psychology that defines the modern character the way Dostoyevski defined Russia. This is not a stretch; Highsmith anticipated the serial killer and located him inside the world that became *Vanity Fair*. A German version of *Edith's Diary* was good, though it lacked the specific torments of an American oscillating between the hawks and doves of Vietnam, and the French made *Deep Water* with Trintingant, which was good although I don't remember why. There's a Depardieu version which isn't a bad film but misses the psychosis of the book. Wenders's *The American Friend*, a free adaptation of *Ripley's Game* is the best of the Highsmith movies because he stays true enough to the plot, and creates an atmosphere which isn't in the book until after you've seen the film, but it works. *The Talented Mr. Ripley*, with such brilliant acting and atmosphere, Ripley's dream of Europe made real, also misused Highsmith; it avoided showing Ripley as a cheap criminal from the beginning, and refused to let him go free at the end, trapping Tom in a murderous homosexuality that Highsmith always kept beneath his surface, it was something he never acts on. Highsmith's courage sent Tom, the man who gets away with murder, to the best hotel in town, the reward for his hard-fought practice. But none of the adaptations are as evil as what Hitchcock did with *Strangers on a Train*, a novel about a man who proposes the perfect crime to another man: to commit each other's murders. And in the book, both men commit their crimes. For Hitchcock to lop off the truth of the book in favor of a safer psychology is a cultural murder.

The result of all of these butcherings is that the appropriation of a great plot and the evisceration of an artist's nerve reduces Highsmith to an eccentric expat with a few nifty premises. And the end of that misdeed of communal entertainment is that she is barely in print anymore.

3) Some combination of Fassbinder's *Ali: Fear Eats the Soul* and *Close Encounters of the Third Kind*. I'm sure I've fucked myself because of this.

4) I'm reading *The Idiot* right now so I'll say *The Idiot*, but earlier this year I read Jonathan Raban's *Passage to Juneau*, when I would have said *Passage to Juneau*.

5) *Strangers on a Train*.

Carrie Fisher

(actress, writer, screenwriter)

1) *To Kill a Mockingbird*.

2) I make a practice of not clinging to unpleasant entertainment experiences.

3) *Groundhog Day*.

4) *Middlemarch*, *Play It As It Lays*.

5) *Daughter of the Queen of Sheba*.

Eric Bogosian

(actor, playwright, screenwriter, *subUrbia*, *Talk Radio*; novelist, *Mall*)

1) Atom Egoyan just directed an adaptation of Beckett's *Krapp's Last Tape* that is about as fine an adaptation as I can imagine. It stars John Hurt, and I guess what makes it brilliant is that it takes a major piece of writing and enlarges it. Although I love Beckett, he's a little like homework for me. John Hurt expanded on every possibility the words presented and Atom kindled the atmosphere with his very patient camera. Watching this movie was kind of like listening to an amazing bell being rung perfectly.

2) I hated *The Getaway* remake of 1994 (based, as was the original Peckinpah/McQueen/MacGraw film, on Jim Thompson's book). This remake smacked of every bad choice contemporary Hollywood can make: softening the sharp edges, missing the point, imitating the actions without any notion of what the story was really about. The very fact that the film got released at all is repellent. And all of this is pretty much true for all remakes of classic cinema. I guess the only thing lower than fucking up great old movies is remaking old TV shows into movies.

3) *Midnight Cowboy* had a pretty major impact on me. Before that time, I, as a young actor, had never seen anyone who looked like me (Dustin Hoffman) playing a lead role in a picture. After seeing that movie, I knew two things: I could be actor, and I was going to live in New York City so I could meet those way-out people in the movie. And I did both.

4) *The Tibetan Book of the Dead* is the most influential book I have read. (Not to be confused with *The Tibetan Book of Living and Dying*.) This is a prayer book used to lead souls through their trials after physical death. It encourages the spirit to walk through (rather than be chased by) the things it fears most.

5) The book I most want to adapt is something I wrote a few years back called *Notes from Underground*. It's the journal of a man who appears to be "normal" and is, in fact, living on the very brink of sanity. It's a tragedy. I wanted to play the role originally but now I'm too old for the part. Robert Downey Jr. would be perfect.

Patrick McGrath

(author, *Spider*, *Asylum*, *Blood and Water*, etc.; screenwriter, *Grave Indiscretion*, adapted from his novel *The Grotesque*)

1) It has to be *Rebecca*, Hitchcock by way of Daphne du Maurier.

2) *Hangover Square*, a gloriously strange and seedy novel by Patrick Hamilton that was treated very unfaithfully, and turned into absurd melodrama, in the adaptation starring Laird Cregar. That and *Moby Dick*, in which Gregory Peck was a most inadequate Ahab.

3) *Touch of Evil*—border as metaphor.

4) *Heart of Darkness.*

5) *The Monk*, M. G. Lewis's great gothic novel that utterly scandalized late-eighteenth century England.

Peggy Rajski

(producer, *Home for the Holidays*, *Little Man Tate*, *Matewan*, etc.; Academy Award-winning director of short film, *Trevor*)

1) In recent memory, *The Remains of the Day*. The book was so interior, and I couldn't imagine how they could adapt it. I was truly surprised that they made it work, and that it worked as well as it did.

2) *Dune.*

3) Clichéd as the choice is, *Citizen Kane* is still a standout for me for its economy in storytelling, and for the awe-inspiring way in which it was shot. *The 400 Blows* stunned me the first time I saw it and opened my eyes to the world of foreign films. I saw both of these films in high school and couldn't believe the impact they had on me. They cut to the core of my being and just took my breath away.

4) *The Reader*, by Bernard Schlink, is one of the most beautiful books I've ever read. I continue to be moved and humbled by its spare power. Same for Willa Cather's *Death Comes for the Archbishop*. These books pulled something out of me that's very hard to put into words. Something shifted in me after reading them, moved me to a deeper place, a deeper knowing about life, death, the complexity and richness of interior life, and the emotional power that comes from acceptance, self-acceptance.

5) Don't really have one that's a burning desire for me right now.

Daniel Halpern

(poet; founder, with Paul Bowles, of *Antaeus*)

1) *Ulysses*, Joyce/Joseph Strick.

2) *The Sheltering Sky*, Bowles/Bertolucci.

3) *Children of Paradise*, Carné.

4) On August 5, 2000: *Don Quixote*, Cervantes.

5) *Nightwood*, Djuna Barnes.

John Savage

(actor, *The Deer Hunter*, *The Thin Red Line*, *Inside Moves*, etc.; co-producer, with Nelson Mandela, *Malcolm X*)

1) *A Tale of Two Cities*, the old black and white version.

2) *The Onion Field*, because I had to do it, and I realized there's no way a character can be fully represented as well as in a book, especially one that's so narrative, although the film was a good attempt at adapting a

great book—a true story about some honorable men and some terrible men, too.

3) *The Hunchback of Notre Dame* with Charles Laughton.

4) *My Antonía*, by Willa Cather. When I read it as a child.

5) *There but for the Grace of God*, by Monsignor Patrick Carol Abbing. Put that in your pipe and smoke it.

Alison McLean

(director, *Crush*, *Jesus' Son*)

1) *Belle de Jour, Solaris.*

2) *Sheltering Sky, The Talented Mr. Ripley.*

3) Really can't answer this one.

4) No one book in particular, but writers (right now) include Adam Phillips, Tim O'Brien, and Jane Bowles.

5) *Moby Dick*; also the *Narnia* books by C. S. Lewis.

Robert Polito

(poet; author of the National Book Critics Circle winner *Savage Art: A Biography of Jim Thompson*, among other books)

1) So many. Once upon a time most feature films originated as novels. These are two terrific ones: *The Unholy Three* (1925 version), directed by Tod Browning from a novel by Clarence Aaron Robbins; and *Fantomas*, directed by Louis Feuillade from the novels of Marcel Allain and Pierre Souvestre.

2) Almost anything by Merchant Ivory.

3) Edgar Ulmer's *Detour.*

4) Oh my God ... *The Changing Light at Sandover* (Merrill), the Beckett trilogy, *The Book of the Body* (Bidart), *Lolita* (Nabokov), Marvell's poems, *Brass Knuckles* (O'Brien), *Down There* (Goodis), *Three Lives* (Stein), *A Hell of a Woman* (Thompson).

5) None of the above ... maybe a Stanley Elkin novel, *The Magic Kingdom*, or Edward Ruscha's *Twenty Gas Stations.*

András Hamori

(producer of many adaptations, including *Crash* and *The Sweet Hereafter*)

1) *Naked Lunch.*

2) *Bonfire of the Vanities.*

3) *Touch of Evil.*

4) Personally, *The Master and Margarita*; professionally, *The Art of War.*

5) I can't answer, I am negotiating for it.

George Plimpton

(founder and editor, *The Paris Review*; author, *The Curious Case of Sidd Finch*, etc.; and actor in dozens of movies, from *Reds* to *Good Will Hunting*)

1) *Bang the Drum Slowly.*

2) *The Old Man and the Sea.*

3) *Citizen Kane.*

4) *Huckleberry Finn.*

5) *The Curious Case of Sidd Finch.*

Howie Sanders

(book agent for the movies at United Talent Agency, co-represents, with Rich Green, writers such as Chuck Palahniuk and Sebastian Junger)

1) This is a very difficult question. I'd have to say *Marathon Man*, *Day of the Jackal*, and *The Godfather* are right up there.

2) I plead the fifth.

3) *The Graduate.* Who can forget the Alfa Spyder, the music, and Mrs. Robinson?

4) *Portnoy's Complaint.* It should be required reading for puberty and bar mitzvah.

5) The idea frightens me. I can't spend that much time alone with myself.

Andrew Hultkrans

(editor of *Bookforum*)

1) Robert Altman's 1973 adaptation of Raymond Chandler's *The Long Goodbye.* Working with Leigh Brackett, who co-wrote the script for *The Big Sleep* in 1946, Altman updates and upends his source novel, placing the mantle of Philip Marlowe, the fast-talking, resourceful private dick previously played by Bogart, onto the stooped shoulders of, well, simply "a dick"—in the mumbling, bumbling form of Elliott Gould. Chandler's mean streets, once "darker than night," are blanched with oppressive sunlight, everybody has a savage tan, pastels are the new black, and Arnold Schwarzenegger appears as the three-line heavy he always should have remained. Only the various interpolations of the title song coursing through the soundtrack remind us where this all began.

Honorable mention: Francis Ford Coppola's *Apocalypse Now*, for a similarly brilliant misuse of another Marlow, and, in stuffed man Marlon Brando's pills-and-pork-addled improvisations—the Horror!—of T. S. Eliot's "Hollow Men."

2) Although I've never been enough of an idiot to actually watch it, my choice would have to be Martin Ritt's 1959 adaptation of *The Sound and the Fury.* I picture Yul Brynner's Jason barking, "Once a bitch, always a bitch," in faux Siamese after his offer of "Shall we dance?" is rebuffed by Caddy, and Quentin wandering around Harvard in a long black overcoat and grinding his teeth (basically how I spent my time there) as ticker-tape subtitles of his endless, circular ruminations on time run along the bottom of the screen. No wonder Faulkner tried to drink himself to death in Hollywood.

3) David Cronenberg's *Videodrome.* Don't ask. Let's just say that when a spent, affectless James Woods says, haltingly, "I'm having some trouble...finding my way around," near the end of the film, I know exactly what he's talking about.

4) Not a book, but a comic book: *Amazing Fantasy #15*, Marvel Comics, the origin and debut of Spiderman, which ends with the maxim "With great power comes great responsibility." Words to live by, even if you're still working on the great power part.

5) *The Crying of Lot 49*, by Thomas Pynchon. Quixotic perhaps, but I think it could be done. I imagine it as a conflation of Cronenberg's *Videodrome*, Alan Pakula's *The Parallax View*, and John Frankenheimer's *Seconds*—all films that begin small, slowly open out onto infinite webs of interconnected conspiracies that promise everything, then close again into darkness, delivering nothing—like an iris, or life itself.

Benicio Del Toro

(actor, *The Way of the Gun*, *Fear and Loathing in Las Vegas*, *Basquiat*, etc.; director-writer, *Submission*)

1) *The Godfather.*

2) I'd have to look at a list of bad films. There are a lot of bad movies. I do believe films from adaptations should stick close to the book, if it's a good book. You take one line out, and the thing goes kaboom.

3) Somewhere between *King Kong* and *Papillon*. I'm talking about movies I saw as a kid. Professionally somewhere between Scorsese, Cassavetes, Gutierrez-Alea, and maybe Tarkovsky. It's hard to separate the director from the film—I'd have to add in Buñuel and Polanski.

4) *The Old Man and the Sea*, personally. Professionally, *Fear and Loathing in Las Vegas* because I got a chance to do a movie based on a masterpiece.

5) I would love to see the song "Meeting Across the River," by Bruce Springsteen, turned into a film.

Harvey Shapiro

(poet, *Selected Poems*; editor, *New York Times Magazine*)

1) Monty Python's *Life of Brian*. A trenchant retelling of the Gospel.

2) *Portrait of a Lady*, Jane Campion's creative muddle.

3) The gangster films I saw as a kid, films with James Cagney and Edward G. Robinson. The gangster was the heroic outsider who needed the city to sustain him and hide him, who lived by his wits, was worshiped by a moll, and came to a bad end. I think I saw him as the artist I wanted to become.

4) Charles Reznikoff's *By the Waters of Manhattan*, because it furnished me, as an adult, with images of the poet I could accept and use—an unheroic, battered man, making his daily quest through the maze of the city, looking for the way.

5) I would most like to adapt two stories by Stephen Crane, "The Open Boat" and "The Blue Hotel."

Victor D. LaValle

(author, *Slapboxing with Jesus*)

1) *Deliverance* is the only film I've seen that was much better than the book.

2) *From Beyond*, an awful adaptation of an H. P. Lovecraft story.

3) *The Five Heartbeats*, by Robert Townsend, is profoundly moving for me every single time.

4) *The Collected Stories* of H. P. Lovecraft.

5) The stories of Breece Pancake.

Robert Pinsky

(poet, translator, former U.S. poet laureate)

1) Maybe Kurosawa's *Ran* and his *Throne of Blood*, if we allow Shakespeare to be a book. Maybe Kubrick's *Lolita*.

2) The Gregory Peck Ahab and Disney *Winnie the Pooh* come to mind. Come to think of it, they are kind of similar.

3) Maybe *Ivanhoe*, maybe *His Girl Friday*, maybe *Bad Day at Black Rock*.

4) Joyce's *Ulysses* or Faulkner's *The Hamlet*.

5) Plutarch's *Life of Alcibiades*. The part may be too outrageously great for any living actor ... It would require aspects of David Bowie, Toshiro Mifune, and Brando.

Heidi Julevitz

(author, *The Mineral Palace*)

1) My favorite adaptation of recent years is Atom Egoyan's *The Sweet Hereafter*. Though I am a fan of Banks, *The Sweet Hereafter*, the novel, had a less than effective narrative structure (chapters of alternating POV), or was maybe simply a less effective work, structure aside. *The Sweet Hereafter*, the movie, meanwhile, had a nonlinear narrative that swooped ahead and then circled back on itself in a way that aptly captured the disconnected, emotionally distant, and bewildered state of a town in crisis. I loved the way the ending referred to a point back in time, returning us to the moment just before the loss of innocence; the film resisted fake, feel-goody redemption, but still sought to abandon us in a happier place (that is nonetheless heavy with impending doom).

2) No comment.

3) Altman's *Nashville*. I admire the way the film moves narratively from chaos and disjointedness to a sort of uneasy union, while emotionally, the movement is from an uneasy union to total chaos, apathy, alienation, and purposelessness, ALL, mind you, presented in a triumphant manner, the "winners" not for a moment realizing what they've lost. I always feel like someone is slowly squeezing my innards during that final scene, no matter how many times I watch it.

4) The book with the most influence on me is almost always the book I've read most recently. Most recently (this summer) I read *Moby Dick* (shamefully, for the first time) and was utterly amazed to discover how narrative drive can be so undeniable in a book that is composed, nearly entirely, of bombastic asides. It just goes to show what little suggestion of plot one actually requires to keep a reader interested in your opinions, for example, on cetology.

5) I would like to see *Two Serious Ladies*, by Jane Bowles, adapted for the screen. Atmospherically, the book straddles the fence between proper (even arrested), ladylike realism and daft, loony surrealism. It seems the book would give a filmmaker a lot of interpretive leeway, while also providing a fairly stable base from which to wander off into the strange, (Jane) Bowlesian stratosphere.

Robert Haas

(poet and translator, former U.S. poet laureate)

1) *The Maltese Falcon* or *Shoot the Piano Player*.

2) A toss-up between Huston's *Moby Dick* and Disney's *Winnie the Pooh*.

3) Too many: *Seven Samurai*; *The Seventh Seal*; *Hiroshima, Mon Amour*; *Woman of the Dunes*; *La Strada*; *Ikuru*; *Bringing Up Baby*.

4) Impossible to say.

5) A. S. Byatt's *Still Lives* or W. G. Seibold's *The Rings of Saturn*.

Jeanette Watson

(founder of Books & Co.; publisher, Turtle Point Press)

1) The recent adaptation of Proust (*Time Regained*). I also liked *Clueless*.

2) I hated *Eyes Wide Shut*, from Schnitzler.

3) The first movie I remember seeing—*Roman Holiday*, with Audrey Hepburn and Gregory Peck, which gave me a lifelong love of romantic movies. I longed to be thin and glamorous like Audrey with large sunglasses, a gamine haircut, and a chic Givenchy wardrobe.

4) A collection of Hans Christian Anderson fairy tales which gave me some preparation for the vicissitudes of life.

5) *A Confederacy of Dunces*—too bad Bill Murray is too old to play the main character!

Corrinne Mann

(producer, *The Confession*)

1) In analyzing this question is the dilemma of—what book did I love? and then, did I love the film version of it? Most films fall short of great books. A great book relies on the vision of one person—the film having to sieve the synergy of adapted material with the amalgamated chemistry of many participants through the eyes of a director whose vision captures a truth you felt when you read the book. *One Flew Over the Cuckoo's Nest*, novel by Ken Kesey, film directed by Milos Forman, is one example. Albeit each medium requires different rigors, the successful film adaptation is not, cannot be, the same reiteration or renactment of the book—but the same truths must penetrate. *One Flew Over the Cuckoo's Nest* captured the ever steady, never punctured, insidious lack of humanity in the book. A rare crystallization—when art, craft, and alchemy create the perfect fusion of what cinema has to offer literature. Other favorite film adaptations: *Lolita*, novel by Vladimir Nabokov, film directed by Stanley Kubrick—with flawless, mesmerizing images and performances, a director who understood how to translate the subtle ironic perversion and obsessions of the novel to moving pictures; as well—*The Accidental Tourist*, *The Tin Drum*, *The Wizard of Oz*.

2) *The Unbearable Lightness of Being*, by Milan Kundera. The book is an elegant and erotic depiction of how time, place, and politics affect the characters' abilities to create and destroy their sexual and romantic pursuits—which the film fails to capture. The film had some intention and interest in approaching the erotic nature of the book—but unfortunately coldly danced on the surface, barely approaching either the warmth of the soul or the cruelty of the ego captured in the book.

3) *Citizen Kane*, *Bad Timing: A Sensual Obsession*, *Wings of Desire*, *All That Jazz*, *Les Enfants du Paradis*. I highly recommend you watch each of these films.

4) *The Painted Bird*, *A Wrinkle in Time*, *Don Quixote*, *The Old Man and the Sea*, *Charlotte's Web*.

5) Would like to see the book *The Master and Margarita* adapted to film.

Susan Minot

(author, *Lust*, *Monkeys*; screenwriter, Bertolucci's *Stealing Beauty*)

1) *The Godfather*, Parts I and II.

2) *Swann in Love* is one of the first that springs to mind, but I know there are hundreds more if I had time to think about it.

3) *The Wizard of Oz.*

4) *The Sound and the Fury.*

5) *Monkeys.*

Danny Elfman

(film-score composer, *Sleepy Hollow*, *Instinct*, etc.; film-score producer, *Edward Scissorhands*, *Batman*, *Good Will Hunting*, etc.; lead singer, Oingo Boingo)

1) It's a tie between *The Innocents*, adapted from Henry James's *The Turn of the Screw*, and Shirley Jackson's *The Haunting of Hill House*, which was released as *The Haunting*. Both were, I think, done in the sixties but I could be wrong. I'm a shitty film historian. I haven't seen *The Innocents* in a long time but I remember being really impressed. Simple, straightforward production but very effective and chilling. *The Haunting* was done by the great Robert Wise. Although it was a little corny in places, all you have to do is look at the new version to see an absolute destruction of a great story in a film. I have to say that I love the Kubrick adaption of Steven King's *The Shining*, although purists who loved the novel hated it. They're wrong.

2) Oh, my God! The list is too long. Where do you start, there's been so many.

3) That's so hard. Other than the ones I mentioned already, I think *The Godfather* and, I hate to be like everyone else, but *Citizen Kane*; Fellini's *8½* and *Juliet of the Spirits* and *Casanova* are triple-tied contenders. Hitchcock's *Psycho* and *Rear Window*. Carol Reed's *The Third Man* is way up there. Scorsese's *Taxi Driver* and *Raging Bull* rate very, very high. Howard Hawk's *Red River* . . . an impossible-to-find Japanese film which I think translated to *The Black Cat*. I'll stop here or I never will.

4) *Crime and Punishment*, by you know who.

5) I just finished an adaptation of a book called *Undying Love* for the screen. My lifelong favorites would have to be, like so many people, *The Master and Margarita*, by Bulgakov, and *Perfume*, by Patrick Susskind.

Stanley Tucci

(actor, director, writer, producer, *Big Night*, *The Impostors*, *Joe Gould's Secret*, etc.)

1) There are a few adaptations that are quite wonderful, *Dr. Zhivago* being one, or, *A Sunday in the Country*, by Bertrand Tavernier, which is adapted from a novel of a different title, and *The Godfather*.

2) I don't have a least favorite anything, just a lot of things I dislike or even hate.

3) There is no one film that has influenced me the most, but some that are high on my list are *A Sunday in the Country*, *Rules of the Game*, *Monkey Business*, *Manhattan*, *The Bicycle Thief*, *La Dolce Vita*, *L'Atalante*.

4) Again, there is no single book, however *Letters to a Young Poet*, by Rilke, *Hunger*, by Knut Hamsun, *Huckleberry Finn*, *A Giacometti Portrait*, by James Lord, come to mind.

5) This time there are too many to mention.

Eddie Bunker

(author, *No Beast So Fierce*, *Animal Factory*, *The Education of a Felon*, etc.; screenwriter, *Straight Time*, *Runaway Train*, *Animal Factory*; actor in more than thirty movies, including *Reservoir Dogs*)

1) My favorite adaptation is either *The Grapes of Wrath* or *How Green Was My Valley*. *L.A. Confidential* was also very good because Ellroy is so difficult to adapt.

2) My least favorite was *Malcolm X*, which lied and distorted truth in favor of political correctness.

3) John Huston's *High Sierra*. And Quentin Tarantino's manner of writing dialogue.

4) A book toward which the revisionists have changed from fulsome praise to calumny, Colin Wilson's nonfiction study of the outsider, in a book of the same name.

5) My own fourth novel, *Dog Eat Dog*. It begs to be a movie.

Jonathan Ames

(author, *The Extra Man*, *What's Not To Love*; performer of one-man shows)

1) *One Flew Over the Cuckoo's Nest*. The book is written from the perspective of the Chief, who is absolutely nuts, but wonderfully so. The book is sort of like *The Great Gatsby* of the insane asylum—the Chief is Nick Carraway and McMurphy is Gatsby. The movie, which obviously can't recreate the Chief's voice, is, nonetheless, funny, mad, and tragic: a kind of strange, glorious twin to the book.

2) When I was kid, I loved the J.R.R. Tolkien books—*The Hobbit* and the trilogy *The Lord of the Rings*, and during this time of my love affair with Mr. J.R.R. an animated film of some part of the trilogy came out and I remember it was dark and murky and a gross disappointment. Kind of heartbreaking, actually. So I hope this new movie they're making is good. And I haven't read Harry Potter, so I shouldn't put him (the books) down, but I wish kids were reading Tolkien instead, which is just a stupid prejudice, and overall, I'm glad children (my son included) are reading, even if it's Harry Potter. That's the good news—young people are reading. But is this another simple prejudice? Being pro-reading?

3) Professionally, I'd have to say it's *La Strada* and *Nights of Cabiria*, because Giulietta Masina's facial expressions in these movies inspired me to create this dance which I used in my one-man show of storytelling, *Oedipussy*. This Masina-inspired piece of choreography was called "A Dance of a Thousand Faces." I also love the way she waves backward in *La Strada* (when she leaves the nuns) and I try to wave backward like that. It's an affectation of mine that I enjoy.

4) Professionally and personally: all the Bertie and Jeeves cycle of stories and novels by P. G. Wodehouse. On a personal level,

they've rallied me out of numerous depressions, and on a professional level, I just admire the work like crazy and would hope to give one one-thousandth of the pleasure to readers that Wodehouse consistently delivers.

5) *A Confederacy of Dunces*, by John Kennedy Toole. I would love to see Ignatius, the hero of the book, come to life. Of course, as with the Tolkien animated film, I would be heartbroken if it was mangled.

Barry Shils

(director, *Wigstock*, *Motorama*; producer, *Vampire's Kiss*; director-producer, HBO's *Real Sex*)

1) I have quite a few, so I'll just say what comes to my mind first. *In Cold Blood*, by Truman Capote. Odd that came up first. I must be feeling murderous. *Valley of the Dolls*, by Jacqueline Susann. I often quote the line "Art films? They're nudies!" *Lolita*, by Nabokov. The Kubrick version, not the new one directed by Adrian Lyne. *One Flew Over the Cuckoo's Nest*, by Kesey. A great film. *The Player*. Michael Tolkin wrote the book and the screenplay. *The Godfather*—can't beat that adaptation. And I can't forget to mention *Rosemary's Baby*, by Ira Levin, movie by Polanski.

2) I thought this question would be real easy, but it's not. I actually remember more that I like than dislike. I don't think I go if I hear the movie version was bad, and even though it's a common saying, "Oh, the book was so much better," in fact it's a real feat to squeeze a story that could take ten to twenty hours to read into two hours. I think the main reason I don't like the film version is when they change too much of the original to make it more commercial, like *Angela's Ashes*, by Frank McCourt, where they tried to give the movie an upbeat ending. *The Bonfire of the Vanities* was a tough one to translate, but I think the movie probably got a worse rap than it deserved. I loved the book of *Dracula*, and although I enjoyed Gary Oldman's portrayal of the lead character, I had big problems with Winona and Keanu doing fake period English accents. *Interview with a Vampire* was also a disappointment. Even with Brad Pitt and Tom Cruise, it lacked the sexual energy of the book. That book actually made me horny in a weird way. I didn't read *The Virgin Suicides*, but the movie ruined my interest in ever doing so. And last but not least, *The Sheltering Sky*, by Paul Bowles. To quote Susan Tyrell, "Bertolucci cut the balls off the book."

3) Again it's tough to pick one, so here's a few—Fellini's *Satyricon* blew my mind when I saw it at the tender age of sixteen. So did *Nights of Cabiria*, and *Pink Flamingos*. The first movie I ever saw in a theater, as a mere babe, was *Some Like It Hot*, and it has remained a great influence. I also love *The Seven Year Itch*. *Written on the Wind*, by Douglas Sirk, is a biggie (I love stories of rich Americans gone bad) and the Technicolor is amazing. Busby Berkeley musicals have also had a profound effect. Can't forget Almodovar's *Law of Desire*, and I've got to pay homage to Kenneth Anger's *Scorpio Rising*.

Documentaries have had a big influence on me as well—such films as *Grey Gardens*, by the Maysles, and the prison doc *Tatooed Tears*, by Joan Churchill. All of Frederick Wiseman's movies. And of course *Woodstock* and *Paris Is Burning* were inspirations for *Wigstock. The Producers*, by Mel Brooks, is currently a big influence—so are *Harold and Maude* and *Sunset Boulevard.*

4) Lots of nonfiction: *The Tibetan Book of Living and Dying*, by Sogyal Rinpoche (impossible to make a movie out of this one). *The Celluloid Closet*, by Vito Russo (a pretty good movie was made from it). Thich Nhat Hanh's *The Art of Mindful Living* (I also have him reading it aloud on tape). Fiction, I love *A Confederacy of Dunces*. James Baldwin's *Giovanni's Room. The Magic Mountain* and *Death in Venice*. William Kotzwinkle's *The Fan Man* and *The Midnight Examiner.*

5) I am currently adapting two books for the big screen. *A Low Life in High Heels*, the autobiography of Holly Woodlawn—the legendary drag superstar of Warhol movies, as well as famous junkie and survivor of the scene. We may change the title to *Walk on the Wild Side* (after the Lou Reed song about Holly and her cronies) since there's a Disney movie coming out called *Low Life and High Heels* (a female action pic with Minnie Driver). How dare they! According to a librarian I met from Beverly Hills, Holly's book holds the record for being the book most often stolen from the library. I'm also adapting *Damned Strong Love*, by Lutz van Dijk, a gay holocaust story based on the life of Stefan K., who survived the camps and currently lives in Poland. I don't want to say too much about it yet. The screenplay will be finished next month. I hope to make the audience cry a lot with this one. I wanted to adapt Jonathan Ames's *The Extra Man*, but Isaac Mizrahi has decided to direct, and he and Christine Vachon outbid me for the rights. Christine, if you're reading this magazine and Isaac has gone back to making clothes, please call me! I have a vision for that book!

Jerry Stahl

(author, *Permanent Midnight*, *Perv*)

1) *The Man with the Golden Arm*, Nelson Algren by way of Otto Preminger. Sinatra's pupils are worth the price of admission.

2) *Portnoy's Complaint*. Hollywood is never lamer than when trying to be "hip." Even the idea of Richard Benjamin with a boner is creepy.

3) *Nightmare Alley*. Tyrone Power goes from big money to biting the heads off chickens—which pretty much sums up my career in Hollywood.

4) *Death on the Installment Plan*. Celine found a way to render his deepest despair screamingly funny. I stole everything I could carry from Celine.

5) *The Book of Job*. I'd set it in contempo L.A., starring Don Cheatle, and make it a comedy.

Buck Henry

("all-around entertainer")

I haven't a clue as to how to answer these questions. In fact I don't believe these questions should have answers and I don't think I would trust the person who could answer them.

Rick Moody

(author, *The Ice Storm, Purple America, Demonology*)

1) I liked *Affliction* pretty well. *Howards End* was probably better than the book. So is *The Godfather. Blade Runner* is adapted from Philip K. Dick, and it's pretty good. The original *Frankenstein* film (James Whale, director) is great. I'm sort of partial to the incredibly weird, dated adaptation of John Cheever's *The Swimmer*, which stars Burt Lancaster.

2) I hated *Remains of the Day*, by Merchant Ivory, and it's a book I really love. I thought *L.A. Confidential* was slick, cynical crap, and I can't really take seriously anyone who liked it. *Crash*, after the novel by Ballard, was ridiculous and hollow, though I like almost every other film directed by Cronenberg. *Sheltering Sky* was a rare misstep by Bertolucci, alas.

3) Well, when I was a kid, lots of monster movies. But *2001: A Space Odyssey* had a very profound effect on me. As did, at different times, *La Dolce Vita, Fanny and Alexander*, most of the work of Werner Herzog, *Naked*, by Mike Leigh, and *Marat/Sade*, by Peter Brook. I once saw *Tommy* on acid and it seemed really personally influential at that moment.

4) Probably it's too long a list, and I'm not sure I could boil it down to one or even ten, but among the many I might list are *The Recognitions*, Murphy (Beckett), *Labyrinths* (Borges), *The Crying of Lot 49* (Pynchon), *To the Lighthouse* (Woolf), *The Bloody Chamber* (Angela Carter), *Pale Fire* (Nabokov).

5) I have often felt that *Two Against One*, the best novel by the incredibly great Frederick Barthelme, would make a really tremendous film. *Revolutionary Road*, by Richard Yates. *Elect Mr. Robinson for a Better World*, by Donald Antrim. I'm forgetting a lot of others.

Bruce Cohen

(co-producer with Dan Jinks of Academy Award winner *American Beauty, Mouse Hunt, The Flintstones*, etc.)

1) *Schindler's List*—a Keneally masterpiece turned into a Spielberg masterpiece.

2) *Midnight in the Garden of Good and Evil*—one of my all-time favorite books came up short on the screen.

3) *The Color Purple* was the first film I ever worked on and inspired me to pursue my dream of making movies.

4) Reading *The Chronicles of Narnia* as a kid kindled my love for reading and storytelling.

5) It had always been *The Mists of Avalon*, but that's now being made as a TNT miniseries.

David Gates

(author, *Jernigan, Preston Falls, Wonders of the Invisible World*)

1) *The Godfather, Godfather Part II*, with Fellini's *Casanova* tied for second with *Strangers on a Train*, though I don't normally think of any of these as book adaptations, which of course they absolutely are. Or how

about *Rebecca*? If we're talking about books I know and like (*The Godfather* is dismally written, and I've never read either Highsmith or Casanova's memoirs) I'd say *The Bride of Frankenstein*. But of course that's so unlike the book that I guess it hardly counts. I like David Lean's *Great Expectations* and that recent *Persuasion* pretty well, and the old *Pride and Prejudice* (with Olivier and Greer Garson). Hell, there's no flies on *The Wizard of Oz*, or *Gone with the Wind* or *Dracula* (the Bela Lugosi/Tod Browning one) or *Fat City* or the James Bond movies either. I mostly stay away from films of books I really care about. I stayed away from *Short Cuts* and the Adrian Lyne *Lolita*; I'll probably stay away from *Jesus' Son*.

2) Well, Patricia Rozema's *Mansfield Park* pissed me off good and proper, so I guess if by "least favorite" you mean the one that most made me want to throw things, that's probably it. The most staggering travesty I've ever seen has to be *Meet Nero Wolfe* (1936), adapted from Rex Stout's *Fer-de-Lance*, but it's so surreally bad that it's a goof.

3) Hmm. Professionally? Probably Hitchcock's *North by Northwest*. I don't know how to assess a film's influence on me personally, but some of the films I've been obsessed with—that is, ones I've seen probably twenty times or more, are: *North by Northwest*, *Godfather/Godfather II*, Hans-Jurgen Syberberg's *Parsifal*, Fellini's *Casanova*, *Top Hat*, *The Man Who Came to Dinner*, *42nd Street*—well it goes on.

4) Professionally: probably Samuel Beckett's trilogy: *Molloy*, *Malone Dies*, and *The Unnameable*, but Ann Beattie's *Distortions* would be right up there, also Carver's *Where I'm Calling From*, Donald Barthelme's stories, Jane Austen's novels, Woolf's *To the Lighthouse*. Personally? I'm afraid it was *On the Road* or something.

5) Well, in another life I'd consider taking a crack at Rex Stout's *The Doorbell Rang*, or *Death of a Doxy*. I could hardly do a worse job with Nero Wolfe than those people did back in the thirties. I love visualizing Richardson's *Clarissa*, but it's probably unfilmable—both because you'd have to jump back and forth between her dying in bed and Lovelace doing whatever, and because Richardson's eighteenth-century sensibility just may not go into a twentieth/twenty-first century medium. In another other life, I might take on *Little Dorrit*. But this is this life.

Charles Wright

(poet, *Negative Blue*, *Selected Later Poems*, etc.)

1) Mike Nichols's *Catch-22*.

2) Anything by Dalton Trumbo.

3) *Ieri, Oggi e Domani*, Federico Fellini.

4) *Confessions of Saint Augustine*.

5) Italo Calvino's *Invisible Cities*.

Ann Hood

(author, *Somewhere Off the Coast of Maine*, *Ruby*, etc.)

1) My favorite film adaptation of a book is *The Cider House Rules*. It captured the nuances of the book in a way most adaptations don't. Perhaps because John Irving wrote the screenplay?

2) I've really thought hard about this question and maybe it sounds like I'm avoiding an answer, but the truth is most film adaptations of books aren't very good, making it difficult to choose just one.

3) Personally, *The Graduate* has had the most influence on me. Everything about it sums up exquisitely the era in which I came of age and that shaped much of my thinking and attitudes. Even the Simon and Garfunkel soundtrack reflects my adolescence.

4) Two books have had the most influence on me personally and professionally because I bought them the same day at the Spring Street Bookstore in SoHo: *Black Tickets*, by Jayne Anne Phillips, and *Shiloh and Other Stories*, by Bobbie Ann Mason. I had recently moved to New York City and was starting to write seriously. These books blew apart many things that were keeping me back—they had fresh voices, both written by women not much older than I was at the time, and opened creative doors for me. I still remember reading them with great clarity—where I was sitting in my Bleecker Street apartment, the way I had to keep catching my breath because I was so excited, how I read entire sentences and paragraphs aloud to myself.

5) For all I know someone has already made a TV movie out of it, but I would love to adapt Anne Tyler's *Dinner at the Homesick Restaurant*. I read that book around the same time as the other two I just talked about and it has an interesting structure that perhaps seems like it would be difficult to adapt into film. But the emotional honesty in that book would carry well into a film.

Fred Leebron

(author, *Out West, Six Figures*)

1) *The Great Gatsby*, with Redford, et al. It caught the heat of that particular summer. *In Cold Blood* (the original one).

2) The relatively recent *Day of the Locust*; it took one of my favorite numbers and gave it a gauzy rather than sharp and piercing quality.

3) Personally: probably *Apocalypse Now*, which crushed me and stayed with me. Professionally, a tie between *Pulp Fiction*, which I loved both structurally and in juxtaposition of humor and violence and the long version of *Once Upon a Time in America*, which blended a vision of what is real and what is projected that the "American" version did not. Also *Fanny and Alexander.*

4) *Revolutionary Road* (Richard Yates), which taught me a lot about the wasted and the hypocritical life, *Dubliners* (Joyce), which followed a trajectory to personal responsibility, *The Metamorphosis and Other Stories* (Kafka), which confirmed paranoia, and Chekhov's stories, which taught me everything. Professionally, *In the Lake of the Woods* (O'Brien) with its profound embrace of ambiguity.

5) I'd like most to adapt *Revolutionary Road* or *Going After Cacciato* or *The Plague.*

Andrej Blatnik

(author, *Skinwraps*)

1) *The English Patient.*

2) *Empire of the Sun.*

3) *sex, lies, & videotape.*

4) *The Roadside Picnic,* by A. and B. Strugacki (filmed by Andrei Tarkovsku as *Stalker!*)

5) *El hombre solo (The Lone Man),* by Bernardo Atxaga.

Ariel Dorfman

(author, *Death and the Maiden* and numerous other plays and novels)

1) Harold Pinter's adaptation of Hartley's *The Go-Between* for Joseph Losey.

2) There are so many that I am loath to distinguish one with my raspberry. Thinking back, *The Brothers Karamazov* must have been the most godawful travesty I ever had the misfortune to watch. (I feel like answering, below, that I'd love to adapt *The Grand Inquisitor*—now that would be a kick-ass film!)

3) *La Dolce Vita*—done by that semi-divine madman Fellini.

4) *Rayuela* (known to the mortals who sadly cannot read Spanish as *Hopscotch*), by Julio Cortázar.

5) *Widows,* by the deceased Danish author Eric Lohmann. Ever since I came in contact with that book (now out of print in the States), I have been obsessed with that river which brings faceless corpses to women who claim them as their dead and face off with the military to bury them—a cross between *Antigoni* and *The Trojan Women,* with the modern and the so-called primitive clashing tragically.

David Leavitt

(author, *The Lost Language of Cranes, Martin Bauman,* etc.)

1) Either John Huston's version of Flannery O'Connor's *Wise Blood* or William Wyler's version of Sinclair Lewis's *Dodsworth* (which starred Walter Huston).

2) Merchant Ivory's version of *Maurice.*

3) Carlos Saura's *Cria Cuervos.*

4) Ford Madox Ford's *The Good Soldier.*

5) Forster's *The Longest Journey.*

James Chapman

(author, *Glass, Daughter! I Forbid Your Recurring Dream,* etc.)

1) *Berlin Alexanderplatz,* a novel I love, is actually equaled by Fassbinder's film version, and that never happens. But this was a book he more than understood—he read it when he was young, and it determined the whole course of his life. You experience his film from the inside.

2) Why not just stay away from stuff made in bad faith? All it does is feed irony. I'd rather think about the opposite—the films that would have been great, had they not been prevented—like Tarkovsky's unmade *Crime and Punishment.* Or any of the thirty films Sergei Paradjanov was refused permission to make, including half a dozen scenarios he wrote while lying on his shelf in a prison camp (put there for committing "surrealism, homosexuality, and incitement to suicide").

3) I've learned more about writing fiction from Godard's post-1968 films than from almost anybody's novels. He gets better every year, and in his world art and commerce never do intersect.

4) I find I can't answer without listing lots of books. But it could be *Portrait of the Artist*, since that showed me, at seventeen, a way to love my alienation, which is what I'd previously despised most about myself.

5) In Paradise we'll sit and watch Sam Fuller's *As I Lay Dying*, Cassavetes's *Journey to the End of Night*, Tarkovsky's *Resurrection*, and *The Waves* by Seijun Suzuki, unless in Paradise we don't need solace anymore.

Greg Villepique

(copy editor; guitarist, Aerial Love Feed)

1) For a faithful translation, Peter Bogdanovich's 1971 *The Last Picture Show*. For a radical transformation, Amy Heckerling's 1995 *Clueless*.

2) Joseph Strick's *Ulysses*: an idiotic idea idiotically realized.

3) Bob Fosse's *Cabaret*, because of the gay Nazi decadence thing, not the Liza thing. Big deal when I was fourteen. Also Alan Parker's *Birdy* and Coppola's *Apocalypse Now*, both of which brilliantly blur the arbitrary divisions between breakdown and transcendence.

4) *Moby Dick*.

5) *The Chicago Manual of Style*, with Joan Cusack as the serial comma, Gary Oldman as the dangling modifier, and Leo DiCaprio as the ellipsis.

Lauren Milne Henderson

(author of many tart-noir mysteries, including *Black Rubber Dress* and *Strawberry Tattoo*)

1) Bertolucci's *The Sheltering Sky*. I'm not generally a Bertolucci fan, but my God, he did a great job with that film. Everything was perfect—even the small changes they made were absolutely right.

2) I loathed the recent version of *Mansfield Park*. If you can't do Jane Austen without sexing her up and changing the plot, keep your hands off her because you are *Not Worthy*. And *Modesty Blaise*—Monica Vitti as a dolly-bird Modesty ... what a great opportunity lost. And much as I worship Terence Stamp, he was NOT Willie Garvin. That's one role for which I would LOVE to be running the casting couch.

3) *Cat People*—mainly the Jacques Tourneur version, though there was some good stuff in the remake. And all those wonderful 1940s film noirs with the devilish femmes fatales behaving as badly as women were allowed to in those days. *Build My Gallows High* with Robert Mitchum, Jane Greer, and Kirk Douglas...I could watch it to death. Ditto *Bound* and *The Long Kiss Goodnight*.

4) *Modesty Blaise* and *Tank Girl*—the comic. Two amazing action heroines, written by guys, at a time when women were turning out wet-as-a-dishcloth whiners or heroines who wanted to be men—Philip Marlowe in a skirt never worked for me. When I started writing my detective series, *Modesty* and *Tank Girl* were my two big influences—though I sometimes describe the books as *Tank Girl*-meets-P. G. Wodehouse on cocaine, so P. G. Wodehouse too. Also *Bridget Jones*, as a purely negative influence—she epitomizes everything I loathe about women's fiction, or

chick-fic as we call it in the U.K. I am currently writing an anti-*Bridget Jones* book and having enormous fun with it.

5) This is such a dodgy question because every single author is going to say "My own," if they're being honest! So, uh, apart from mine . . . *Modesty Blaise*. I'd like to do it properly, and I think I could. Just give me Carrie-Anne Moss (from *The Matrix*) and a whacking great budget. And the Willie Garvin casting couch, of course. But the second-best would be Hemingway's *The Garden of Eden*. It would make an amazing film; I'm surprised no one's done it already.

Jim Lewis

(author, *Sister*, *Why the Tree Loves the Ax*; recently adapted his own short story, "When God Dips His Love in My Heart," for Francis Ford Coppola's American Zoetrope)

1) There are three categories, I think. First, minor books—that is, those which have no extraordinary literary merit—which seem to be readily adaptable, sometimes into great movies. Thus, Kurosawa's *High and Low*, based on Ed McBain's *King's Ransom*, and Charles Laughton's *Night of the Hunter*, adapted by James Agee from a novel by Davis Grub. Second, canonical books transformed by very loose adaptation into brilliant movies, as *Heart of Darkness* became *Apocalypse Now*, *Emma* became *Clueless*, and Xenophon's *Anabasis* became Walter Hill's *The Warriors*. Finally, and this is very rare, great books adapted fairly faithfully into great movies, like *Lolita* and Huston's *The Dead*. *Who'll Stop the Rain*, from Robert Stone's *Dog Soldiers*, may belong here, too, though the movie isn't perfect.

2) *The Great Gatsby* certainly ranks high, though I don't know if the script itself was bad, as opposed to, say, the acting or the cinematography. There are perhaps too many others to count.

3) Those I mentioned above. Also, Powell's *Peeping Tom* and Herzog's *Every Man for Himself and God Against All*. And *The Killing of a Chinese Bookie*, and *La Jetée*, and *House of Games*; and Jerry Lewis's *The Nutty Professor*, and *Repo Man*, and *Pennies from Heaven*, and *The Sweet Smell of Success*.

4) As a novelist, far too many books have mattered to me for any one to merit being singled out. As a screenwriter, Manny Farber's *Negative Space* has taught me more about film than anything else I've read.

5) Just off the top of my head: *The Thousand and One Nights*—though not as a period piece; *The Hank Williams Story*; Richard Rhodes's *The Making of the Atomic Bomb*; some of Isaac Bashevis Singer's more supernatural, mystical stories; Russell Hoban's *Riddley Walker*, and Melville's *The Confidence Man*.

Adina Hoffman

(film critic for the *Jerusalem Post*; author, *House of Windows: Portraits from a Jerusalem Neighborhood*)

1) The Taviani brothers's *Padre Padrone*, which is a film about the hunger for words. Based on the autobiography of the linguist Gavino Ledda, who grew up an illiterate Sar-

dinian shepherd, at an almost complete remove from other human beings, it's one of the best and most moving examples I know of an adaptation that manages to embody the elemental, preverbal potential of film as it argues fiercely on behalf of articulate speech.

2) Confining myself to the last decade alone—an especially fertile period for senseless movie adaptations of great books—I'd pick Roland Joffe's rightfully dumped-on *The Scarlet Letter*, with Demi Moore as a bumping and grinding Hester Prynne and Gary Oldman as her studly, hard-rock-star-styled Dimmesdale. What stops this travesty from being merely awful in that entertaining Hollywood Cliff Notes way (or merely dull, in the tasteful, stuffy Merchant Ivory tradition) is the active hostility toward Hawthorne that one feels coursing through the script. The problem is not that Joffe and his scriptwriter, Douglas Day Stewart, somehow misunderstand the original or that they venture too far in a sympathetic reinterpretation: they seem actually to hate this (amazing) book's guts, and to believe that their own happy, soft-core rehash is much, much better. In fact, it couldn't be worse.

3) *The Wizard of Oz*. Not because it's a great or even a good movie (I haven't seen it since I was a child, so I can't honestly say), but because it was the first film I ever adored. Well before I'd ever heard of Pauline Kael, it taught me the necessity of passionate engagement with the form, what she calls Movie Love.

4) There isn't just one. I'd begin a longer list with three books that would make terrible movies: Ezra Pound's *ABC of Reading*, James Agee's *Let Us Now Praise Famous Men*, and Claudia Roden's *A Book of Middle Eastern Food*.

5) I have no aspirations to write scripts, though I'd love to see an intelligent adaptation by someone else of Thomas Roszak's novel *Flicker*, which is itself all about the deep, dark, total, almost otherworldly pull of the movies.

Amanda Davis

(author, *Circling the Drain*)

1) That would be a tie between *The Sweet Hereafter* and *The Ice Storm*. In both cases I liked the books and loved the movies. I felt they did what so many adaptations are unable to do: respect the book, yet range free within the filmic medium.

2) Recently, *The Talented Mr. Ripley*, which is a phenomenally creepy book and was a lukewarm mediocre movie.

3) I had some sort of storytelling epiphany watching *The Ice Storm*. It sounds dumb to write that, but for some reason watching that film explained to me the essential difference between a novel and a story—between the scope of what's covered and what questions are raised or answered.

4) Professionally, probably Annie Dillard's *The Writing Life*, which I tend to turn to whenever I feel overwhelmed or stuck or in need of inspiration, and Evan S. Connell's *Mrs. Bridge*, which is an incredible amalgamation of moments, each small and precise

and essential to the story as a whole, and which made me believe it was possible to be a writer who loved such moments and still write a novel. And two books that I've felt very influenced by recently are *The End of Vandalism*, by Tom Drury, which is a wonderful spare generous funny novel about a small town in Iowa, and Barbara Gowdy's *Falling Angels*, which is a harrowing but exquisite novel about three girls growing up in an insane family. I think both of these books might be out of print.

5) Maybe *Falling Angels*. I am so interested in the three sisters and their nutty mother and the way they raise each other. It would make for a devastating film. Or *Hunts in Dreams*, a more recent book by Drury, which I think is incredibly cinematic and funny and moving.

Larry Gross

(screenwriter, *48 Hours*, *Streets of Fire*, *Another 48 Hours*, *Geronimo*, all co-written with Walter Hill; *This World, Then the Fireworks*, adapted from Jim Thompson's novel)

1) There are so many. Recently, Raoul Ruiz's astonishing *Time Regained*. Ruiz manages Proust's world brilliantly. He slices into the continuous present of film-time to make a thematic—rather than plot-driven—interpretation of the novel *In Search of Lost Time*. He understands that a straightforward linear melodramatic approach to the material would lose Proust's essence. He understands that the film must be somewhat difficult to access, and must solicit a constant interpretive agility on the viewer's part. That we have to think while we feel. By being more aggressively and unconventionally cinematic, Ruiz is paradoxically deeply faithful to the inner nature of Proust's writing.

Another recent fave: Barbet Schroeder's *Our Lady of the Assassins*, an adaptation of a Latin American novel published to great acclaim in France but not yet available in America.

Going back in time a bit: Karel Reisz and Judith Rascoe's version of Robert Stone's *Dog Soldiers*, released under the title *Who'll Stop the Rain?*, Frankenheimer's *The Manchurian Candidate*, Huston's *Maltese Falcon* and *The Treasure of the Sierra Madre*, Welles's take on *The Trial*, and just about all of Kubrick's adaptations, but especially his ingenious handling of *Lolita*. A case of a film masterpiece only associated with its director but in fact an adaptation of a novel is Truffaut's *Jules and Jim*.

2) There are so many. The Roland Joffe-Demi Moore *Scarlet Letter*, with its astonishing tacked-on happy ending definitely is a low point.

Amazing that one of our greatest directors, John Ford, did two of the worst adaptations of all time, *The Grapes of Wrath* and *The Fugitive*, a botched version of Greene's *Power and the Glory*.

Amazing that the novelist who probably influenced screenwriters more than any other, at least in the thirties and forties, almost always had his novels turned into lousy films. I'm referring to Hemingway. Both versions of *A Farewell to Arms*, even the one directed by the great Frank Borzage, are just awful. The adaptations of *For Whom the Bell Tolls*, *Adventures of a Young Man*, taken from the Nick Adams stories, and *The Old Man and the Sea* are worse. The two decent films from Hemingway material, Siodmak's *The Killers* and Hawks's *To Have and Have Not*, have literally nothing to do with their literary sources.

The most revelatory cases of bad adaptations are the many terrible versions of Tolstoy's *Anna Karenina*. While you read Tolstoy, his clarity and plainness of language naturally make you think, this stuff would turn into a great movie. Almost all the versions are admirably scrupulous and well-intended. But an interesting thing happens. They focus entirely on the novel's plot as it pertains to Anna and Vronsky, and they either eliminate or diminish the Levin-Kitty story and all the connectives between the two plots. When this happens the Vronsky-Anna story, no matter how faithfully rendered, suddenly starts to look surprisingly trivial. One more proof, if one were needed, that Tolstoy's art is far more intricate than it appears on the surface.

3) *Citizen Kane. Citizen Kane.*

4) *Moby Dick*. Professionally, James Agee's collected film reviews from the 1940s, *Agee on Film*, were lent to me when I was sixteen by an uncle of mine. Agee's journalistic response to Chaplin, Keaton, Griffith, Huston, Dreyer, Rossellini, Vigo, and others revealed that there was a highly cultivated humane way of taking movies seriously without being pretentious or humorless. I stopped thinking of myself then as just a fan of movies and decided one could unashamedly be dedicated to them. A year or two later I bumped into Pauline Kael's first and, to my mind, finest collection of criticism, *I Lost It at the Movies*. It contained her response to *On the Waterfront, Grand Illusion, Yojimbo, Breathless, Shoot the Piano Player*, and Ray's *Apu Trilogy*. Reading this book confirmed the instruction of the Agee book. Films could be more than entertainment, they could be a whole life's work. Movies always get to us in a childish, atavistic way, especially, of course, when we're children, and it takes some special event to make you feel that they can be part of your adult life. These two books were it for me.

5) There are so many: Dickens's *Bleak House*, which has an opening description of London drenched in fog that seems like a description of the most glorious crane shot in the history of film. Dostoyevsky's *The Idiot*. Myshikin, Rogozhin, and Nastasy Filiponova are three of the greatest roles ever created to be put in a movie. More recently, Mario Vargas Llosa's tight, elegant murder mystery *Who Killed Palomino Molero?*; Madison Smartt Bell's ingenious bunch of short stories thematically linked, *The Year of Silence*; Peter Handke's *Short Letter, Long Farewell*, which would make an edgy road movie; and Frederick Barthelme's *Brothers*, which has fantastic comic dialogue.

TODD HAYNES

[on art and melodrama]

INTERVIEWED BY

JON RAYMOND

Winner of countless awards and prizes, darling of discerning filmgoers the world over, Todd Haynes makes the job of glamorous indie auteur look almost easy. His meticulous, politically engaged body of work ranks among the most beautiful and uncompromised of any director working today.

Haynes first gained notoriety in 1987 for *Superstar*, an ingeniously crafted biopic of seventies icon Karen Carpenter. Using Barbie dolls to recount the singer's tragic submission to anorexia, the film's miniaturized stage sets and haunting soundtrack of Carpenters music immediately established it as an underground classic; to this day it circu-

lates among eggheaded indie kids like some kind of illicit drug.

Haynes's next movie, *Poison* (1991), extended his path of formal and political experimentation, offering a triptych of genre shorts based, respectively, on the prison romances of Jean Genet, the cinema verité of the television news documentary, and the pulp stylings of the fifties horror film. Funded in part by the NEA, *Poison* made Haynes a poster boy for the New Queer Cinema and a field marshal in the early nineties culture wars. As one senatorial wife was quoted to say upon watching *Poison*, "It made me want to bathe in Clorox."

Next came *Safe* (1995), Haynes's critically acclaimed meditation on "environmental illness," a slow-burning melodrama tracing the deterioration of an L.A. housewife (Julianne Moore) caused by an undiagnosable disease. Applying the space-age textures of Kubrick's *2001* to the banal surfaces of the haut bourgeois domestic sphere, *Safe* is already recognized as an American masterpiece—it was voted the best film of the nineties last year in a *Village Voice* critics' poll.

Velvet Goldmine followed in 1998, a ravishing experiment in the milieu of glitter rock and an extended essay on the construction of rock-and-roll selfhood. Recipient of a special artistic award at Cannes and nominated for an Oscar for its costumes, the film has gone on to inspire more than forty Web sites among devoted fans worldwide.

But the thing about Todd Haynes is that he's such a golden boy you don't even begrudge him his copious success. He's so modest and down-to-earth and just incredibly nice that you only want more happiness and conquest to come his way. He's the kind of guy who overhears a cashier at the health-food store fawning over *Velvet Goldmine* and ends up going to the kid's birthday party later that night.

Lately, Haynes has been gearing up for his next project, a period-precise reinterpretation of fifties melodrama starring Julianne Moore. Picking up on the legacy of Douglas Sirk, and more so on Rainer Werner Fassbinder's reinterpretation of Sirk (most explicitly in his remake of *All That Heaven Allows*, *Ali—Fear Eats the Soul*), Haynes will again set up camp in the world of suburban dread and longing, this time heading straight for its Eisenhower-era heart of darkness.

Jon Raymond talked to Haynes in Portland, Oregon, where he currently lives.

Jon Raymond: A lot of people talk about the relationship between film and literature, but you often seem to proceed as much from critical sources as literary ones. Are there any theoretical texts you find yourself coming back to for inspiration? Any critical theorists whose ideas guide you toward new projects?

Todd Haynes: Freud, definitely. Not so much as a way of finding projects, but more as a way of developing them. I look to his work for certain strategies and structures—and they are often psychic structures—that have a kind of dynamic narrative element to them, that may bring a kind of parallel insight to a theme I'm interested in. That sounds super vague; I'll give you an example. The article "A Child Is Being Beaten" is something I've dried up by reading so many times.

JR: Probably the most explicit application of it being in *Dottie Gets Spanked* (Haynes's PBS-commissioned short about a young boy obsessed with a Lucy-like TV comedienne).

TH: Yeah, but it started with *Superstar*. The article describes this amazing period of pregenital orientation in little girls, mostly referred to as the clitoral stage, which is a point where little girls are in full control of their environments and bodies, and exhibit a kind of direct access to their own pleasure. This is glimpsed in the patients' narrative fantasies about certain little boys being spanked, and the total sexual charge they get in imagining it. In these narratives, the little girls are the creators of the dreams, and the administrators of all the conflicts and characters within the dream. They play all the parts in this little psychosexual theater.

I couldn't stop thinking about this in relation to anorexic behavior, which is also predicated on this incredible pleasure of total control. In the anorexic imagination a person is in complete control of their body and their world to the point where their own control replaces sexual desire or the need for satisfaction. They are pulling all the strings.

JR: Intriguing. Sounds like it might have something to do with directing a movie, too. Do you remember seeing your first movie?

TH: I saw my first movie, *Mary Poppins*, when I was three, and it initiated a kind of obsessive relationship to cultural material, and desire, that has probably never really ceased. I drew thousands of pictures of Mary Poppins for the next several years. I performed the songs constantly after dinner.

JR: Oh yes? What would you have Mary Poppins doing in these pictures?

TH: Everything. *Everything*. All kinds of things with the umbrella and parrot. No.

It was really intense, actually. The film induced an obsessive creative response in me. I remember desperately dressing up my mom in the Mary Poppins clothes. "Please, Mom, put this hat on! Put this lipstick on! Put this umbrella on! Make your feet go like that!"

JR: Were there other obsessions, besides *Mary Poppins*?

TH: The next huge, huge obsession was with Zefirelli's *Romeo and Juliet* in 1968, when I was seven. At the time, I fully connected it to hippie youth culture, which was part of its promotional campaign.

JR: Right, you get to see Juliet's boobs and stuff.

TH: Totally. And I remember watching the movie in the movie theater, and these two girls with their long dark hair parted in the middle, sobbing convulsively, ready to kill themselves. Their feet were black from walking up and down Ventura Boulevard barefoot, which is what you did if you were a hippie in 1968, and their toes were up on the seat behind us. I was like, "Whoa. This is powerful stuff."

So I was obsessed by *Romeo and Juliet* and for the next several years I was totally "into Shakespeare." My first movie was *Romeo and Juliet*, which I made when I was nine. I played all the parts, except Juliet. I actually tried to do Juliet one time, with double exposure—I have a test roll—but in the end I got a friend to play her. My sister played the nurse offscreen. We did the whole thing. I would be Romeo on one side of the camera, cut to me as Mercutio on the other. I made all the costumes out of little towels; I would paint them with tempera, cut a hole, make a tunic.

Usually when I was into something I would either perform my own version at school or write a play. I was very into *Henry VIII*, and the *Six Wives* thing, too, which was happening on BBC. I was into those period things. *Anne of a Thousand Days*. *Mary, Queen of Scots*. I wrote a play called *The Roving Eye* about Henry VIII in sixth grade. It was going to be a musical, actually. I collaborated with this guy, Mike, whose last name I can't remember. It was supposed to be a collaboration where he was going to come up with all the songs, but it didn't come to fruition.

JR: So it was never produced.

TH: No, the financing fell apart. That homeroom teacher just didn't come through with it.

JR: And now, many years later, you are working on a Sirkian melodrama, set in the fifties. What brings you to that?

TH: The melodrama as a body of films and a series of discussions about representation in film has been important to me since college. There is a political tradition

The melodrama is about people entrapped and enclosed. It is set in claustrophobic rooms within claustrophobic houses within claustrophobic towns, and usually its subjects are women at the service of traditional families.

there—articulated most beautifully in the translation of Sirk into Fassbinder, and also in a lot of the postfeminist critical writing of the 70s—that identifies what appears to be the most apolitical kind of film imaginable with a structurally, formally potent critique of social oppression and victimhood. That's really what the genre has always been about. Unlike the free open space of the western or film noir, the melodrama is about people entrapped and enclosed. It is set in claustrophobic rooms within claustrophobic houses within claustrophobic towns, and usually its subjects are women at the service of traditional families.

JR: *Safe* being an eloquent updating of that.

TH: Right. So although melodrama is something I'm thinking about more overtly now in a fifties context, I think those interests have affected other films, and *Safe* is probably the most obvious example. But probably *Superstar* too. Basically my two films that are about women are all about melodrama. It was almost inevitable that at some point I would get to Sirk in a more overt and loving way.

Also, I just wanted to make an incredibly sad movie, about people who try to find love and fail. In a weird way, despite the hyperbole and excess of melodrama, it is the most directly realistic, truthful expression of human disappointment available.

JR: Is this return to melodrama in any way a response to the flamboyance of *Velvet Goldmine*?

TH: Not necessarily. Although I've always been drawn to cultural moments of rupture and breakage and transgression, I have a really hard time feeling like I can or want to provide that experience for an audience in a film, to give the audience its transgression in a package. Because in a large way, in a dominant way, culturally, that is what cinema has always done, in a very safe, traditional space. You go and experience sex and crime and illicit behavior in the dark theater and then you leave it and go back to your family. It comes back to an idea that

Fassbinder stated so beautifully, about cinema "not being able to give you the revolution." Basically he didn't believe that cinema can show you the revolution, but can only show you the conditions that make it necessary, which is something I've always instinctively felt to be true—that the best a film can do is deprive its audience of an answer, or the truth, or how the director really, truly feels and what he wants you to think. A film can only show its agenda by inference, and by showing the necessity of doing something other than what is happening up on the screen. So that implies that most of my films will be sad films about dominant culture, and not so much about counterculture.

Something else I was not thinking about consciously while writing the script, but which I have subsequently come to, is how this period we're in now, socially and culturally, bears so much resemblance to the fifties. We haven't been this stable as an economy since then, and although we don't carry a lot of the same unquestioned assumptions about family and the creation of suburbia and so forth, we do seem to be turning inward in various ways. Our technology and computer culture seems to be creating a greater and greater disengagement from cultural and political awareness. We're luxuriating in this hypertechnological society that has all these options and distractions and toggle buttons and Palm Pilots. And the "Interweb" is all over the place. There are so many ways to numb and distract and diffuse now. Just call up the person who delivers anything you want to your house in half an hour.

JR: Oh, yeah.

TH: Oh, yeah. I guess it's not all bad.

JR: So the themes you're developing in your melodrama draw on this parallel between the fifties and now.

TH: Right. The combustion of the little melodrama that I'm working on has to do with imposing on the so-called innocence of the fifties themes that we don't usually associate with that time, like racial ambivalence and sexual orientation.

JR: Themes that were latent in a lot of the melodramas at the time.

TH: True, sexual orientation and race as well, but in strangely unarticulated form. For instance, lately I've been looking at films from the 1949-50 period, during which time there was a real liberal swell of concern around racial representation. Right at that time—which we don't think of because we just blur the fifties into all that "postwar" American era—right at that time, as a result of a new sense of conscientiousness, and the fact that blacks had served in the military and were entitled to a different kind of status upon returning home, there was this attempt in Hollywood to be more complex in the representation of race. But it disappeared immediately as the civil rights movement became this omnipresent home-turf battle, and movies again became completely disengaged. The only really complex depiction of racial issues after that is Sirk's *Imitation of Life*, which is so strangely and symptomatically unresolved.

JR: How do you mean?

TH: It's just full of ruptures, and a really pronounced element of overcruelty. There is a sort of inelegance to the narrative movement—which is found in all melodrama, really—that triggers a level of unconscious psychic discrepancy in the viewer. The excesses and extremes of *Imitation of Life* may not relate directly to the reality or surface experience of our lives, but there is something about their severity and inappropriateness that is so true on a deeper level. There is definitely something in that movie that it can't really contain.

JR: So what were some movies in the 90s that made you cry?

TH: *The Thin Red Line*. I think it is the most mournful, elegiac war film I've ever seen. It brings up a kind of looming sense of meaninglessness, as well as major philosophical questions about war, without ever naming them or stating them. I saw it the first time and found it gorgeous and lopsided and just a big, delicious, heavy imbalance of things. And I'd heard after that first viewing how it was so much longer and how entire plotlines were cut out and I thought, Oh, I really felt that, but when I saw it a second time I really felt that its structure was sound and it had a balance to it that I thought was really interesting.

I also cried at this movie called *Losing Isaiah*. It was a little Hollywood melodrama with Jessica Lange and Halle Berry about this total ghetto, crack-addict girl who has a baby and hides him near a trash can. When she gets back she finds the kid has been picked up and taken to a hospital and ultimately adopted by Jessica Lange. Years later, Halle Berry comes back, cleans up, goes to school, gets a house, gets a lawyer, and starts to fight for custody of the kid. There's this amazing part where she wins and gets the kid back, but by that time the little boy has already been raised in this totally comfortable, middle-class, conscientious, loving environment. Being taken back by his mother, who's doing everything in her power to get her act together and who you totally feel for, but who just simply doesn't have the money, totally traumatizes him. He wants his "mommy" back, and it's this incredibly sad movie because there's no resolution. Everyone is right and everyone is wrong. The kid is in pain. It's a perfect melodrama.

The Fellowship of the Craft

From Woody Allen to Paul Mazursky, a wink and a nod

Ours is an age of homage, of artists "quoting" one another: T. S. Eliot's "The Waste Land" is perhaps the most famous modern tissue of connections or collage of fragments with which the fevered artist shores up his or her vision of the world, creating a community of readers and kindred spirits. Vaughan Williams takes a medieval theme by Thomas Tallis and turns it into haunting music for the twentieth century; John Coltrane quotes Charlie Parker, and jazz moves in a new

BY CHRISTOPHER MERRILL

Poets and novelists nod at one another like friends passing in the street, burying their admiration for another's style or vision in rephrased lines only the initiated recognize.

direction. Painters adapt the brush strokes and imagery of artists they admire, while poets and novelists nod at one another like friends passing in the street, burying their admiration for another's style or vision in rephrased lines only the initiated recognize. Such gestures reinforce the fellowship of the craft. This is a way of paying homage to inspirational spirits who help us get our work done. Art issues from the catacombs, to which it often then returns: for that is where the secret springs of inspiration are found.

It is no different in the world of film. You will recall the heartrending scene from Paul Mazursky's *An Unmarried Woman* (1978) in which Michael Murphy's character confesses to his wife that he is in love with a younger woman, a schoolteacher he has been seeing for more than a year. His wife, a role expertly played by Jill Clayburgh, is so shaken by his revelation that she cannot respond—theirs is a good marriage, or so she has believed. Murphy fills the silence in an awkward fashion: "I met her in Bloomingdale's, for Christ's sake," he says, sobbing. "She asked me if I liked this shirt that she was buying for her father." The details, of course, are cruel—and all too believable: this is how far too many of us act at such moments. Insisting he does not want to hurt her or their daughter, all the same Murphy destroys the story of their lives together with another story, which is devastatingly banal.

Clayburgh's expressions tell it all: at first solicitous when he breaks down on a New York City street, she then stares at him, speechless, taking in each sordid detail of his story. Her shock gives way to anger, and soon she finds her own reserves of cruelty, the map by which this heretofore lighthearted woman will discover the darker regions of her own identity and thus become a stronger individual. "I'm so sorry," he says sheepishly. "You tell Patty [their daughter]," she replies, "You tell Patty that you're sorry." "I'm in love with her," says Murphy in a pathetic manner. "Is she a good lay?" says Clayburgh, announcing in the midst of her grief that she will survive his story—and someday write her own.

In *Manhattan*, which appeared in 1979, Woody Allen pays homage to this remarkable moment when he stages a scene with Michael Murphy in Bloomingdale's. Murphy, an English professor, and Diane Keaton, a lovably pretentious journalist, discuss the difficulty of going on with their affair. "It's just ridiculous," she whines. "You're married. Listen to me. I'm beginning to sound like I'm one of those women. It sounds terrible. I hate it." This scene might have been set anywhere, but Allen goes to Bloomingdale's in order to tip his hat to Paul Mazursky. Indeed, Allen develops one of Mazursky's central ideas—that narratives can begin and end in the most mundane places—by exploring the other woman's story, which is as sad and tawdry as it is comic: "I'm beautiful, and I'm bright, and I deserve better," says Keaton. Perhaps. But the filmmakers share a secret about the human heart: namely, that it is capable of profound delusions. Witness poor Michael Murphy: in *An Unmarried Woman* the schoolteacher leaves him, and in *Manhattan* he betrays not only his wife but also his best friend, played by Woody Allen. That he ends up with Diane Keaton is, at best, a mixed blessing.

Great artists always work within the context of their kindred spirits, the community which challenges and inspires them. Paying homage to someone who shows us a way through a stanza or a scene is how we give thanks to the Muse, who demands our gratitude. "But at my back I always hear/Time's wingèd chariot hurrying near," wrote Andrew Marvell, and T.S. Eliot thanked him thus: "But at my back in a cold blast I hear/the rattle of the bones, and chuckle spread from ear to ear." Woody Allen celebrates Paul Mazursky's work in Bloomingdale's—an appropriate context for the end of the American century—and the effect is the same: delight for the initiated and another thread added to the fabric that artists and writers, filmmakers and composers weave together, the fabric called community.

This scene might have been set anywhere, but Allen goes to Bloomingdale's in order to tip his hat to Paul Mazursky.

Cinema Verité

by

Daniel Halpern

In the cinema verité of the sixties the beautiful
        protagonists always came so close,
so close to the everlasting

        sunset they were so desperately scripted
to ride into. And we, passive onlookers,
        pressed forward in our collective seats

and rooted for them, individually
        and collectively. In the end it went poorly
for those we cheered. As if in imitation

        art led us down its artificial path,
every branch blossoming, the thyme walks
        kicking up the herbal scent, the insects insane

for the goodwill so well distributed.
        Good news has the metabolism of a hummingbird,
its instrument not long attuned to this world.

        Bad news won't extend the prognosis, but time
slows down at its intervention.
        The news, because it's finite, is never good

for long. But when the sun rises over the hills,
        the colored scents of August and the autumnal months
find current and pass on the air. We're okay.

        It's the most we can expect, the temperature
of objects in various weathers, the satisfaction
        of things fitting together, whether in the hand

or mind. We're happy to sit down, properly attired
        to a meal at day's end, knowing the days
are numbered but the evening is long.

Marlon Brando from the book *Hollywood Candid*

JAILBIRD WRITERS:

THEY HAD THE STORIES HOLLYWOOD WANTED—AND PLENTY OF TIME TO WRITE THEM

They made me a screenwriter

In the 1936 Warner Bros. picture *San Quentin*, Pat O'Brien plays a newly appointed warden. Early on he is seen visiting a prisoner named Simpson, known in the joint as the Writer.

WARDEN: "Writing in here, eh?"
SIMPSON: "Want to read?"
WARDEN: "I'll wait till it's published."
SIMPSON: "I didn't start getting acceptance until I got here."
WARDEN: "Maybe they're impressed by the address."

In the next shot, the warden stops in front of another convict, Dogan, who is in for forgery.

DOGAN: "I'm a writer, too."
WARDEN: "Writing other people's names on checks—yes, I know."

BY PHILIPPE GARNIER

No fewer than eight writers worked on this production. The story cost was high, especially for an original: $18,901, almost as much as what the star of the picture was getting, and certainly more than what the other featured players cost the studio ($2,750 for Humphrey Bogart and a paltry $450 for Ann Sheridan). Humphrey Cobb and Peter Milne ended up with the writing credits for this routine Lloyd Bacon crime picture, but the original story had been written by John Bright and Robert Tasker. Bright was the most well known of the two: in the early thirties, he and his partner Kubec Glasmon had been so successful with their stories for James Cagney that Warners featured their names prominently on publicity material for the exhibitors, an unheard-of practice at the time. But then, *The Public Enemy* had been a huge hit, and Bright went on writing movies for Cagney until he ran afoul of Darryl F. Zanuck, the Warner Bros. chief of production, over the casting of Loretta Young as a proletarian girl in *Taxi*. When Bright tried to rally to his cause *Taxi's* co-writer and Pulitzer prizewinner Kenyon Nicholson, a man Zanuck was in awe of, Zanuck called him a stool pigeon. Upon which Bright tried to throw Zanuck out of his office window, only to be restrained by his male secretary. Bright was fired when his option period ran out. But if the cocky young Bright knew the underworld only vicariously (through Glasmon, an ex-pharmacist whose drugstore was a gangster hangout in Chicago), his new partner, Tasker, was the real thing: the jailbird writer in *San Quentin* was literally based on himself.

Both Booth and Tasker, who are serving life terms at Folsom for robbery after a botched escape from San Quentin, have recently been taken under the literary wing of H. L. Mencken.

There had been a time, between 1927 and 1929, when Tasker and fellow inmate Ernest Booth had such a grasp on the Hollywood market for crime stories that they split the pie between them, Tasker sticking to prison stories, Booth to knockover yarns and tales of gangsters' molls. Booth alone made more than twenty-eight thousand dollars out of Hollywood while inside. The gravy was indeed so thick that other cons in both

San Quentin and Folsom wanted in: a December 9, 1931, *Oakland Tribune* article states that "Joe Macklin, ex-jockey and tough guy, has been ordered back to San Quentin where he had gained fame as a writer, to serve eight years remainder of his sentence as a parole violator, for selling morphine. Freed last April, he'd been serving fifteen years for sticking up a crap game." The writing craze inside got so out of hand that the authorities had to put their foot down. A March 29, 1928, *San Francisco Examiner* article opened with an exasperated quote from Judge C. E. McLaughlin, a member of the State Board of Prison Directors: "We're running prisons, not literary bureaus. The board has no time or disposition to read this material and see that it is in proper shape."

New regulations did not prevent cons from writing in their spare time, but from submitting their stories while still in jail, the report went on. "Both Booth and Tasker, who are serving life terms at Folsom for robbery after a botched escape from San Quentin, have recently been taken under the literary wing of H. L. Mencken, editor of the *American Mercury*. Warden Smith disclosed today that three motion picture concerns are now negotiating for film rights to one Booth *Mercury* article entitled 'We Rob a Bank.' And Warden Holohan at San Quentin confirmed that a dozen convicts were preparing material with an eye on the outside market. It all started with the *Bulletin*, and that short-story contest in which Tasker won first prize, out of 400 entries from prisoners." Started in 1924 by Tasker and others, the *Bulletin*, San Quentin's literary magazine, kept on going well after the ban, but declined sharply after its two luminaries got sprung by their famous literary mentor. It got scrapped for good in June of 1936, by Court Smith, the new warden: "It had gone high hat in recent years, and few inmates read it. Now it is mostly written for outside consumption. Only the convict writers seem to read it behind the walls." The funds allotted to the *Bulletin* went to the *Sport News* instead and to the organization of boxing matches.

But for a time, the "outside consumption" included almost every story editor in Hollywood, with Paramount-Publix as the main clearinghouse. On November 12, 1927, for instance, Booth wrote Mencken: "A million thanks for that Famous Players connection. The commercial side of this business is rather amusing to me. I had two movie offers within two days, and I find myself curiously indifferent to them." Mencken had sent them advance proofs of Booth's story "Ladies of the Mob." In an earlier letter, Booth had described the fever: "The whole prison is busy with pen, pencil, typewriter and charred sticks. Art, advancement of letters, contribution to the human progress and all that play no

'Our intention is to build up a San Quentin school that will rival the Chicago school of writers which produced Ben Hecht and others.'

part in the excuses given by the men for writing: 'I want the dough,' or 'If I could only get a coupla centuries...'" But at Mencken's suggestion that he hire Mr. Hardy as an agent, Booth turns serious (letter of May 31, 1927): "There are five of us, including John Backus, who have been working for two years. I am the last member. Our intention is to build up a San Quentin school that will rival the Chicago school of writers which produced Ben Hecht and others. Rather ambitious, but not impossible, for the fellows in here must write, it affords the only release they've got." Two years later, the tone is even more professional. Writing to Mencken of his latest story, "Ladies in Stir": "Also, if you have a proof to send to the Paramount studio. Mr. Oliver H. P. Garrett in a recent letter tells me the movies are hot for such material."

Of the two star writers of the California penal system, Ernest Granville Booth is certainly the more colorful, even if he left a lesser mark on film history than his fellow inmate Robert Tasker. We know Tasker, if we know him at all, mainly through the romantic image his old partner John Bright left of him in his writings and interviews. Tasker's name is also to be found in the society columns of newspapers, as well as on more than a dozen film credits. Whereas Ernest Booth, alias Ernest G. Granville, alias Roy W. Reeves, alias Ray Reeves, cut a large swath mainly across police blotters. He switched numbers like others do P.O. boxes. His number at the Los Angeles City Jail was 44016, at the L.A. County jail it was 349077. For the FBI he was suspect number 12558. At San Quentin he was prisoner 42601, at Folsom 13332, at the Oakland City Jail he was 9530, in Portland 3192, in Stockton 4258, and in Berkeley 497. Those were the numbers of a career criminal, which even Mencken ultimately found "discouraging."

Born in 1899, Booth started his career at fourteen with a break-in that landed him a two-year juvie stretch in Ione, near Sacramento. Having barely turned eighteen, he was next arrested in Oroville for stealing a car. In 1924, on the day he married Valdera Milliken, he knocked over a bank in Oakland, threatening the clerks with an "ammonia bomb," as the local press put it. He spent his honeymoon alone in Folsom. He was ultimately sentenced to a twenty-years-to-life term and was transferred to San Quentin, where he met Tasker, who by this time was already editor of the *Bulletin*. Both were soon writing for Mencken, who loved the romance of rough trade even more than discovering new talent. Although Mencken privately thought Tasker "much lighter stuff than Booth," he also found him a better writer and prospect for parole.

In a letter to the writer Jim Tully, Mencken said he pulled strings with "a few governors he knew" and managed to have Tasker released on parole in December 1929. He still had doubts about the more hardened Booth. In November 1931, Booth's wife, Valdera, his brother, and Warren Mulvey, a shyster and excellmate of Booth's, were arrested in the prison administration building in Sacramento while attempting to steal and replace Booth's prison record with a fake one. The dim plot landed the brother in prison for ten months; Valdera got a suspended sentence; Mulvey went back to Folsom for five years. John Fante, the California writer and protégé of Mencken, knew the prison doctor at Folsom, and wrote to Mencken in March 1937 about another spectacularly inept caper from Booth: "It seems Booth has been trying to convince the medicos that he belongs to the TB ward. According to the doc, he went so far as to bring to the hospital the sputum of a bona fide sufferer, claiming it to be his own, but the deception was discovered. Now, ironically enough, Booth has got tuberculosis! The doc is not very sympathetic, feeling that, now that Booth is a sick man, the best place for him is Folsom."

The parole bureau thought otherwise, releasing him in the spring of 1937. Reporting on this, the *Oakland Tribune* ran a picture of him with the caption "HE'LL BE BACK." Booth settled in Placerville with his wife and child, and there he wrote treatments for Warner Bros. But he found this tough going, and the paltry fifty-dollar checks he sometimes got from Burbank were a startling change from the heady days of the late twenties. Paramount-Publix had shelled out fifteen thousand dollars for his *Mercury* story "Ladies of the Mob" (William Wellman made the film, starring Clara Bow and Richard Arlen). In 1930, *Stealing Through Life*, the autobiographical book Knopf had published a year earlier, had netted Booth a cool eleven thousand dollars. Rowland Brown wrote a script based on the book, with hopes of directing it, but the film was never made. However, the 1931 picture Paramount made of another one of Booth's *Mercury* stories, "Ladies in Stir"—retitled *Ladies of the Big House*—was such a success for its director, Marion Gering and its star, Sylvia Sidney... that the pair went on to make five more films together for the studio, then headed by Sidney's lover B. P. Schulberg. But in 1937, the terms of his parole forbade Booth from writing about the only thing he knew, crime and prison. Instead he had to sweat over patriotic shorts like *Fremont the Pathfinder* and eighteen-day wonders like Penrod's *Double Trouble*, one in a series of Penrod programmers for juveniles churned out at Warners by Bryan Foy and his "B hive." A year later, however, his parole over, Booth was living on Russell Avenue in Hollywood and spinning yarns with telltale names like *This Man Must Die* and *You Might Be Next*. He served as technical adviser on *Men of San Quentin*, and fellow studio hack Horace McCoy wrote a script out of Booth's play *Women Without Names*, which Robert Florey directed for Paramount. But all this time Booth was already supplementing his movie income the only way he knew how, the hard way. In 1941 he was questioned in the murder of Florence Strickler, a dowager who was found by her husband bludgeoned to death and stuck in a closet of their Silverlake house. Strickler, a "drugless doctor," had treated Booth for his recurring TB. A black gardener, hired on the recommendation of the ex-con, had gone missing. Booth was released after spending two days in jail for carrying a gun.

In 1947, he was reportedly on the verge of publishing again: *Young Captain Bligh*, his first nonprison book, about the early life of the Bounty commander, and the more familiar-sounding *Sirens Screaming*. However, the jig was up, as this March 18 flash in the *Daily Police Bulletin* indicates:

> Suspect in company of John J. Sedlak—probably driving Studebaker sedan, 1946; registered to Eulah Sedak, used on several hold-ups. Suspect uses narcotics and is armed with a .32 or .38 caliber blue steel revolver. Known associates are in Hollywood and around Third & Figueroa—Hold—We will extradite.

Booth was finally arrested by the FBI at Musso & Frank's. The police description reads like something out of James Ellroy:

> WMA—48 years old, 5ft11, 160 lbs—blue eyes, brown-grey hair, receding hairline, high forehead, slender build, hollow cheeks (TB), dimple in chin, turkey neck, slightly stooped, walks

> with slight limp. Usually wears blue pin-striped suits. When operating, talks with gruff voice. Has been employed by Warner Bros. studio and as camera repairman for Don Blietz Camera Shop in Hollywood. Has habit of flashing large bills.

Booth had been wanted for questioning on an old 1943 case, a burglary at the Portland Cement Company involving $250,000 in stolen bearer bonds. But the police found he'd also been behind a series of bank robberies in and around Los Angeles, including the Atlas Federal Savings and Loans in Pasadena, from which he took twenty-one hundred dollars. A judge set his bail at fifty thousand dollars, and by July 1947, he was BACK IN ALMA MATER, as several newspapers gloated. The story went coast to coast, as this *New York World Telegraph* headline attests: NOW HE CAN PEN SOME MORE FICTION. Ernest Granville Booth didn't finish his new twenty-year stretch, dying in San Quentin of tuberculosis in 1951. Upon his last arrest, his twenty-sixth, the *New York Mirror* had written: "E.G.Booth always had difficulty deciding whether to write about crime or go out and commit one. He tried both, and both occupations paid him well."

Upon acceptance of his first story in the *American Mercury*, "My First Day," Robert Tasker sent Mencken the requested biography:

"E.G.Booth always had difficulty deciding whether to write about crime or go out and commit one. He tried both, and both occupations paid him well."

> Born in North Dakota on November 13, 1903, raised in Canada, finished high-school in Portland in 1921. One year later I'm in California, go through a bad patch, buy a gun—there you have it. I'm now serving a five-to-life sentence in San Quentin for armed robbery. Don't hesitate to call me whatever you want: thief, hood, knockover artist. It's all the same to me. As to where I'm from, I can't really say—except maybe from here."
>
> (This was signed *Robert Joyce Tasker, number 39962, S.Q., Cal.)*

Robert Tasker (portrait 1936)

Tasker had robbed Sauer's Dance Palace in Oakland on Saint Valentine's Day. He'd thrown a handful of bills onto a tablecloth and left with the bundle, but had been easy to find by the police because he'd just walked a few blocks and hung out; the gun they found on him was empty. The caper had all the hallmarks of a rebellious gesture, and years later his writing partner John Bright did not hesitate to paint Tasker as a romantic hero of the class wars. But this was the year of the Leopold and Loeb case, and the national press was up in arms against "psycho-crimes." The judge threw the book at Tasker. In the 1951 novel Bright wrote based on his friend's life, *It's Cleaner on the Inside*, Bright claimed Tasker robbed the dancehall just to enrage his rich, conservative father. Tasker did cut a romantic figure, with the smooth good looks of a matinee idol (Lew Cody, say), but he was no Robin Hood. In one of many letters he wrote to Mencken that are now held by the New York Public Library, Tasker asked him to send the payment for his story "A Man Is Hanged" directly to his father in Waterville, Ontario, adding: "I'm rather fond of the old chap, and I can think of no nicer manner of sending information of another success." This clearly refutes Bright's take on the father-son relationship, and other checkable facts confirm Bright as a notoriously unreliable witness of his times, both in interviews and in his lively unpublished memoirs, *Arsenic and Old Faces*.

In September 1927, the writer Jim Tully visited several prisoners in San Quentin, including actor Paul Kelly, in for beating another actor to death over the actress Dorothy MacKaill. Tully later reported on his prison excursion in the *Mercury*, describing Tasker as "twenty-four, tall, good looking, a sheik type for society girls and stenographers, with black hair carefully combed." Tasker had just had his novel *Grimhaven* published by

Robert Tasker (right) being handcuffed in Rowland Brown's *Quick Millions*

Knopf, and in December 1929 he was released on parole. Mencken had even finagled a bogus job for him at *Photoplay*, the leading fan magazine. The terms of his parole forbade him from writing on crime for another two years, but in April 1931 he could be seen, handcuffed, on movie stills in theater lobbies all across the nation. Rowland Brown, a screenwriter then directing his first picture at Fox, had given him a small but vivid part in *Quick Millions*. Brown was a connoisseur of tough characters: he had sparred with Jack Dempsey, and knocked him down; in his native Ohio he had rubbed elbows with members of the Purple Gang and worked in a speakeasy. Brown was also the first director to dress gangsters like princes and give George Raft a good part (before *Scarface*). In *Quick Millions*, Raft is the aloof lieutenant of trucker-turned-racketeer Spencer Tracy, who has him killed. A shifty-looking character named Lefty is ordered to give Raft "a nickel finish." "As Lefty, Tasker has only two lines but is seen in his garage filing the number off a gun, handing escape money to Raft before shooting him in the back. But the police are somehow in on it, and Lefty is handcuffed and hauled away.

Even before this, Tasker had probably had a hand in another, more prestigious crime picture. According to Bright, Tasker had written *The Big House* (1930) with veteran writer Frances Marion, who had Thalberg's ear at Metro. Bright also claimed that the fast-working Tasker did more than help her on the script, which is possible, as she was then between marriages (she'd soon wed George Hill, director of *The Big House*). Tasker was uncredited and Marion won an Oscar for best screenplay, the first year in Academy history that an award was given in this category. In her memoirs, *Off with Their Heads*, Marion mentions a "research visit" to San Quentin, which lasted only three hours and was mostly a photo opportunity for publicity purposes. A trusty with a stammer had presented her with flowers, perhaps giving her the idea for the Roscoe Ates character in the film, Wallace Beery's cellmate. As for the rest, even the San Quentin warden was flabbergasted at Marion's accuracy and sense of detail. Let's just say that Tasker's obits in both *Daily Variety* and the *San Quentin News* credit him for *The Big House*, and leave it at that.

Tasker could have used an Oscar, though, as first efforts outside were unprofitable at best. His second novel had been rejected by Knopf, and he was still without a studio job. By December 1931, however, he was in clover, having married Lucille Morrison, whom the society pages described as "an actress and socialite." Bright described her as a "catastrophe," and Tasker as his "shit-pill heiress": Lucille's father owned a laxative factory, the Fletcher's Castoria Company. They moved into a swank bungalow at the Mi Casa, a luxurious apartment building on Havenhurst next to the Colonial, where William Powell and Carole Lombard lived. Hired by RKO in 1932, Tasker, with Samuel Ornitz, helped Rowland Brown prepare *Hell's Highway*, a penitentiary picture. He also wrote *Secrets of the French Police* and *The Great Jasper* with Ornitz, a future member of the blacklisted Hollywood Ten, who introduced him to Bright. "Between us," said Bright, "we completed his radical education."

In effect, Tasker replaced for Bright the writing partner he had recently lost in Kubec Glasmon. But these two were more compatible: they were the same age, shared the same leftist politics, and liked the same things—namely Mexican girls and gambling. Together they freelanced around town, placing a story at Fox with the Sol Wurtzel unit and writing two pictures at Universal (A *Notorious*

Gentleman and *The Accusing Finger*). They were at Warners writing *San Quentin* when they asked their agent, Zeppo Marx, to get them out of their contract. Bright later wrote in an article how B. P. Schulberg, now an independent, had suddenly gone radical, as others get religion, and wanted to line up a number of "socially significant" projects with the likes of Lillian Hellman and Clifford Odets. He had to settle for Saroyan, Bright, and Tasker; the only result of this cockeyed fever was the lackluster *John Meade's Woman* (1937), with a story by Bright and Tasker and screenplay by Vincent Lawrence and Herman J. Mankiewicz. Mostly, Bright and Tasker were aping their new boss, whose creative credo, according to them, was "nags, gin and cunts." By day they drank at Lucey's, across the street from the Paramount lot, scheming to adapt great proletarian novels like B. Traven's *The Death Ship*. By night they were at the Clover or at the Century, or losing money at high-stakes poker games, often to the same moguls who gave them their paychecks.

Tasker shed his heiress in 1934 and he eventually took up with a sensational-looking Mexican girl. In 1938, Tasker and Bright embarked on another epic adventure, *Back Door to Heaven*, which was to be the director William K. Howard's comeback picture but turned out to be his somewhat muffled swan song instead. Howard had been a big man once, holding his own at Fox with the likes of Ford, Hawks, and Borzage. He'd earned salaries of up to four thousand dollars a week. Now he had to get the financing himself from Floyd Odlum, owner of American Airlines, who attached a "drinking clause" to his contract. With good cause—*Back Door to Heaven* was to be shot in Astoria, New York, on the old Paramount stages, without too much supervision, and the movie crew read like an old alky reunion: Wallace Ford, Patricia Ellis, and the inauspiciously named Johnny Walker, who caused less disturbance with his drinking than with his morning epileptic fits. In

By night they were at the Clover or at the Century, or losing money at high-stakes poker games, often to the same moguls who gave them their paychecks.

He had beaten up his wife's lover, a man very close to the chief of police. He knew they were going to come for him, and he had sworn long ago he'd never go back to jail, let alone a Mexican jail.

Ohio, Howard had gone to school with Charles Makeley, who later ran with Dillinger. Sent to death row for killing a cop, Makeley had attempted to escape with a pistol made of soap, blackened with shoe polish. He was killed in the attempt, but the scene remains for eternity in *Back Door to Heaven*, as Bright and Tasker incorporated what the Irish director told them of his old school chum. The film was a flop.

Tasker's own demise was equally dramatic and fraught with rumors. In 1942, already drafted, he'd gone south to join Nelson Rockefeller's goodwill program in Latin America, but essentially forgot to come back from Mexico City, where he'd been assigned. Several wartime Mexican pictures bear his name, including *Dama de las Camelias* and *Los Miserables*. On December 8, four days before Lupe Velez's suicide in the same town, *Daily Variety* wrote that Tasker had been found dead at the age of forty-three in the swanky Chapultepec palace he'd taken with Gladys Flores, "granddaughter of the former president of Costa Rica." An empty tube of Seconal was found by his bed. The day before, according to his wife, they had quarrelled and he had threatened to kill himself. Predictably, rumors flared up on the busy Hollywood-Mexico shuttle. According to his brother Sam, Rowland Brown was one of the last people to see Tasker alive. Tasker had been frightened because he had beaten up his wife's lover, a man very close to the chief of police. He knew they were going to come for him, and he had sworn long ago he'd never go back to jail, let alone a Mexican jail. Bright maintained that he had it "from a famous homosexual Mexican actor" that Tasker had been smothered with a pillow.

The *San Quentin News* was the only paper to mourn "Robert J. Tasker, famous San Quentin Author," adding that he had succeeded in making of the *San Quentin Bulletin* a literary magazine "of splendid intellectual appeal."

Four Poems

by
David Lehman

January 25

Sex wasn't a digression
It was the destination
The plot begins in awe
ends in failure
and is filmed in black and white
with Barbara Stanwyck
At the bars, Marxism was out
Existentialism was in
and their preferred form of escapism was
death penalty news & updates
a trumpet solo
the record spinning
the needle moving
two cigarettes in the ashtray
and this prayer I make to thee
O Love deliver me from evil
with skin wounds only
and Lee Wiley's voice
"for I don't stand a ghost
of a chance with you"

August 13

It's Hitchcock's hundredth birthday (say that fast)
and as luck would have it this August 13 is a Friday
I'll celebrate with Bill Evans and "Autumn Leaves"
tonight I'll see *Shadow of a Doubt* (a man falling
out of a train) last night I saw *Frenzy* (the impotent
killer's tie clasp in the dead girl's fingers) and
tomorrow night Claude Rains will confess to his
fierce mama that he is married to an American spy
Ingrid Bergman in *Notorious* where the uranium
is the McGuffin evil does exist meanwhile I'll take
the side of objects as Francis Ponge would put it
the key she slips into Cary Grant's gloved hand
and at the tennis court every head moves back and
forth following the ball except one

December 12

Gertrude Stein said
the film audience is not
the theater audience no
the film audience is not
an audience that's awake
it's an audience that is
dreaming you must keep
this in mind when watching
movies even movies on TV
with all the lights on say
Le Jour se lève with Jean

Gabin as the king of Gitanes
in Paris in 1971 with Lew
I wanted to write the book
and lyrics of a musical
about her and Alice and
Hemingway and Picasso
and Matisse and their wives

DECEMBER 21

He was in favor of
anything that gets you
through the night,
tomorrow night,
the longest night
of the year with
the brightest full moon
in one hundred
and thirty something
years. It called for
a celebration. He
felt like James Cagney
in the glory of being
killed at the end of *White Heat:*
"Made it, Ma. Top of the world!"

AMONG THE PINAFORES

E.M. Forster as Costume-Drama Fodder

"It will be generally admitted that Beethoven's Fifth Symphony is the most sublime noise that has ever penetrated into the ear of man." So begins chapter five of E. M. Forster's *Howards End*, along with Proust's account of the Vinteuil septet one of the most beautiful meditations on music to be found in modern literature. Six people, related in various ways and loosely comprising a family, are sitting in the Queen's Hall in London, listening to a performance of the Fifth Symphony. (Numbers matter to Forster; it is no coincidence that the Fifth Symphony is played in chapter 5.) With acuity and fleetness, he gives us their responses:

Whether you are like Mrs. Munt, and tap surreptitiously when the tunes come—of course, not so as to disturb the others; or like Helen, who can see heroes and shipwrecks in the music's flood; or like Margaret, who can only see the music; or like Tibby, who is profoundly versed in counterpoint, and holds the full score open on his knee; or like their cousin, Fréulein Mosebach, who remembers all the time that Beethoven is "echt Deutsch"; or like Fréulein Mosebach's young man, who can remember nothing but Fréulein Mosebach: in any case, the passion of your life becomes more vivid, and you are bound to admit that such a noise is cheap at two shillings.

BY DAVID LEAVITT

A Scene from the film *Howards End*, based on the novel by E.M. Forster

The concert progresses, and as it does, very little happens outside the characters' minds. But within their minds—what reactions! As Helen observes, "How interesting that row of people was! What diverse influences had gone into the making!" Later, in a moment of abstracted panic, she flees the theater, bearing with her the umbrella of the young man sitting next to her, a clerk called Leonard Bast whose voice will soon join the others, turning the sextet into a septet like Vinteuil's. This inadvertent act of theft will prove to be the fulcrum on which the novel turns, leading Leonard to seek out the Schlegels, who will involve him with the Wilcoxes, who will seal his fate.

How to translate such a scene into cinema? That was the question I asked myself about a decade ago, when I learned that the famous team of Merchant, Ivory, and Jhabvala was going to be making a film version of *Howards End*. After all, bringing to cinematic life an episode in which very few words are spoken, and no one moves, is no mean feat. For the language of cinema, as I learned from the director John Schlesinger the one time I tried to write a screenplay, is essentially gestural. "Too much talk!" was always his complaint about the script I was working on for him. Coincidentally, the scene in the screenplay that he liked best had no dialogue; it was a study of faces, during which the two principal characters watched a performance of Dido and Aeneas at Carnegie Hall. And how else but through gesture could one get across the import of a passage like this one?

> "No; look out for the part where you think you have done with the goblins and they come back," breathed Helen, as the music started with a goblin walking quietly over the universe, from end to end. Others followed him. They were not aggressive creatures; it was that that made them so terrible to Helen. They merely observed in passing that there was no such thing as splendour or heroism in the world. After the interlude of elephants dancing, they returned and made the observation for the second time. Helen could not contradict them, for, once at all events, she had felt the same, and had seen the reliable walls of youth collapse. Panic and emptiness! Panic and emptiness! The goblins were right.

This passage is crucial to the novel in that it explains Helen, investing with motive the recklessness that will soon become her leitmotif. A few paragraphs later "that tense, wounding excitement that had made her a terror in their nursery days" provokes her to leave the Queen's Hall.

> Helen pushed her way out during the applause. She desired to be alone. The music summed up to her all that had happened or could happen in her career. She read it as a tangible statement, which could never be superseded. The notes meant this and that to her, and they could have no other meaning, and life could have no other meaning. She pushed right out of the building, and walked slowly down the outside staircase, breathing the autumnal air, and then she strolled home.

Such a sequence would pose a challenge to any filmmaker. How would Merchant, Ivory, and Jhabvala handle it? I wondered. Would they render the concert, á la Schlesinger, without words? Would they use voice-overs? Or would they surprise me by finding a means of translation so clever and so unexpected as to astonish?

Well, in the end, they did surprise me, though not in a remotely positive way.

Here, then, is how Merchant, Ivory and Jhabvala have rendered chapter five in the film version of *Howards End*.

We are in a small concert hall—smaller than the Queen's Hall. There is no orchestra. Instead, at a piano, sit an uncredited Simon Callow and a woman with large quantities of black-gray hair; they are playing a four-hand transcription of the opening movement of Beethoven's Fifth Symphony. In the audience Helen sits next to Leonard. Helen alone. No Margaret, Tibby, Aunt Juley, Fréulein Mosebach, or Fréulein Mosebach's young man, as in the novel.

By replacing the orchestral concert with a lecture, Jhabvala had hoped to find a dramatic means of incorporating some of Forster's verbal ideas into the screenplay.

After a few seconds the pianists stop playing, and Simon Callow, rising from his bench, gives a speech:

> It will, I think, be generally admitted that Beethoven's Fifth Symphony is the most sublime noise ever to have penetrated the ear of man. But what does it mean? One can hardly fail to recognize in this music a mighty drama, the struggle of a hero beset by perils riding to magnificent victory and ultimate triumph. That's described in the development section of the first movement. What I want to draw your attention to now is the third movement. We no longer hear the hero but a goblin. Thank you. Mother...

This speech bears careful analysis. In essence, it cobbles together bits and pieces from the concert scene, beginning with an almost verbatim transcription of the opening line and ending with the appearance of a goblin. And yet much more is altered than left alone! Forster's account of the symphony's first movement—"Gusts of splendour, gods and demi-gods contending with vast swords, colour and fragrance broadcast on the field of battle, magnificent victory, magnificent death!"—becomes the rather banal "struggle of a hero beset by perils riding to magnificent victory and ultimate triumph," while Helen's subtle distinction between the "heroes and shipwrecks of the first movement" and the "heroes and goblins of the third" becomes the lecturer's "We no longer hear a hero but a goblin." Most distressingly, given the allergy to cliché that is such a hallmark of Forster's prose, the two halves are glued together by the leaden "But what does it mean?"

Why is this? My guess is that by replacing the orchestral concert with a lecture, Jhabvala had hoped to find a dramatic means of incorporating some of Forster's verbal ideas into the screenplay. (Not incidentally, a lecture would also have been substantially less expensive to film.) And yet the decision to give these words to a pompous speechifier has a corrosive effect on them.

Consider, for instance, the opening line. In the written version, a hint of the vernacular ("noise" instead of "music") softens the impact of what might otherwise seem merely a piece of grandstanding. Moreover, the sentence echoes the opening line of *Pride and Prejudice*—"It is a truth universally acknowledged, that a single man in possession of a large fortune must be in want of a wife." Austen, as it happens, was Forster's favorite writer, and it is her modest voice that we hear at this moment in the book: a far cry from Simon Callow's booming, Scotch-accented baritone.

Even more injurious to the novel is the heedlessness with which Jhabvala fuses ideas that in the novel belong to distinctly different characters. It was one of Forster's most noteworthy strategies to draw back periodically from the action at hand in order to offer commentary of his own; this is certainly the case with the opening paragraph of chapter 5, in which the six auditors are observed, as it were, from on high. And yet later on the narrative is handed—almost literally—to Helen:

> For the Andante had begun—very beautiful, but bearing a family likeness to all the other beautiful Andantes that Beethoven had written, and, to Helen's mind, rather disconnecting the heroes and shipwrecks of the first movement from the heroes and goblins of the third.

With three words—"to Helen's mind" — Forster indicates a clear transition from omniscient narration to a single character's intimate point of view. In the film version, on the other hand, both the "sublime noise" and the shipwrecks come from Simon Callow. More importantly, the "heroes and goblins" that belong to and in a certain key sense define Helen's imagination are taken away from her. For Helen's decision to flee the auditorium, if it is to make sense at all, must owe entirely to her reaction to the music. In the film, by contrast, she leaves because she is bored; to make the point vivid, Ivory has her check her watch not once, but twice.

So now Helen is checking her watch, and Simon Callow's mother is playing a passage from the symphony's third movement, and Callow is pacing the stage and talking. "A single, solitary goblin walking across the universe again and again," he pontificates, as the camera fixes on Helen, looking unconvinced, and Leonard, looking blank. All at once she picks up his umbrella and leaves. At first Leonard doesn't notice. An old man with a white beard raises his hand to ask a question.

> Questioner: Why a goblin?
> Speechifier: I beg your pardon?
> Questioner: Why a goblin?
> Speechifier: It's obvious. A goblin signifies the spirit of negation.
> Questioner: But why specifically a goblin?
> Speechifier: Panic and emptiness. This is what a goblin signifies, you see . . .

"Panic and emptiness"—a crucial phrase that recurs on several occasions throughout the novel—is here grafted onto a windbag's stodgy non-answer, made part and parcel of the "spirit of negation" to which Callow—unequal to his elderly interrogator—must lamely resort. Even Helen herself seems to dismiss the goblin and all it implies as unworthy of her attention.

It is at this point that the film moves beyond mere misguidedness and begins to manifest a real contempt for Forster's vision. All at once Leonard realizes that Helen has made off with his umbrella. As he gets up to follow her, she disappears into the rain, to the accompaniment of a booming fragment of the Fifth Symphony. Yet no sooner has she arrived at Wickham Place, and a sopping Leonard stepped through the door to beg restitution of his umbrella, than she is demanding his opinion of the lecture, the title of which, we learn, was "Music and Meaning":

It is at this point that the film moves beyond mere misguidedness and begins to manifest a real contempt for Forster's vision.

What did you think of the lecture? I don't agree about the goblins—do you?—but I do about the heroes and shipwrecks. You see, I'd always imagined a trio of elephants dancing at that point—but he obviously didn't.

While this speech is effective to the extent that it dramatizes how much the Schlegel sisters, with their flow of talk, flummox poor Leonard, it is also insidiously slanderous of Helen—even more so than Callow's callow lecture, since in this case the words come out of her own mouth. That she "disagrees about the goblins"—her own goblins—only brings home the point that this Helen is a flustered and muddle-headed child, not the visionary, undisciplined rebel that she is in the novel, and that she will grow into (to be fair to Jhabvala) as the film progresses. And yet how much is lost as a consequence! For in the novel, the scene in Queen's Hall serves as nothing less than a précis of the grand themes that will carry *Howards End* to its inevitable and tragic denouement: the clash between intellect and instinct; the impotence of talk; the grave matter, in Lionel Trilling's words, of "who shall inherit England." In the film, on the other hand, music—the art Forster cherished above all others—becomes merely the occasion for a slight and basically unfunny set piece: an opportunity for Helen and Leonard, in the parlance of Hollywood, to "meet cute."

Why have I chosen to focus here on only this one episode from *Howards End*?

Instead these books merely provide a period backdrop for mannered British actors to emote against.

Many other aspects of the film are deft and feeling. Several of the actors, most notably Emma Thompson as Meg and Adrian Ross Magenty as Tibby, give wonderful performances, and a few scenes—Jacky and Leonard's intrusion upon Evie's wedding, the final reconciliation between Meg and Mr. Wilcox—make for cinema of a high order. And yet something is deeply wrong here. For the sort of misrendering that mars the concert scene cannot be written off as an erroneous slip, or blamed merely on obtuseness. On the contrary, it seems to have been part of a conscious strategy, the intention of which was to muffle Forster's voice and blunt his vision, leaving us with the impression that this most intimate of authors is as decorative, touchy, and faintly ridiculous as Simon Callow nattering on about the spirit of negation. Alas, the only spirit negated here is Forster's own.

It is not my intention, here, simply to condemn the film of *Howards End*, nor to argue that the filmed adaptation of great novels is a priori a doomed enterprise; indeed, one need only recall John Huston's film of Flannery O'Connor's *Wise Blood* or, more to the point, Charles Sturridge's delicate and sincere film of *Where Angels Fear to Tread* to realize that great novels can be made into good films. And yet if a director or screenwriter is going to succeed in translating a novel into such a radically different medium—and often a medium that came into being only after the novel was written—he or she must first of all express a genuine respect and, if possible, fondness for the writing. And this is what I miss in most of Merchant Ivory's films: fondness. I never got the feeling that any member of the team really liked *Howards End*, or *A Room with a View*, or *The Remains of the Day*. Instead these books merely provide a period backdrop for mannered British actors to emote against. As Americans, we have the same appetite for them that we have for Britcom night on PBS, for *Keeping Up Appearances*, *To the Manor Born*, and *Waiting for God*, shows which in effect tell us that there'll always be an England, and not the England of *Trainspotting*, or even *The Full Monty*; instead this is a world where Miss Marple pours out, and Hyacinth Bucket (pronounced Bouquet) mans the white-elephant table at the church "Bring and Buy." How ironic that Forster—England's most trenchant critic and prophet—should of all writers have become fodder for such a voyeuristic and distinctly American fetish.

F. Scott Fitzgerald

An excerpt from the classic novel of Hollywood
—THE LAST TYCOON—

Stahr smiled at Mr. George Boxley. It was a kindly, fatherly smile Stahr had developed inversely when he was a young man pushed into high places. Originally it had been a smile of respect toward his elders, then as his own decisions grew rapidly to displace theirs, a smile so that they should not feel it—finally emerging as what it was, a smile of kindness sometimes a little hurried and tired but always there, toward anyone who had not angered him within the hour. Or anyone he did not intend to insult aggressive and outright.

Mr. Boxley did not smile back. He came in with the air of being violently dragged through no one apparently had a hand on him. He stood in front of a chair and again it was as if two invisible attendants seized his arms and set him down forcibly into it. He sat there morosely. Even when he lit a cigarette on Stahr's invitation one felt that the match was held to it by exterior forces he disdained to control.

Stahr looked at him courteously.

"Something not going well, Mr. Boxley?"

The novelist looked back at him in thunderous silence.

"I read your letter," said Stahr. The tone of the pleasant young headmaster was gone. He spoke as to an equal but with a faint two-edged deference.

"I can't get what I write on paper," broke out Boxley. "You've all been very decent but it's a sort of conspiracy. Those two hacks you've teamed me with listen to what I say but they spoil it—they seem to have a vocabulary of about a hundred words."

"Why don't you write it yourself?" asked Stahr.

"I have. I sent you some."

"But it was just talk, back and forth," said Stahr mildly. "Interesting talk but nothing more."

Now it was all the two ghostly attendants could do to hold Boxley in the deep chair. He struggled to get up; he uttered a single quiet bark which had some relation to laughter but none to amusement, and said:

"I don't think you people read things. The men are dueling when the conversation takes place. At the end one of them falls into a well and has to be hauled up in a bucket."

He barked again and subsided.

"Would you write that in a book of your own, Mr. Boxley?"

"What? Naturally not."

"You'd consider it too cheap."

"Movie standards are different," said Boxley hedging.

"Do you ever go to them?"

"No-almost never."

"Isn't it because people are always dueling and falling down wells?"

"Yes—and wearing strained facial expression and talking incredible and unnatural dialogue."

"Skip the dialogue for a minute," said Stahr. "Granted your dialogue is more graceful than what these hacks can write—that's why we brought you out here. But let's imagine something that isn't either bad dialogue or jumping down a well. Has your office got a stove in it that lights with a match?"

"I think it has," said Boxley stiffly, "but I never use if."

"She has two dimes and nickel and a cardboard match box. She leaves the nickel on the desk, puts two dimes back into her purse and takes her black gloves to the stove, opens it and puts them inside."

"Suppose you're in your office. You've been fighting duels or writing all day and you're too tired to fight or write any more. You're sitting there staring—dull, like we all get sometimes. A pretty stenographer that you've seen before comes into the room and you watch her—idly. She doesn't see you though you're very close to her. She takes off her gloves, opens her purse and dumps it out on a table."

Stahr stood up, tossing his key-ring on his desk.

"She has two dimes and nickel and a cardboard match box. She leaves the nickel on the desk, puts two dimes back into her purse and takes her black gloves to the stove, opens it and puts them inside. There is one match in the match box and she starts to light it kneeling by the stove. You notice that there's a stiff wind blowing in the window—but just then the telephone rings. The girl picks it up, says hello—listens—and says deliberately into the phone 'I've never owned a pair of black gloves in my life.' She hangs up, kneels by the stove again, and just as she lights the match you glance around very suddenly and see that there's another man in the office, watching every move the girl makes—"

Stahr paused. He picked up his keys and put them in his pocket.

"Go on," said Boxley smiling. "What happens?"

"I don't know," said Stahr. "I was just making pictures."

Boxley felt he was being put in the wrong.

"It's just melodrama," he said.

"Not necessarily," said Stahr. "In any case nobody has moved violently or talked cheap dialogue or had any facial expression at all. There was only one bad line, and a writer like you could improve it. But you were interested.

"What was the nickel for?" asked Boxley evasively.

"I don't know," said Stahr. Suddenly he laughed, "Oh yes—the nickel was for the movies."

The two invisible attendants seemed to release Boxley. He relaxed, leaned back in his chair and laughed.

"What in the hell do you pay me for?" he demanded. "I don't understand the damn stuff."

"You will," said Stahr grinning. "Or you wouldn't have asked about the nickel."

EPISTLE

F. Scott Fitzgerald to Thomas Boyd

THREE UNPUBLISHED LETTERS FROM FITZGERALD'S CORRESPONDENCE WITH TOM BOYD, A FELLOW SCRIBNER'S AUTHOR. BOTH WERE IN HOLLYWOOD IN THE EARLY 1930S, WRITING FOR THE STUDIOS.

Great Neck, Long Island } Prelude

Dear Van + Tom —

The book is marvellous, both in content and exterior, in close-ups and long shots. I have never heard of the gentleman with whom it is chiefly concerned but presume him to be one of our cleaner American humorists. } Gay Opening

Seriously I'm reading it now and enjoying it immensely — as I should the definitive biography of my favorite poet; thank you both immensely for the present and for the remembrance. } More Serious Stuff

Tom's namesake Earnest is coming out over New Years. Saw our own Mencken here in N.Y. today. If you want a good laugh see the screen version of the B. + D. } News + Section

My love to both of you + to your wives and children with the august thanks and blessings of } Climax

Yours Ever

F. Scott Fitzgerald } Fade Out

Released by Fitzgerald – Artcraft
To 4th + Cedar Sts.

~~Great Neck~~ — (Force of habit)
c/o A. D. Sayre
6 Pleasant Ave, Montgomery, Ala.

Dear Tom:

Sorry I've been so long in writing.

(1.) Enclosed find check for books. There is a rumor ~~that it is~~ the first of Abelards letters + has been published in English before. Is there any Truth in this?

(2) The ~~Hearst~~ price was $1750.00 per story. It totals $10,500.00

(3) Glenn Hunter is going to do This Side of Paradise for Paramount. They paid me fifteen thousand dollars cash for it. So you see I'm now a purse proud millionaire + as good a business man as Hergesheimer.

(4) "The Vegetable" (my same play) comes out on April 15th or 20th. In a previous

(2)

version Hopkins turned it down. No one has seen this version — it is the 6th & like all the others, absolutely perfect. It will sell 20,000 in book form & be eagerly bid for by 20 managers — and run one solid year in New York.

(5) Perkins is a wonder — the brains of Scribners since the old man has moved into another generation. I'd be glad to review Thru the Wheat. I wrote one blurb for it & will try another. I'll see that Wilson reviews it.

(6) I shall never write another document-novel. I have decided to be a pure artist & experiment in form and emotion. I'm sure I can do it much better than Anderson.

(3)

(7) The butler would let you in with pleasure. We get home around April 1st & you'll have to spend at least a night with us.

(8) I am offended that Peggy thinks my productive days are so nearly over that I should go to Scribners as a sort of Grant Overton. I assure her I'm not dead yet. Does she imagine that such jobs are well paid?

(9) I reviewed Grace's book. Thought it was magnificent of its type. Liked it better than Babbit as I never could sufficiently tolerate the middle-class booster Babbit & get near him.

(10) Thanks for the Doran book. I am enjoying it immensely. I feel

(4)

I should return it to you as obtained under false pretenses but I have no attention of doing so.

(11) All these "marvellous" places like Majorca turn out to have some one enormous disadvantage— bugs, lepers, Jews, consumptives or philistines.

(12) I wrote Glenn Hunter's next picture "Braver + Braver". Also he's to play in "This Side of Paradise" A pleasant affiliation as he's a nice kid. Paramount are now paying him $156,000 a year and two years ago he was starving in Central

(5)

Parks

(3) you're wise to stick with one publisher. Nobody's ever gained a damned thing by switching around unless they've actually been treated like a son of a bitch

(4) St Paul with three weeks more of winter must be hell. Down here it's heaven. Commend me to Peggy.

Yours Prosperously

F Scott Fitzgerald

(No figures in this letter are for publication)

F.S.F.

14 Rue de Tilsitt
Paris, France

Dear Tom:

You malign me. I am a faithful and punctillious correspondent. I wrote you that I was crazy about *Points of Honor*. Since then I have read them both over (I must have given away 2 doz. copies of *Through the Wheat*) and I think they are about my favorite modern books. Feeling the war, as one still does over here, they grow in stature.

I am anxiously awaiting *Samuel Drummond*— of course in choosing a field that so many men + women from Zola + Hardy to Sheila Kaye-Smith have tilled you set yourself a problem — that is you must bring twice as much freshness, data and communicable emotion to it to make it absorbing, as those who like Geo. Elliot first saw something in the subject, were required to do. No doubt you have — I hope so and I'm looking forward with enormous interest. Did you agree with me that *The Apple of the Eye* was a big fake?

Was your description of Mrs. Sinclair Lewis sincere or ironic? I've always heard she was a pretentious fright.

Sorry you didn't like *Gatsby* — and thank you for being so nice about concealing the fact (I mean this); I think you're wrong but time will tell.

Ever your Friend Scott

Watch for a book by young Ernest Hemminway.

by Deanne Stillman

STUDIO OPTIONS DESERT, THEN DISAPPEARS

Two young girls sliced to the bone by a deranged Marine in the sweltering Mojave Desert... Sound like a good film pitch to you? You bet. So where's the movie?

This is a desert tale. Like many such tales it involves strange characters and entities who may or may not have ever existed. And like many such tales, it is written on the wind, surely born of a desert djinn and thus requiring no argument or reaction. It happened exactly as I tell it, even the part about the Guardian Angel in the SUV and the Homeless Hag with the Grocery Cart on Wilshire Boulevard who may or may not have been ghosts. Shortly after the Gulf War in 1991, I wandered into a story that took over my life. Two girls—who might have been referred to as average in mainstream publications had such publications ever chosen to write about them—had been brutally murdered (each sliced to the bone thirty-three times) by a marine in Twentynine Palms, the desert hamlet I had been visiting for years whenever I fled Los Angeles. The story rang me like a church bell on D-Day and I resonated right back; such was my genetic, emotional, and geographic coding that the choice to follow the story had been made long ago.

Los Angeles Times

SUNDAY

APRIL 28, 1996

THE SPIN
BILL BOYARSKY

Journalists and Public Need a Strong Shield

Deanne Stillman didn't expect to wind up in a thorny legal fight over reporters' rights when she began her investigation of a vicious double murder in the desert community of Twentynine Palms.

Stillman, a contributing writer to Los Angeles magazine, spends a lot of time in the desert, hiking in Joshua Tree National Park and hanging out in Twentynine Palms, a community dominated by a large Marine base.

Reading the local paper one day, she spotted a story about the murders of 15-year-old Mandi Scott and Rosalie Ortega, 20, her friend. Each had been stabbed 33 times with an 11-inch kitchen knife. Marine Valentine Underwood, 34, a Gulf War veteran, was charged with the deaths, and faces trial for murder.

"It resonated with me on every level," Stillman said.

Stillman was drawn to the desert. So were Mandi, her family and her friends. Mandi had a problem-filled youth. So had Stillman. "I grew up as a misfit and I identified with her problems," said Stillman. "I knew this was a story I was going to tell. I felt it called me."

Stillman traced Mandi's life up to her death by tracking down family and friends. It took her 3½ years to get the story, which appears in the April issue of Los Angeles.

But her own story didn't end when the magazine came out. The lawyer for the accused Marine demanded Stillman's notes, tape recordings and other materials.

Although my background was not as dire as theirs, I had endured a riches-to-rags childhood which had led me at an early age to meet girls of a similar caste. I knew that often, these girls held wandering communities of rootless people together; when they met with catastrophe, as often they would, their communities—over time—would disperse, reconfigure, or sometimes disappear. They took care of their brothers and sisters, took care of other kids in the neighborhood, mothered their parents (usually their mothers; the fathers were generally not on the premises), mothered their own children, took care of the children of their friends. They would leave no legacy on the national register, these noble girls who led these wretched lives; they were not black and therefore their plight was taken up by no one of influence, least of all liberals, their appearance in the public arena confined to statistics in surveys about teenage pregnancy or drug use, or noisy panels on afternoon talk shows.

What had happened to the girls? What had sealed their doom? From the moment I first heard of them, I had to know. And so began my ten-year-long quest. I started asking questions. I called the lawyer for the man accused of the double homicide. He said his client didn't do it. I tracked down the mother of one of the murder victims. She didn't want to talk. I read the autopsy reports, the court records. A few months later, I received a call. It was Debie McMaster, whose world I had tried to enter a while ago. She wanted me to visit her where she tended bar, talk about her daughter Mandi. It wasn't long before I disappeared into the desert land which I had dreamed of ever since I could remember.

Although I grew up on the ever wintry shores of Lake Erie, I was hardly ever there; as far back as I can remember I was reading Zane Grey and accounts of Cochise and Geronimo, vanishing into the red rock and mesquite of western literature while everyone around me was ice-fishing or partaking in league night at the Kingpin Lanes. It was my father who first fueled my spiritual wanderlust; as I would sit in his immense library before a Promethean fire, he would read Edgar Allan Poe's "El Dorado," the sad poem about the questing knight who roams across life's sands, comforted by the journey itself and the pilgrim who urged him "to ride, boldly ride." This was a moment that fully informed my life, I later realized, even as it saved me. When my parents got divorced, my mother, my sister, and I moved from a distinctly nondenominational upper-middle-class suburb where no one talked about God because they were Protestant, to the working-class, Catholic part of town, where everyone's parents worked at a tool-and-dye plant and gathered for meals under the watch-

It was my father who first fueled my spiritual wanderlust; as I would sit in his immense library before a Promethean fire, he would read Edgar Allan Poe's "El Dorado,"...

ful eye of a crucified, tortured savior nailed up and dripping blood over the dinner table ("Christ who?" I innocently asked when told by a Catholic friend that the Jews had killed Him). I escaped to a vast, welcoming West of the imagination, finding refuge on the path to El Dorado. I wore fringe and cowboy boots. I sent away for seeds from Kaktus Jack's. I read encyclopedia entries about the James gang and Doc Holliday, pioneer diaries of survival and hardship. I wrote my own stories of flight, always disappearing in a swirl of magic dust. It was not just my own heartbreak from which I fled. For the first time in my life I met children who wanted, who suffered, who had macaroni and cheese, not filet mignon, for dinner, who had not seen Monet's Water Lilies in Cleveland's world-famous museum and never would, children who dreamed at night but forgot all about it in the day. Their parents lived from paycheck to paycheck, which, along with the word divorce, was a concept I did not fully understand, although as time passed, more and more "divorcées" and their children would land on this side of town. Almost everyone had a terrible secret; our neighborhood was poor but abundant with the tears of unspeakable sorrows.

Years later I moved to Los Angeles. I liked it; for all its fabled disconnect, everything about the place seemed the inevitable result of some weird joke. Like every enclave of castles in the sand, L.A. was overrun with fakirs. Dreams rose and fell with the caprice of a studio djinn. Deal-proferring bedouins named Steve wandered the dunes, searching for temporary oasis. But it wasn't long before I began heading for the real thing, the Mojave, where the glitter was refracted not in the sheen of a limousine, but in flecks of obsidian and pyrite and quartz; the Mojave, where the silence was not the thunder of an unreturned phone call but the flap of a butterfly's wings in the springtime. And then one day I opened a door, a portal; I entered a particular desert tavern to quench my thirst, and came the fork in the road, the choice already made, the story overheard, the terrible tale of the two girls sliced up by one of the few, the proud. The paths of my life had now become one; for the next ten years I would follow a trail of tears deep into the Old Testament scenery of the Mojave, deep into the nooks and crannies of the hidden lives of those who lived there, knowing that someday I would bear witness, someday I would write a book about the unlucky girls with shattered dreams and families who lived in the shadows of the world's largest Marine base, a place where children took care of other children and plotted their own routes of escape, just a few hours from the dream factory itself, Los Angeles.

From that moment on, I spent hours, days, at the Oasis, where Mandi's mother Debie tended bar. I listened to marines who loved the Corps, marines who hated the Corps, marines who hated the government for what happened in Beirut and Somalia, marines who easily consumed a dozen pitchers of beer in one sitting but always said yes, ma'am and no ma'am even as they were stumbling back to the barracks so they could sleep it off and then get up in the morning to protect the country, safeguard our rights. I visited shacks in the middle of nowhere to introduce myself to the victims' friends, kids who were so shell-shocked by life that they didn't, couldn't, finish a sentence or a thought or sometimes even

Action Council for 29 Palms, Inc.

9 April 1996

Deanne Stillman
Los Angeles Magazine
11100 Santa Monica Blvd, 7th Floor
Los Angeles, CA 90025

Dear Deanne,

The volunteer members of the Action Council have asked me to write you concerning your article in the April issue of Los Angeles magazine. We are sure that you and your editor have received many phone calls and letters from citizens of this community, both civilian and military, expressing their shock and anger at the article.

We feel that you have betrayed the hospitality shown you by the citizens of 29 Palms who met you during daylight hours. They were sure that you were more interested in what was on top of Jumbo Rock rather than what was under it.

But it is the unauthorized use of our copyrighted mural "Desert Storm Homecomimg and Victory Parade" that has us most concerned. The mural is a proud and joyous reminder of the safe return of our Marines and Sailors from Saudi Arabia. The dark, foreboding tones of your photo have turned this into a most depressing depicition of the occasion.

You and your editor had a monetary and a philosophical motive for doing the article the way it was done. Popular Detective could have done it better.

Sincerely,

Larry Briggs
Chairman

cc: Editor, Los Angeles Magazine

a greeting because why bother? One dwelling would lead to the next phone booth which in turn would lead to a crash pad. A week later phones would be disconnected, sources would be in jail, some just disappeared. I would start all over again, walking new paths, retracing the old, circumscribing a web of evil that left nothing and no one out. Everyone I met—adult and child alike—had a terrible tale of woe involving violence, abuse, parental neglect, time in rehab, strange

The desert promised me safe passage. So on I journeyed. There was something really awful afoot in the promised land, and it was not on 60 Minutes.

run-ins with veterans of various wars. So deep was my submersion that the attorney for the accused killer subpoenaed my notes—six years' worth—arguing in a pretrial motion that perhaps I had come across information which exonerated his client. California, as I learned, has very broad First Amendment shield laws, and after several lengthy sessions in San Bernardino County Superior Court, the judge ruled that I was not required to relinquish my notes. Along the way, my work had also caused concern among the merchants of Twentynine Palms (a book about the murders would be bad for tourism, they suggested repeatedly and vociferously in *The Desert Trail*, the local weekly), as well as within the Naval Criminal Investigative Service (the federal agency which investigates—and ultimately spins the official story of—marine crime). A book about the murders would make the Corps look bad, several officers suggested to me over the years. By the time *The Desert Trail* referred to me as an "Antichrist" from a big city who would "crucify"their small town, the signals had become clear. There was danger. There were those who advised me to quit the path. I thought about this. I consulted my advisers—the plants and critters who have served me well since the day long ago that I began dreaming. The desert promised me safe passage. So on I journeyed. There was something really awful afoot in the promised land, and it was not on 60 Minutes.

Alas, I did not have the deep pockets of such an investigative outfit. To fund my dig, I divested myself of unnecessary things and a large apartment. I borrowed money from friends and relatives. I not only robbed Peter to pay Paul, but beat him up, cut off his air supply, and kicked him in the groin in order to keep Paul at bay. It wasn't enough. Who would finance my desert crusade?

Enter Tina Brown, stage left. In 1993, after two years of research, I approached *The New Yorker* and was commissioned by the then heat-conferring editor to write an article about the children of the desert who drift from town to town with what's left of their families, often following the military. A year and a half passed and Condé Nast covered my hefty expenses. My editor called. Where was the article? Tina had been wondering. She had just read about a fashion shoot in Twentynine Palms, he said, and I translated the remark thusly: as Versace goes, so went barrels of ink; can you deliver the piece right now? I had not finished, I replied. There were some bikers I needed to find. Not to mention some Crips and Bloods. You see, I explained, many of the players in my story did not have listed telephone numbers or known residences, or for that matter, a desire to be interviewed. Okay, he said, but hurry up if you can. Tina's very high on this. Meanwhile, my agent was building a fire, talking about the piece to various studios so that by the time I turned it in, six months later, they were ready to bid, the desert denizen's dream of privacy blown before I had set pen to paper. The calls poured in the moment my piece landed at *The New Yorker*'s doorstep; it seemed that every producer in town had heard publication was imminent, and could they get in on the game? I passed the calls to my agent and thus did the bonfire grow.

But once again the desert had a big, hearty, silent laugh; it played another joke—this time on me. Amid the ensuing blaze, my piece was rejected; evidently, it was in competition with what my editor referred to as "another murder-in-the-heartland story" (*New Yorker* staff writer John Gregory Dunne's piece about Brandon Teena, another subject which, as it would happen, burned brightly for years and was finally memorialized in the Oscar-winning movie *Boys Don't Cry*). But according to the grapevine, Tina liked my story so much that she called her *Vanity Fair* protégé Michael Caruso, then editor of *Los Angeles* magazine, and suggested that he take a look. He liked it and bought it immediately, and it won a Maggie Award for best news story in 1996. However, having expected to option a *New Yorker* article and instead being offered something from *Los Angeles* magazine, the studios reacted to the apparent bait-and-switch, and quickly swam away. Again, the problem: how to finance the crusade?

Enter a book publisher, downstage. Two months after my article ran, I was offered a contract from Avon Books to write a book based on my article. The studios returned and the expected bidding war ensued. Enter TriStar, stage left. The studio won my signature and a small piece of my heart, acquiring my nonexistent book with me assigned to write the screenplay in a sweet deal billowing desert-style with a strange and alluring back-end money mirage and inscribed in big letters across page 3 of *Variety*.

And so the mission continued, but not without a peculiar detour. To avoid starvation while finishing my book, I had to write and deliver the screenplay, kind of a West Coast Guggenheim way of financing the arts. Of course, in the parched and desperate environs of the desert, people do much more than buy things that don't exist; they pay writers to make up endings to true stories that have yet to conclude. "We'd like you to write a *Norma Rae* for the nineties," the people at the studio said. "We want a tough woman like the one in your story." They were referring to Debie, who had filed a wrongful death suit against the Marine Corps for an outrageous act of negligence—the leatherneck who killed her daughter had been arrested for previous sex crimes and according to some was supposed to have been in jail on the night he murdered the girls but was permitted to range through town because he was a star on the marine basketball team.

"Has she argued the case yet?"

"No," I would say, "she's filed some papers."

"She'll win, won't she?" I would shrug. "We'll rework the ending later," they would continue. "This is an Oscar part for an actress, especially the courtroom scene at the end. We're thinking about Julia Roberts. Madeline Stowe's agent has been calling."

Of course, the screenplay was due as quickly as I could write it, before the book. The studio was concerned that other studios would option and make a similar story, now that everyone knew about mine. (Unbeknownst to me, at the same time, TriStar was developing *Erin Brockovich* for Julia Roberts, another true story about a tough-talking system-confronting chick derived from a conversation the wife of a studio executive had evidently had with her chiropractor.) For the next nine months, I wrote the screenplay, and continued my research. Of course, the screenplay ended with a dramatic courtroom scene in which the mother of the murder victim forcefully, eloquently, and emotionally argues her case, displaying complete knowledge of the civil code after a few visits to the library and calling a high-ranking marine officer as a surprise witness, whom she devastates on the witness stand with questions that a real judge would rule inadmissible. Ultimately, she is awarded a precedent-setting multimillion dollar award from the government, and the Corps is ordered to alter its recruitment policies so as to weed out potential felons. (As it stands now, a judge has yet to rule on whether the case can actually go to trial. It has been thrown out on a technicality involving service of a witness; the issue of whether the particular service was done properly is under appeal. Moreover, Debie McMaster is no longer representing herself, having hired an actual lawyer. And the Corps—presumably—is still recruiting people who cannot control their urge to do violence in a nonwartime situation. However, lest you scoff, if the case is allowed to proceed, should a federal judge have the courage to rule against the government, the case could alter military policy).

Soon after I turned in the screenplay, TriStar vanished, subsumed in a commercial storm of converging elements, with many of its key players, including my producer, cast out and sent whirling into the void like so much desert flotsam.

Does Tina Brown exist? I'm not convinced. Was there really a TriStar? Who knows? Anyone can concoct a letterhead. But I wrote my book and it's coming out this April, the time of year in the desert where if you get really quiet and still and you sit for a while, you can hear the crack of a hatchling's egg, you can watch the lily of a Joshua tree unfurl and open. Now that the journey is complete, I've come to see the various midwives along the path as desert spirits, imaginary Hollywood characters who entered my life in a blast of heat, the friction attracting coin and hangers-on and well-wishers and all manner of desert opportunists who found refuge, however brief, in certain pockets of my own dream, making it possible for me to tell a story I could not shake, one that had its own need for revelation.

Now that the journey is complete, I've come to see the various midwives along the path as desert spirits, imaginary Hollywood characters who entered my life in a blast of heat, the friction attracting coin and hangers-on and well-wishers and all manner of desert opportunists who found refuge, however brief, in certain pockets of my own dream ...

Yet there are two more who figure conspicuously in my tale. For all their importance, I do not know their names, nor, I suspect, shall I ever see them again. And I did see them, I swear, although they seemed to appear out of a fog that swirled up off the Pacific and eastward into Santa Monica and down through the corridors of Wilshire Boulevard at dusk on a winter day. I had hired someone to edit my manuscript before I delivered it to the publisher. I had just picked up the final revision from her house and placed it in an open envelope which I left sitting on top of my car. I drove off, happy that the trail was reaching its end. As I rounded a corner onto Wilshire and toward the beach, I heard the sound of fluttering papers outside my window. I looked and saw my entire manuscript skittering page by page across the pavement, down Wilshire for several blocks, sucked by the winds of a gathering storm, cast further astray by the wake of passing traffic. I jumped the curb and jammed the brakes, hopped out of my car and ran into the street, stopping trucks and cars as it started to drizzle and gust, picking up the pages of my book one by one before they were stolen by the weather. A woman in an SUV stopped at a light and joined me. "Don't worry, we can do this," she said, directing traffic as I darted in and out of cars, picking up pages even as they were run over by buses and jeeps. Up and down Wilshire I ran, chasing paper, as motorists slowed down and watched. The weather was winning, it seemed. But then came another helper, an ancient hag with a grocery cart who materialized out of the gathering storm and headed into the street to retrieve the remaining pages, now gusting around streetlights and toward distant neighborhoods. "We'll get them," she said, "it's okay." A while later, she handed me a pile of pages from her cart, every Post-it still in place, not a page missing, each editorial notation still legible under the tire tracks. I gave her what little money I had, a few bucks left from my studio gig, scrip in this company town.

The next day I turned in my book, meeting the last of what had been many missed deadlines, the last one before my publisher cancelled my contract (and incidentally, my original publisher had vanished too; it was now William Morrow, which had merged with Avon, and then both were purchased by HarperCollins. Like my book, my editor survived the corporate mayhem and in a way she is another player on this sandy stage, for I have only had elemental encounters, heard the voice, seen the notations.). "Thanks, desert," I said after I dropped my manuscript at the post office, thinking of the old guy in *The Treasure of the Sierra Madre* as he bid the mountain farewell and headed back to civilization with its treasure. After ten years of wandering in the Mojave, I had officially cast my book to the winds. ☗

The man who was made of netting

by Katherine Vaz

Manny Valente bought his daughter a cape that would stun everyone into silence. It cost him ten thousand dollars, half of which he had taken from the "Miscellaneous" account at his brother-in-law's furniture company, where Manny kept the books. He had been writing himself one-hundred-dollar checks every week for a year, and Frank, his brother-in-law, had not noticed. The petty-cash fund was large. Besides, Frank was busy spending several hundred every week taking clients to lunch. Manny planned to replace the money as soon as humanly possible.

Whenever he saw his daughter, Gemma, huddled in her room, what he had done felt splendid; this time luck would not fail him. A Hollywood scout—a cousin of a friend of a friend, something like that—had heard that dozens of girls in amazing capes turned out every spring for the Portuguese Holy Ghost Festival in Monterey, and he was coming to have a look. The festival's organizer, Maria Duarte, was told that a movie was in the works, about a miracle striking a girl in a procession. She was supposed to levitate or get the stigmata; stories about spiritual calamities were popular now. Some producer must have said, Hey, we'll make it Portuguese, they already have those parades and the costumes are great, and we haven't touched those people since *Mystic Pizza*, and that one made Julia Roberts a star. All of this was fine with Manny—Gemma's cape was going to catch the eye of the scout. Every family was in an uproar about this Hollywood lottery, but Manny was calmly assured about winning.

The night before the festival, he did not sleep well, and when he rushed to his daughter's room in the morning, he was surprised to find her still in bed. Her cape, sheathed in plastic, was hanging on the outside of the door of her pine wardrobe. "Gemma?" he said. "Time to get ready. Aren't you excited?"

A woman wearing a Holy Ghost Festival cape

She turned over in bed, a sullen, leaden mass, and ignored him. Where had his child gone? When was it exactly that she had left him?

"Gemma?" he said. "Your cousin is probably already waiting for us downtown."

"Oh, God, leave me alone," she said.

He had been there at the first scan of her: on the sonogram, she began as nothing but a white spiral with a feathering attached. Already that was her, real, a mysterious coil, clashing with his idea of her. When Manny was a child, his mother had pointed to a pregnant woman and said, "She's taking the time to knit her baby's bones together," and even when he was married at eighteen and about to be a father, that image stayed with him. He pictured knitting needles clicking some cells into a spine, then ribs, and then came the glomming on of more cells that knew how to knit up a person with a spleen and nipples and a predisposition. He loved the soft down that made a seam on the back of his daughter's neck, and everybody else's as well—that was an inspired brushstroke of creation that had blessedly, finally, nothing to do with any function and everything to do with arousing compassion, especially when you saw it on a person who was sleeping.

He went into the bathroom to dampen a towel to wash her face. The towels were so old that the flowers and fruits on them appeared to have been held up against flowers and fruits so real and potent that they had bled faint impressions onto cloth. When Manny's wife had run off years ago with a rich, older man, she had said, "Everyone is replaceable, Manny. Everything and everyone." He found her parting comment so vile that he held onto things—clothing and linens, pots and pans, plants—until they disintegrated.

He found Gemma up and encased in sweatclothes, sunk heavily on the end of her bed. Her black hair looked yanked by unseen hands.

"Daddy," she said, "would you do my hair in a French braid?"

He had no skill with beauty. He did not know any of the terms. "What's that?" he asked.

"Grandpa knew," she said. "What's your problem?"

"I don't have a problem, Gemma," he said. "I'm in a good mood. Why are you wearing those clothes? Get into your gown." He handed her the towel and told her to scrub her face. Other parents were calling in hair stylists and makeup artists and were generally going mad because of this scout. He should have planned for some help like that. Another mistake—part of his lacking any talent in matters of grace. Gemma was seventeen but looked like an unhappy, fat thirty-year-old. He would control his temper and cheer her up, or all the money and art on earth that she might carry on a cape would not win her to anyone.

"Show me how to do a French braid," said Manny. "If Dad learned, I bet I could."

"Oh, forget it. Christ."

"Christ got busy and sent me instead." Manny didn't blame Gemma for missing his dead father; he wanted him back, too. She had lived with her grandpa during the years when Manny's gambling was bad, but that was over now. He'd made a vow to her to quit.

When Gemma had on her silk white empire dress and high heels, Manny took the wrapping off the cape, and even Gemma stared at it for a minute and could say nothing. It was changeable fabric, the kind that had a warp that was one pattern and color, and a weft that was another. The cape had a lengthwise gold weave with rusts and reds that looked like tongues of fire, and the opposite weave was brilliant white. On the whole sweep of it, sequined doves held ribbons attached to fish in a sea that was a froth of lace. He had gone to Dotty Flores, who lived in Merced and did nothing but make Holy Ghost capes, and he had said, "It has to be better than anything you've ever done." After she'd huffed and said that

He held out his hand to help Gemma step from the car. Queens and their attendants in capes and crowns milled around, sequins flying and parents shouting . . .

---

everything was her best, he'd said, "Make this more than everything." He handed over his ten thousand dollars, and she opened the lids of bins and crates, and the room gleamed as if the tide had drawn back from a wreckage of treasure chests, pearls draped here and there, braids, laces—he did not have the vocabulary to describe these things. Dotty Flores needed to teach him the term "changeable fabric."

He took the cape off its hanger, and the slats of light through Gemma's blinds changed it from white to red, then white to rust, as if it were a living thing, and the fishes' eyes sparkled and so did the eyes of the birds that were meant to be the Holy Ghost, and he put it on her and tied the gold ribbons that looped down over her heart.

"This weighs a ton, Daddy," said Gemma.

"You know the saying, 'Beauty knows no pain'?"

"No."

"How about the French saying, 'One must suffer to be beautiful?'"

"We aren't French."

He helped her gather up the long train so that they could drive to the plaza in Old Town near the Bay. Manny wished that the waterfront could look less tarted-up and more like what it used to be, the place of Steinbeck, with wonder or some shock of actual life seeped into everything, including the rickety wharf. He and Gemma lived inland. His sister, Glória, was married to Frank Silva, Manny's boss, and they lived with their daughter, Lily, in their house on a bluff.

He held out his hand to help Gemma step from the car. Queens and their attendants in capes and crowns milled around, sequins flying and parents shouting and trains being spread out with their plastic underliners to protect against the ground. The brick plaza was lit up with violent color, flowers, screams, biers with Our Lady of Fátima or Saint Anthony and the Paraclete doves, and paper and tin ornaments waving in the damp, salted breeze; baroque overload—all good, all just right; Pentecost was the feast when the Holy Ghost appeared as tongues of fire over the heads of the apostles huddled frightened in a room. Suddenly the apostles caught on fire and burst out into the world.

And now here was Gemma, out of her room on a bright Sunday. He unfurled his daughter's train, and a little girl stopped to stare. She said, "Oh, you must be the main queen."

"Not the main one," said Gemma, and she smiled. "I'm one of the queens today, though."

Manny could feel the stirring in the air, the last-minute fussing and glances over the shoulder, an air of: Where is he? Where is our special guest, the starmaker? He recognized the Dutras, the Batistas, the Bettencourts, and Amélia Pavão, a rich girl. He couldn't help it; he needed to survey the competition. He guessed that Amélia's cape also cost about ten thousand dollars—the wealthy families paid two to five to eight or ten thousand. Girls like Clara Medeiros wore borrowed ones. Amélia's gown was lovely, but Gemma's was stunning. People were studying it in awed silence, and he felt relief and a sudden blaze of confidence.

A woman wearing a Holy Ghost Festival cape

"Here comes Lily," she said.

Manny's niece ran to them and threw her arms around Gemma and said, "Your majesty!" The girls giggled. Lily's cape was elegant but plain, red silk with jewels on the perimeter and a short train.

"Where's the Hollywood guy, Uncle Manny?" said Lily. "Everyone's trying to guess who he is."

"Oh—" He tried to sound as if he had forgotten about the scout. "I think he's going to show up at mealtime."

"When we're picking meat out of our teeth?"

"That's what I've heard," said Manuel. He adored his niece as much as he disliked working for her father. She was generous in her attention to Gemma. There was a lightness about Lily that was not weightlessness but a grip on the power of light. She played the flute and knew ballet and was on the speech team at Monterey High, and although she wasn't a knockout, with her wide face, high forehead, and large teeth, she had a way of opening up those huge features and enjoying herself. Manny was made aware, as he looked at her cape, that this was another kind of beauty, the kind that knew what it was and therefore, being essential, did not have to try too hard.

Lily's parents emerged from the crowd. Frank required a wide berth and walked heavily in his boots. Glória's face was drawn. At some point, Manny had lost his sister, too. When had that occurred? When she married Frank? She was plastered with makeup and wore round plain earrings that struck him as aggressive.

"Uh oh," said Lily. "Here comes the wrecking crew."

Frank arrived and shook Manny's hand, and he kissed Gemma's cheek and began studying her cape.

"Nice," he said, looking at Manny. "Very nice."

"Hello, Manny," said Glória, and closed her eyes and screwed up her face to kiss the air near him.

"You haven't been to Artichoke Joe's for a round of blackjack, have you, Manuel?" said Frank.

"Shush, Frank," said Glória.

Manny kept his breathing even, but heat glowed out of his skin and Lily and Gemma could see it. He should have known that Frank would wonder where he had gotten the money for a cape like this.

"No," said Manny, "that part of my life is over. You know that. I promised my girl."

Frank shrugged. "A joke. Man-well."

The procession lined up, with teenagers holding banners—Luso-American Sports Club, Knights of Columbus, Monterey I.D.E.S., Irmandade de Espírito Santo, the Brotherhood of the Holy Ghost. Queens, senior and junior, were here from Monterey, the Bay Area, and the valley towns, with attendants who held onto

He heard sighs and "ooh," and "oh, heavens," and "God," as if everyone were making love suddenly to someone invisible.

the loops stitched into either side of every cape so that it could be held out on display at its grandest width.

"Time to go!" said Lily.

Frank and Glória went to join the procession, but Manny decided to stay on the sidelines, to keep Gemma from being nervous. He leaned over to kiss her and whispered in her ear, "Go knock everyone dead."

It would all have been worth it, even if Frank caught him, even if he couldn't get the money back into the books in time: all worth it. Because people stood aside and inhaled sharply as if *they* were having trouble breathing when two girls took the side loops and fanned out Gemma's cape. He heard sighs and "ooh," and "oh, heavens," and "God," as if everyone were making love suddenly to someone invisible. Gemma's face brightened and opened as she stepped behind the Monterey banner, and right then she was lovely, too.

"Daddy!" she called out. And she didn't say, "Thanks, Dad," but that was all right. That was all right. She said, "Wouldn't Grandpa love to see me now?"

He said, and hoped it was loud enough for her to hear over the din, "I'm sure he's seeing you, darling."

Manny did not believe in heaven, but if anyone could graft another world onto this one, it would be his father, who had been a gardener and expert grafter in Agualva, or White Water, on the island of Terceira in the Azores. Manny had been born in Monterey, where he helped his father take living pear blossoms and thread their limbs inside bottles, so that whole pears would grow inside glass. They tied the bottles throughout the trees everywhere they could in Monterey, and the breezes made people say, "Listen. It's the music from those bottle-tree people." It had been a good thing to do with his father, who stuttered badly and stopped speaking. Manny never knew quite what to do with the weight of that silence.

Gemma never had that problem. She and her grandpa had shared a devotion to the movies. It made up for them not being able to tell their own stories back and forth. They went to films so often that Gemma's eyes got uncomfortable outside of dark rooms, and she squinted through daylight. Sometimes, back when Manny was gambling—driving as far as Reno because he'd once been lucky with keno at Harrah's—he would go to the movie theater in town to find them with their heads together, watching the screen. He would stay near the exit. Even then, he could not get rid of his betting spirit: if I count to ten, Lord, and she turns around, she'll come home, and if she doesn't, Lord, then fine, she's better off with my father for a while.

Her weeping at the funeral had cracked Manny in so many places that a tap from someone would have finished him off.

He followed the parade through downtown, past the old customs house toward the church, where everyone would file in for Mass. He would stand outside; he hated church. But he liked to see the *vara* go by, the four-sided corral of poles decorated with garlands. Amanda Sousa, the main festival queen, was walking inside the *vara* with her court. At the steps of San Carlos, the boys carrying it lifted it high and collapsed the poles together into a lintel for everyone to walk beneath.

"Uncle Manny!" Lily cried out. She stuck out her tongue and laughed. She was having a great time and blew him playacting kisses, pretending to be a queen. In fact, she did have a monied but beneficent air—not so different from Queen Isabel of Portugal, who had started the whole idea of Holy Ghost cults long ago. Manny liked very much that far away now in California, they were still doing as Isabel had asked: she declared that each year, at Pentecost, the poor and hungry had to be fed for free, and the nobility should give them robes and crowns and sit down with them.

"Gemma!" he called, watching his daughter head for the church.

She also blew him a kiss, getting into the act. Being around Lily was good for her. Today you could make a lucky *promessa*, a barter with the Holy Ghost, and he made one: Please, her name in lights. I will help pay next year to feed everyone, if You do that.

He would wait until next year to rejoin those who said that the expense and competition with the capes was getting away from the idea of being humble and feeding everyone. For now, he felt perfectly clear. A person looking at him, out in the hot sunshine, would see that he was slight, with a thin mustache, and it might be surmised that he had a tendency toward ailments of the nerves, but would that person guess that he was forgiving this aspect of human nature, to compete, to dress up, to try to be regal? Would that person know he was finding it noble and touching that this vow to feed one another for at least one day had remained unbroken since the time of Queen Isabel? How perfectly astonishing, when you thought about it, that people could keep a promise for over six hundred years.

He became bothered when Humberto Vargas, one of his old bookmakers, came up to him in the parish dining hall and said, "What am I, the devil, you say two words to me you're going to hell?"

"Yeah. Something like that."

"Nice cape your girl's got. Been taking your business elsewhere?"

"No," he said, "I haven't."

"Sure," said Humberto, "sure." He clapped a hand on Manny's shoulder and walked away, leaving Manny furious, and then anxious. Maybe playing around with the numbers in Frank's office books counted as gambling. Not a loan. Had he already broken his promise to Gemma? His breathing got shallow. For that matter, what about the business of making a deal with the Holy Ghost? Do this magic trick, and if I get lucky with some net profits, I'll pay You back? A dice roll with heaven. Did that count?

Men and women in red aprons were seating people at the long tables and passing bowls with slices of French bread and mint. Everyone took one and waited for the pans of meat, cabbage, and broth to go down the table, and they ladled that over the bread and mint to make a soup. Manny scanned the room, trying to find Gemma. He saw the main queen, Amanda, talking to her father, Joe Sousa. A lot of the food and decorations were donated, but Joe had offered to take his turn this year picking up most of the expenses, and he looked agitated but pleased, like a father at his daughter's wedding. A long line stretched out the door, and in the far end of the dining hall, in the open kitchen, men were drinking beer and stirring vats. People were chatting and laughing and arguing and helping each other pass things, and they were sharing wine and Styrofoam cups filled with pickled lupini beans. Someone had gone to the trouble of covering the white paper tablecloths with decals of stars. He wanted to find Gemma, to be with her; the scout was supposed to arrive at any second, and everyone knew it; heads were lifting and turning.

Maria Duarte came up behind him and said, "By yourself over here, Manny?"

Farther away, a single man occupied a third net-boat, not fishing, just off by himself: community, romance, and solitude.

"I'm looking for Gemma. You did a great job. Big crowd this year."

"I ever have to put this day together again, I want a whistle and a whip."

They watched covered tureens of the *sopas* being handed out through the kitchen's window, getting loaded onto trucks to go to the housebound, or the people who were too sad about their dead to come out. "It's a good thing, all of this," he said.

"It'll be a better thing when Mr. Hollywood shows up," said Maria.

"Not here yet? I was wondering."

"We're all wondering." She did a Mae West wiggle. "Maybe he'll say, Forget these young chickies, honey, it's you we want."

A shout went up for Maria, and she left him by himself again. On one wall, the Vieira brothers had made an elaborate mural out of netting. They had taken old fishing nets and bunched them up and twisted them into the shapes of people and boats and fish. They had shaped a lighthouse out of netting and given it an orange light over net-waters. In one net-boat, a crowd was hauling in a catch; in a net-rowboat, a man and woman sat together, not working. They had to be in love. Farther away, a single man occupied a third net-boat, not fishing, just off by himself: community, romance, and solitude. He was glad that the Holy Ghost festival would happen up and down the valley for a whole season, in other communities, but he was especially glad that the scout had chosen Monterey as the one to visit. Monterey had the ocean backdrop, the view, the clear air, the fishing history, and this mural with the people made of netting.

Gemma tugged at his elbow.

"Got a place saved for me somewhere?" he said. "I'm starving."

"Daddy," she said fiercely. "I saw you talking to Humberto."

"For half a minute. Right? It wasn't what you were thinking."

"How do I know that?"

"Because I made you a promise."

"Big deal. You've made lots of promises."

He caught his breath and closed his eyes a minute before opening them. "I am looking you in the eye and telling you the truth," he said.

"I've heard that one before," she said. He lost her in the crowd, couldn't see where she and Lily and Frank and Glória might be sitting, but now he wasn't hungry anyway, he was feeling short of air. He passed the bar, where the television was playing the Giants game. He stopped at the bar and said, "Give me a red wine," and Joe Almeida took his money and poured his drink. The Giants were behind, 3-2, against the Cardinals. He had another red wine before going outside.

He shouldn't have done that. He was getting light-headed, and he'd risked Gemma catching him with his eye on a baseball game right after talking to Humberto. She would never believe he had resisted placing a bet. His hands were trembling. Because he'd had an urge to do exactly that, make some fast money to put back in Frank's petty-cash fund so that he could be past any chance of unpleasantness.

He went outside. He could get some shrimp or crab at the *tasca* set up near the auction stage. Booths were selling ceramic plates and T-shirts that said, Kiss Me, I'm Portuguese and Monterey I.D.E.S, 2000 A.D. Another booth offered *fado* and *chamaritta* cassette tapes, and another had the bazaar: Old ladies tightly rolled hundreds of square-inch scraps of white paper that they then bent in the middle. Manny was tempted to pay a dollar for five out of a fishbowl and unroll them to see if he had one with a number that would match a prize. Most of the stuff was junk—white-elephant donations—but there was also a money tree. This was innocent festival play, but he never knew what would send him into that old desire. Rose Bettencourt was behind the counter and said, "Manny, cheapskate, buy some chances."

"No thanks, Rose," he said. To make conversation—she was always moaning about her health—he added, "Good job rolling all those papers, what with your arthritis."

She held out her hand and said, "Arthritis? Get over here."

"Jesus, Rose. Relax. What, you want to arm wrestle?"

"Come here and test my grip."

"No."

"I don't see this hand dropping." She stood there as if she'd said hello and he was being rude. He went to shake her hand and be done with her, but her grip

Manny knew he was panicking, drunk on an empty stomach; his chest began to heave. He had lost his ability to put on a good poker face. He told himself to calm down.

was brutal. She had a shock of iron hair and a bosom like a rock ledge. He would be a bad guy if he overpowered her, but a weakling if he didn't. What was it with people? Always ready to squeeze you until your bones broke.

"Hey, you win," he said.

"Ha," she said, letting him go. "Okay, I give you now some free chances. You're a good sport."

"Nothing there I want to win, Rose."

"We got here a money tree and potholders and waffle irons not outta the box. My booth don't need your insults."

She thrust the chances into his hand, and he was clutching them when Frank showed up and said, "That's a nice money tree."

He held up the chances in his hand and said, "This is a charity booth at a festival, Frank, and these are a gift. Aren't they, Rose."

"My lips are sealed. I say I'm giving away free chances, I get my ass run outta the business."

"Listen, Manny," said Frank. And then Manny disappeared into some chamber where he was submerged and the sound of Frank's voice was barely getting through. Something about Frank planning to bid on a painting to be auctioned by Aquatic Galleries. An underwater artwork. Frank was going to bid on it for the office, an empty space over a reception table. "You'll need to write me a check from petty cash tomorrow," said Frank, "and then we'll be having an outside auditor come in and look through everything so we can get that loan."

"What loan?" said Manny.

"You getting senile? We talked about it last week, remember, for the new wing I'm adding to the store? Lamps, plates, linens. Everything you could want indoors, I'm thinking. Not just furniture."

Manny knew he was panicking, drunk on an empty stomach; his chest began to heave. He had lost his ability to put on a good poker face. He told himself to calm down. Frank was his boss; he often bought things for the office from petty cash. He was not trying to trap or test him. But why was Frank bringing this up now, with Manny standing there with a fistful of bazaar chances?

"Manny? You hearing me?"

"Why wouldn't I be?"

Across the lawn, men on the auction stage were setting up crates of produce, flats of peppers and figs for the first round of bidding. People were gathering on the benches. Manny saw Gemma without her cape on, and he said, "Excuse me, Frank," and went to her, the wrapped little paper chances falling from his wet fist onto the lawn. He said, "Gemma? Honey? Why aren't you wearing your cape?"

"Because it's four million degrees out, Daddy. Lily isn't wearing hers, either."

"You know," he said, lowering his voice, "that scout might already be here. Wouldn't it be nice if he sees you in it and—well, anything could happen for you."

"I wish you'd stop that."

He never knew what to say to her. Her grandpa couldn't speak to her either, but their speechlessness was profoundly full of stories and images, as if inspiration and aspiration, the twin glories of movies, were caught in the breath and lit up on screen. Manny had a craving to win this day that made him dizzy, as if desire and heat like this were too much for his frame.

"Daddy?" said Gemma. "You look terrible."

"No," he said. "No, I'm fine, darling."

But she went to find her cape hanging from a tree branch, and for a moment, his eyesight swimming, it looked like a white-to-red enormous flower being plucked out of the tree; Gemma might as well have cracked open one of the pear-blossom bottles and the long captured, long-trapped, long-repressed plant had exploded out, not pear-colored but bloodred and cloud white. She put on the cape, and people backed away, looking at her.

Frank sat with Glória and Lily at a distance, on another bench, as the auctioneer, Carlos Dutra, began prattling. Manny reminded himself that today was the day for everyone to be fed, and he hadn't eaten. He could still go to the dining hall, but he did not want to miss the scout. The sound of numbers, amounts, people bidding higher and higher, Frank's voice chiming in, increased the sense that his head was liquid and sloshing back and forth, and he had a thought so ignoble, so horrifying, that he clutched his hands because they were going to fly up as if to get as far as possible from his mind: he could ask Gemma for a loan. They could raid her money-market fund, her college money, and put five thousand dollars back into the petty-cash fund, and he could find a way of explaining to the outside auditor the consistency of the error; he would invent a hundred-dollar-a-week need for more office supplies. That would work.

Gemma sat next to him again, wearing her cape, and her hand reached up to wipe the side of his face.

"Daddy?" she said.

He looked up and saw the auctioneer offering an enormous seascape, and Frank's voice was in counterpoint to the voice of a woman who also wanted it: one hundred, three hundred, five hundred; the audience was gasping and applauding. Manny got up and said to Gemma, "I'd better get something to eat, precious," and on his way to the *tasca* with seafood, a small woman in a blue shift, probably a cousin of the Sousa family, said to him, "Show me the nearest food, I'm dying," and he said, "Come with me." The woman was scary-skinny, like all the Sousas, and he said, "Let me," and he bought her a plate of crab fritters and shrimp and scallops with garlic. "This is the good stuff, so we pay for this, to help raise money," he said, thinking that he should eat, too, but he couldn't. Strange; his appetite was there, but the effort of feeding himself seemed too much. He heard Frank's voice, offering eight hundred dollars for the painting, and he saw himself writing the check for it. He was already onto tomorrow and wanted today to be finished, the results in.

"This is nice of you," said the woman, and slid her dark glasses onto the top of her head. She ate with a plastic fork, and when she finished, she said, "Thanks for feeding me in such grand style. These are the best scallops I've ever had."

"Right out of the ocean," he said. "That's the beauty of Monterey."

She thanked him again and said that she wanted to watch the auction for awhile.

He stayed inside the little shed and watched the cooks frying clams in hot oil, and when he walked outside again, the bidding was over and Frank was smiling. Eight hundred dollars for a seascape. What was it like, to have that kind of money? He wondered again if Frank already knew the truth and was trying to frighten

It took all of his strength to let Gemma alone to do the talking. He had a sense that barreling over there now, talking to the bald man with the briefcase, would tip fate the wrong way.

him into an admission; that would be just like Frank, to require a beseeching for forgiveness. Then Manny was startled: a large bald man with a briefcase was talking to Gemma.

All the planning, and week-by-week writing of those checks—and now the moment was here, just like that, time collapsed. The man walked around Gemma, who held her cape out for him to take in. He stepped back to view it, and Manny said, "Thank you, thanks, next year I'll pay everything, I'll feed everyone," but that brought the panic back, too, because Frank might fire him tomorrow or press charges, and Glria would certainly side with Frank and not him. Money, to Glória, was much thicker than blood. But Gemma was going to be in pictures, and he could live with finding another job. That would be for the best anyway. He would be inspired to do better for himself, now that Gemma was taken care of. He might still have a brainstorm between now and facing the outside auditor, some way of explaining the ongoing one-hundred-dollar debit. Frank's company was doing well. No one needed to be punished with jail, but now that didn't matter; Manny could do time, if he had to.

It took all of his strength to let Gemma alone to do the talking. He had a sense that barreling over there now, talking to the bald man with the briefcase, would tip fate the wrong way. Gemma was grinning, nodding at the man.

Manny waited until he saw the bald man shake Gemma's hand and walk away. Gemma sat down again to follow the auction: someone had donated wooden toy trucks. He tried to read her face but couldn't. A man shouted, "Ten dollars," then came twenty, twenty-five, thirty dollars. Manny found the man with the briefcase on a bench, and he forced himself to walk slowly until he was next to him, and he said, "I saw you admiring my daughter."

"That's quite a cape," he said. "Something else."

"Yes," said Manny. He had a speech ready, a shameless one; he was ready to beg the man to select Gemma. He waited for the man to say who he was, that his

Lily was lit up, open, happy, inflamed, eager; not the most stunning girl but the most alive presence—far and away the most spirited, the one most likely to find an inspired moment with a camera eye on her.

---

daughter would be on a plane to Los Angeles next week, and Manny could forego pleading and say in a dignified manner that he understood the role would be small but that didn't matter, when the man said, "Looks like the scout has found her girl."

"What?" said Manny.

The man pointed toward the small blond woman, who was standing next to Lily, Frank, and Glória. Manny's sister had her hands over her mouth to cover her squealing. Gemma had walked over to them, and the blond woman was lifting up the cape. Gemma looked happy. Lily's face was radiant, as always, but now it was an intensification of radiance, a thing made more itself by being found.

"I thought you were the scout," said Manny.

"No," said the man. "No. Why would you think that?"

What, thought Manny, I fed that tiny woman scallops, now she has to put my daughter in the movies? How could a savior be so thin and small? More than that, he had not considered the possibility that Frank, who already had so much, should win this time, too.

Gemma ran to him and said, "Daddy! The lady wants to rent my cape. She says it's the most beautiful cape in the world! She wants Lily to wear it in the movie."

"You should wear your cape. It's yours."

"It'll still be mine," said Gemma, "but I'm glad it'll be Lily wearing it. She loves the stage. You can tell. I get stage fright."

"You'll get over it."

"My cape is going to be there for everyone to see," said Gemma, reaching for her father's trembling hand. He was staring at Frank and Glória and Lily celebrating, and Gemma said, "Thanks, Daddy."

He looked at her and bowed his head. What had he ever done, to be rewarded with such a generous girl? He did not know what to say, because numbers were crowding out any words: he had a few hours before the auditor would be staring at Manny's work. Frank could be in a fine mood, his daughter tapped by the great outer powers, and Frank would still send his brother-in-law to jail. At some point, Manny would have to tell Gemma the truth, and he would have to agree with her: Lily was lit up, open, happy, inflamed, eager, not the most stunning girl but the most alive presence—far and away the most spirited, the one most likely to find an inspired moment with a camera eye on her. He had known Lily her whole life and not quite seen that, but this scout had figured it out in minutes. He despised the clarity and fairness of it; of course Lily was meant to win all along.

Still—he and Gemma could go to the movies together, when his debt was somehow paid. If he had to go to jail, it would not be forever. If the film were ever finished, they could sit together in the dark theater and listen to everyone sharply inhale to see such a dazzling thing. They would know, the two of them, where it had first come from. There would be a point in the movie when his niece would turn away from the camera, and only the cape would be on view; the star right then could be anyone. What would be the harm, if he said to his daughter in those rapid few seconds: There you are. That's really you, darling.

That night he lay awake, wondering how he would face the terrors of the next morning, everything he had done laid bare. He was rehearsing how to ask Glória, and Frank, and Gemma, for forgiveness, when he heard Gemma shrieking.

He ran to her room and switched on the light. She was having a nightmare, she said; someone was holding her down where she could barely breathe, and she'd been trying to get to the surface and wake up but couldn't. She was sitting up in bed now, shaking.

"I can tell you what that is," he said. "Your grandpa explained it to me when I was a boy. It's called o pesadelo com a mao furada. That means the Nightmare with the Drilled Hand."

"Yes, it was like a hand over my face," she said. She was sweating. He sat on the edge of her bed.

"Is it like having Grandpa here with you, to learn this?" he asked.

She nodded.

"It feels as if the hand holding you down has only a drill mark in the palm, and

Mostly it happened while he was figuring the net totals for his rich brother-in-law, when he felt porous and as string-like as the lines on the pages of his accounting books.

you inhale all panicky through it while you're trying to swim up to where you can be awake."

"Yes," she said, "that's it."

"It makes you feel horribly alone. But my father used to tell me, it will give you compassion when you find out everyone in the world goes through it."

"Does it happen just once?" she asked.

He told her that the Nightmare with the Drilled Hand was a trial of childhood, so that she would think it would go away soon and never return. That was a lie. He had had many Nightmares with the Drilled Hand since he had fallen in love three years before with a married woman. Their affair had only lasted six months. But sometimes, even now, he was so struck by the image of this woman locked naked in his embrace that it staggered him. He might be in a line at the bank and would have to grip the velvet rope. He might be in a grocery store and would need to brace himself against a ledge of produce, his head down as he waited for his lungs to fill back up. Mostly it happened while he was figuring the net totals for his rich brother-in-law, when he felt porous and as stringlike as the lines on the pages of his accounting books. What was he then, eight hours a day, except some fishing snare meant to catch errors? How do we all manage it, he often wondered, walking around as self-possessed as we do?

"Daddy," Gemma said, and put her arms around him, "I thought I was going to die."

He held his daughter close.

The truth, he knew, is that love never comes again in the same way, and often it never comes again at all. And even when the gift of it is there, in your arms, something in love cannot resist leaning toward your ear to whisper. It whispers that it's a temporary blessing, it always is, and soon it will be—not gone, not that, that would be more of a relief; it will be dissolving into the very air around you, the air that becomes a labor to breathe.

AN EYE FOR AN I: FROM NOVELS TO FILMS

PHILIP KAUFMAN, MASTER OF VISUAL STORYTELLING

BY ANNETTE INSDORF

When reading a book, each of us assumes the role of filmmaker. As words turn into images in our minds, we become not only the characters but the camera eye. Perhaps that's why we rarely find a filmed version of a novel as satisfying as the book: the mental movie we make is necessarily more personal than the highly selective and condensed version of the director. Moreover, the very elements that make a novel shine—rich prose, tone, rhythm, subjectivity—are the hardest to transpose to the cinematic medium.

Philip Kaufman, director of *The Unbearable Lightness of Being* and *Quills*

In early December of 1999, I attended a screening of the almost-final version of *The Talented Mr. Ripley*, introduced by writer-director Anthony Minghella. Since he also adapted *The English Patient* for the screen, Minghella had a solid basis for proclaiming, "The nature of adaptation is that it betrays as much about the adapter as about the source material."

Successful adaptations "betray" a great deal about gifted filmmakers—namely their concerns, from stylistic to thematic and moral. When William Trevor saw Atom Egoyan's film of his book *Felicia's Journey*, he called it a "brilliant interpretation of the novel." As a *New York Times* article pointed out, "the choice of words is precise: interpretation, not realization. Even when Egoyan could have transcribed the book exactly, he chose to transform it instead."

When it comes to cinematic transformation, Philip Kaufman may be our most gifted contemporary American director. A visual stylist who is truly literate, a San Franciscan who often makes European films, Kaufman is not easy to categorize. Nevertheless, *The Right Stuff, The Unbearable Lightness of Being*, and the recently released *Quills* explore not only Kaufman's concern with the complex interactions of the individual body and the social landscape, but how film language works.

How does a camera tell a story? How does cinematography approach the nuances of verbal narration? How do composition, lighting, visual texture, and color function as narrative devices? These are some of the questions that need to be raised when we look at how—or how well—novels become films.

THERE HAS ALWAYS BEEN A SYMBIOTIC RELATIONSHIP BETWEEN BOOKS AND MOVIES, AND MANY OF THE GREATEST LITERARY WORKS ARE INDEED "CINEMATIC."

There has always been a symbiotic relationship between books and movies, and many of the greatest literary works are indeed "cinematic." Those who get excited about the parallel tales of Paul Thomas Anderson's *Magnolia* should be aware not only of the pioneering work of Robert Altman and Jean Renoir with collective protagonists, but of D. W. Griffith's; he, in turn, was influenced by the parallel montage in the literature of Dickens and Flaubert.

The relationship between an author (or wordsmith) and a director (or image maker) is complex and shifting. One way to characterize it was offered by Alberto Farassino:

> Even if they have always traveled in the same boat, and have often exchanged favors, writers and filmmakers are used to shoving each other around and often try to push each other overboard. It is an old game: the former disparage the cinema in the name of the purity of literary works; the latter invoke the autonomy of the two languages, even if they don't disdain to exploit the title, the fame, and the narrative substance of the book.

But then again, don't all narrative films adapt a verbal tale? Isn't there always a story set in words—an idea, a treatment, a script—before the images overtake linguistic constructs? The novelist E. L. Doctorow wrote:

> Film de-literates thought; it relies primarily on an association of visual impressions or understanding. Movie going is an act of inference. You receive what you see as a broad band of sensual effects that evoke your intuitive non-verbal intelligence. You understand what you see without having to think it through with words.

From their very beginnings, movies embodied a paradox: they were often based on literary sources (such as nineteenth-century novels), yet they unfolded in silence. Words existed only as intertitles, and primarily for limited dialogue. By the 1930s and '40s, with the advent of sound, films became more loquacious— especially comedies, which depended on rapid-fire dialogue. By now, moviemaking has grown sophisticated enough to express in primarily visual ways.

One of the best examples of visual storytelling is *The Unbearable Lightness of Being*, directed in 1987 by Philip Kaufman (whose filmography includes *The Wanderers*, *Henry and June*, and *Rising Sun*) from a screenplay he co-wrote with Jean-Claude Carrière (Buñuel's frequent accomplice whose script collaborations also include *The Tin Drum*, Daniel Vigne's *The Return of Martin Guerre*, Milos Forman's *Valmont* and Peter Brook's *Mahabarata*).

Its source is Milan Kundera's novel of 1984, which is filled with seemingly unadaptable philosophical asides about eroticism and morality. Nevertheless, together with the cinematographer Sven Nykvist (best known for Ingmar Bergman's films), Kaufman created an engaging visual tale as well as a complex meditation on voyeurism, politics, and morality.

"People would always say to us that the book seemed impossible to adapt. And they were right," Kaufman acknowledged. "The film is a variation on the book, a thread that comes from the book and leads back to the book. Maybe people who see the movie will refer to the book for references and reverberations."

Set in 1968 Prague, the movie begins like an erotic comedy, turns into a political tragedy, and ends in a domestic pastoral. Printed titles introduce us to Tomas (Daniel Day-Lewis, before his international success in *My Left Foot*), a young surgeon. Unlike Kundera's first-person narration, the film opens with a refusal of the spoken word. Self-consciously and humorously, at first the film seems to be silent, although doves coo after we hear laughter behind a closed door.

That Tomas is an irresistible playboy is evident from his recurring line to women, "Take off your clothes." When he first utters these words to an attractive nurse, Kaufman's rich treatment of voyeurism commences; the camera reveals that this scene is being watched by a patient and orderlies on the other side of the hospital window.

This gentle self-consciousness continues in Tomas's scenes with the stunning artist Sabina (Lena Olin), as a mirror accompanies their lovemaking. Later, during a frankly erotic scene, she straddles the mirror which is on the floor and asks Tomas, "What are you looking at?" He replies, "Your eyes."

Kaufman does indeed replace the "I" of Kundera's text with the "eye" of cinematic storytelling—an appropriate substitution for a work that alludes more than once to Sophocles's *Oedipus Rex*. And it is eye contact that brings Tomas together

Lena Olin as Sabina in *The Unbearable Lightness of Being*

with Tereza (Juliette Binoche, long before *The English Patient*) when he visits her town to perform an operation. Here is how the novel presents their initial contact: "He had first met Tereza about three weeks earlier in a small Czech town. They had spent scarcely an hour together. She had accompanied him to the station and waited with him until he boarded the train."

Subsequently, Kundera muses on destiny:

> The town had several hotels, but Tomas *happened* to be given a room in the one where Tereza was employed. He *happened* to have had enough free time before his train left to stop at the hotel restaurant. Tereza *happened* to be on duty, and *happened* to be serving Tomas's table. It had taken six chance happenings to push Tomas towards Tereza, as if he had little inclination to go to her on his own.

Kaufman makes the locale a spa town, redolent of steam baths, where an off-screen massage evokes sounds indistinguishable from sexual moans. At the center is a swimming pool, where Tomas observes six men around a floating chessboard—an image of male strategy that is suddenly disrupted by the graceful dive of a female body. Tomas's gaze follows Tereza's underwater glide through the pool, and then to the screen behind which he watches the silhouette of her naked body as she dries herself with a towel. Tomas then follows her through the mist-filled corridors of the spa into the cafe where she is a waitress.

There, her eyes (in a subjective shot) find Tomas, who pretends to be reading. By the time they finally speak, the atmosphere is charged with simmering sexual attraction. In a departure from the novel, their eyes suggest desire—or free will—rather than chance. Or perhaps enhancing the novel, Kaufman anchors the metaphysical in the gloriously physical.

Tomas must return to Prague that evening. Tereza is hooked. She shows up on his doorstep one day, and the surprised Tomas flirts with her almost amusedly, while she responds with violent passion. For the first time, he lets a woman stay overnight in his bed, and she later gets him to marry her. Despite Tereza's touching vulnerability, peasantlike charm, and love for Tomas, he continues to philander, especially with Sabina (who helps Tereza get work as a photographer).

When the Russians invade Prague, masterful scenes seamlessly cross-cut newsreel footage with grainy black-and-white images of Tereza and Tomas in the streets amid tanks. (Tereza's photographs are all stills from actual footage taken in 1968.) In the light of the new dictatorship, *The Unbearable Lightness of Being* seems to be asking whether sexual license is a substitute for political freedom. (This

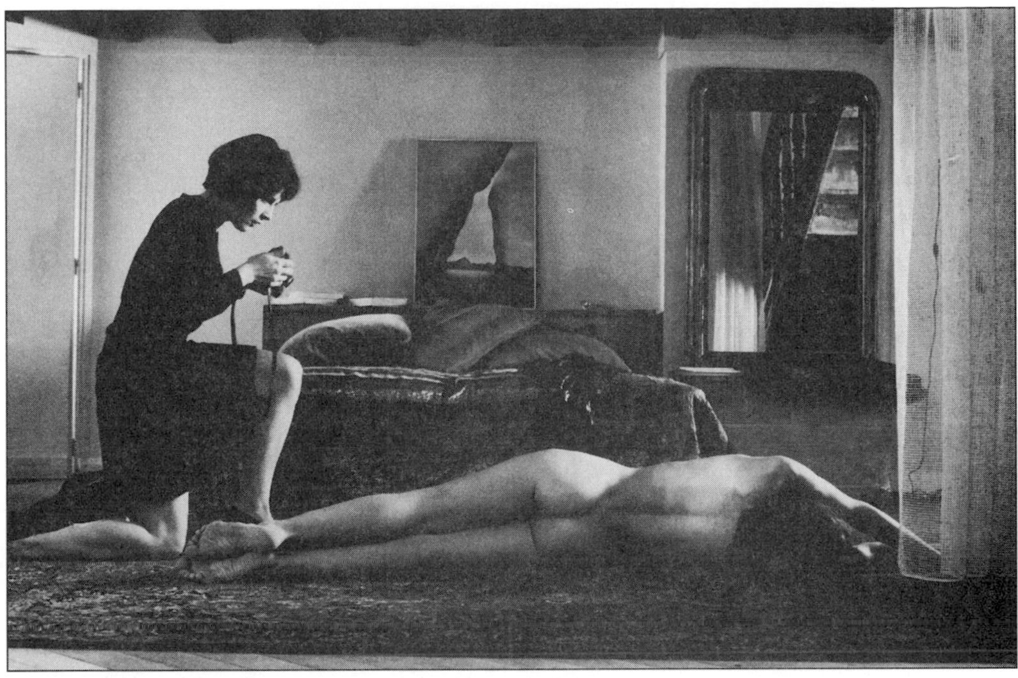

Juliette Binoche and Lena Olin in *The Unbearable Lightness of Being*

is somewhat literalized by the montage in a later Prague scene: Kaufman cross-cuts between a woman stripping for Tomas and photos of her with political leaders.)

Tomas and Tereza leave for Geneva—as has Sabina, who embarks on an affair with Franz (Derek de Lint), a handsome professor. The voyeurism is downright playful when they make love in a train compartment, whose sole other passenger pretends to be sleeping; as the man puts on his glasses before seeming to close his eyes, he becomes a benign audience surrogate, almost inviting us to peep along with him.

In another remarkable sequence that makes us aware of the voyeurism inherent in the cinematic experience, Tereza visits Sabina, ostensibly because she needs shots of female nudes to get photographic work. When Sabina first takes off her clothes for Tereza, she can't bear to look at her. But later she does, and then she in turn tells Tereza, "Take off your clothes," before snapping pictures of Tereza's nude body. It seems as if Tereza is attracted to Sabina, using the camera as a defense mechanism. But is this because she knows that Tomas loves Sabina's body, and the camera represents his eyes?

Tereza subsequently leaves Tomas and returns to Prague, supposedly because she feels too dependent on him: "The weak returns to the country of the weak," she admits. But he follows her, and they must remain in Prague. Because he once wrote an article criticizing the government, he can't get his job back without signing a retraction. He says no, even after the Interior Ministry official (Daniel Olbrychski) coaxes him to do so (a foreshadowing of Day-Lewis's character's refusal to sign a confession in *The Crucible*). If Tomas initially seemed like an amoral Don Juan, he becomes a political hero when he refuses to sign. (Tereza develops into a heroine as well, albeit temporarily, when she furtively gives her photos of the Russian invasion to foreign journalists.)

KAUFMAN SAID OF THE NOVEL TO AN INTERVIEWER, "IT BEGINS WITH A STATEMENT OF A THEME AND THEN GOES BACK AND FORTH. I DIDN'T WANT TO LOSE THE MUSIC. I TRIED TO FIND POETIC RHYTHMS THAT WOULD MATCH KUNDERA'S RHYTHM, BUT FOR THE SCREEN."

Tereza finally decides to even out the adulterous score of the marriage, and goes to the apartment of an engineer (Stellan Skargard) who picks her up at the bar where she works. Later, realizing from a former ambassador who now sweeps the bar (Erland Josephson) that she might have been set up for blackmail, she makes Tomas move with her to the countryside, where they stay with the jolly Pavel (Pavel Landovsky).

All seems blissful, but Sabina—now in California—receives a letter saying Tomas and Tereza have died in a car crash. Then we cut back to Tomas and Tereza alive, on the road, fading to white before the ostensible accident. Do they really die? Has an accident been set up because they were once opponents of the Communist regime? We will never be certain.

Using the music of Czech composer Leos Janácek, Kaufman provides a structure that could be called musical: we move from andante to adagio, from light—visually and thematically—to dark, and from quick cuts to longer takes (as is true of Truffaut's *Jules and Jim*, another splendid adaptation that traces the attempt of characters to love more than one person at one time).

While Kundera's book has a musical form as well—a kind of theme plus variations—the experience of the two works is quite different. Kaufman said of the novel to an interviewer, "It begins with a statement of a theme and then goes back and forth. I didn't want to lose the music. I tried to find poetic rhythms that would match Kundera's rhythm, but for the screen."

He created striking visual equivalents for Kundera's words. Sabina straddling the mirror visually suggests the lightness of being, especially when Tomas lifts her.

Geoffrey Rush as the Marquis de Sade and Kate Winslet as Madeleine in *Quills*

Later, in Geneva, she creates a sculpture from mirror shards—in the form of a female body, with Sabina's signature bowler hat on top—which shares the frame with her undressing. Reflecting the air openly, her art is a virtual embodiment of lightness.

Tereza's lightness, on the other hand, is expressed by her floating in the swimming pool: the point of view alternates between objective (we see Tereza) and subjective (we see through her eyes). In this context, how appropriate that when Tomas is reduced to menial work after refusing to sign the retraction, he becomes a windowwasher, often suspended on high floors.

Kundera urged Kaufman to "eliminate" whenever possible, well aware that an adaptation of his novel could not be faithful. The director recalled that when the writer asked him if he should be on the set, he said no. Kundera acknowledged, "You are right. For me it would be like a father watching his daughter make love." "But for me," Kaufman continued, "it would have

Joaquin Phoenix as the Abbé Coulmier in *Quills*

been as bad … like watching a father watch me while I made love to his daughter."

Kaufman therefore enjoyed a degree of freedom that permitted him to shift the focus of the book from a philosophical rumination to a love story. As in his latest film, *Quills*, the director substitutes an "eye" for an "I," celebrating the visual that takes flight from the verbal.

Quills tells the story of the Marquis de Sade (Geoffrey Rush) in the asylum of Charenton, a provocative portrait of the artist as an aging pervert in a repressive and violent world. Doug Wright's script (based on his Obie Award-winning play) places us in 1794 Paris, the time of the guillotine.

In the opening scene, the marquis watches from behind a window as a beautiful young woman is about to be decapitated. The descending blade is cross-cut with his quill. That he writes in red ink suggests that his prose is not so much purple as bloody—the color of the violence around him. Whatever he pens, no matter how pornographic, can ever be as brutal as what the authorities unleash.

Like *The Unbearable Lightness of Being*, Kaufman's latest adaptation foregrounds voyeurism; with characters often framed at cell windows, *Quills* poses questions about freedom, internal as well as external. The marquis is not only imprisoned, but—because he is seen as a threat to society—increasingly dispossessed of his belongings and his means to write. Nevertheless, his defiant stare at most of his visitors is a testament to his triumphant lucidity.

When his quills, ink, and paper are removed, he writes on his bedsheets with a chicken bone dipped in red wine. When these too are taken, his own blood becomes the ink (recalling the red text of the opening scene), his nails the quills, and his clothes the paper. The less he has to write with, the more aggressively he manages to compose his stories.

We, the privileged spectators, watch the marquis through the perspective of two sympathetic inhabitants of the asylum. Madeleine (Kate Winslet), a chambermaid who smuggles out the marquis's writing with his linens, is a free spirit. The Abbé Coulmier (Joaquin Phoenix) is a well-intentioned liberal, a young priest who prefers for his inmates to paint or write their demons than embody them.

As the film progresses, the inmates fall increasingly under the marquis's spell, and he comes to seem less a degenerate scribbler than an intimator of people's darker urges. Because he sees through everyone's pretensions, he writes his cynically bawdy tales (already cinematic in their conjunction of drawings and text). From this source material as well as Wright's play, Kaufman—once again—gives us an eyeful. ■

Geoffrey Rush as the Marquis de Sade in *Quills*

by ANNE BEATTS

SAY IT AGAIN, SAM

Wise Words from the Silver Screen

IN MEMORY OF MICHAEL O'DONOGHUE

Movies are the filter through which we see the world. If we are all in Plato's cave, then movies are the shadows on the wall which tell us about life. Ever since Jolson ad-libbed "You ain't seen nothing yet!" words heard on the silver screen have burrowed into our brain cells like a virus and invaded our dreams, both sleeping and waking.

They have permanently shaped our personalities, tastes, attitudes, and worldview. And why not? Philosophy found in the pages of a textbook can hardly hope to compete with words murmured by lips that are three feet high and belong to a movie star.

It's no accident that motion pictures were almost permanently christened "talkies" instead of "movies" by the public. Back then the words were just as important as the pictures that moved. Today, in the age of blockbusters, dialogue sometimes seems like a lost art. The most memorable lines date from a vanished era. Yet even in the present day, every so often a true gem shines through.

Here, then, is a treasured collection of aphorisms from the best and worst that Hollywood has to offer.

AFRICA

"A woman on safari! Never!"

—Stewart Granger as Allan Quatermain

King Solomon's Mines, 1950

AFTERLIFE

"There are worse things awaiting man than death."

—Bela Lugosi as Count Dracula

Dracula, 1931

AGING

"Just old age. It's the only disease, Mr. Thompson, that you don't look forward to being cured of."

—Everett Sloan as Bernstein

Citizen Kane, 1941

ALCOHOL

"There comes a time in every woman's life when the only thing that helps is a glass of champagne."

—Bette Davis as Katherine "Kit" Marlowe

Old Acquaintance, 1943

ANTICIPATION

"The longer they wait, the better they like it."

—Marlene Dietrich as Frenchy

Destry Rides Again, 1939

BIRD-WATCHING

"You don't fuck with the eagles unless you know how to fly."

—John Belushi as Bluto

Animal House, 1978

CHAUVINISM

"There's no place like home."

—Judy Garland as Dorothy Gale

The Wizard of Oz, 1939

CHIVALRY

"Chivalry is not only dead, it's decomposed."

—Rudy Vallee as John D. Hackensacker III

The Palm Beach Story, 1942

COMEDY

"Words with a K in them are funny."

—Walter Matthau as Al Lewis

The Sunshine Boys, 1975

COSMETICS

"When you're in love with a married man, you shouldn't wear mascara."

—Shirley MacLaine as Fran Kubelik

The Apartment, 1960

COURAGE

"With enough courage, you can do without a reputation."

—Clark Gable as Rhett Butler

Gone With the Wind, 1939

DATING

"Girls don't pay. Guys pay."

—Candy Clark as Debbie

American Graffiti, 1973

DEPRECIATION

"It's not the years, honey, it's the mileage."

—Harrison Ford as Indiana Jones

Raiders of the Lost Ark, 1981

DISCRETION

"It's better to be a live coward than a dead hero."

—Claire Trevor as Gaye Dawn

Key Largo, 1948

DIVORCE

"That's the only good thing about divorce. You get to sleep with your mother."

—Virginia Weidler as Little Mary

The Women, 1939

DUELING

"For the woman, the kiss: for the man, the sword."

—Erik Rhodes as Alberto Beddini

Top Hat, 1935

ETIQUETTE

"I never shake hands with a left-handed draw."

—Sterling Hayden as Johnny Logan

Johnny Guitar, 1954

ENTERTAINMENT

"Not even the best magician in the world can produce a rabbit out of the hat if there isn't already a rabbit in the hat."

—Anton Walbrook as Boris Lermontov

The Red Shoes, 1948

EXISTENTIALISM

"This is this."

—Robert DeNiro as Michael

The Deer Hunter, 1978

ETERNITY

"A kiss on the hand might feel very good, but a diamond tiara is forever."

—Marilyn Monroe as Lorelei Lee

Gentlemen Prefer Blondes, 1953

FAME

"Your face can be on a magazine cover one week and in the ashcan the next."

—Jeanne Crain as Vicki

Vicki, 1953

FASHION

"You can't show your bosom 'fore three o'clock."

—Hattie McDaniel as Mammy

Gone with the Wind, 1939

FEELINGS

"Sentiment comes easy at fifty cents a word."

—Clifton Webb as Waldo Lydecker

Laura, 1944

FIREARMS

"I knew one thing—as soon as anyone said you didn't need a gun, you'd better take along one that worked."

—Robert Mitchum as Philip Marlowe

Farewell, My Lovely, 1975

FOOD

"Life is a banquet, and most poor suckers are starving to death."

—Rosalind Russell as Mame

Auntie Mame, 1958

FUNERAL ARRANGEMENTS

"Live fast, die young, and leave a good-looking corpse."

—John Derek as Nick Romano

Knock on Any Door, 1949

FURS

"You may as well go to perdition in ermine. You're sure to come back in rags."

—Katharine Hepburn as Terry Randall

Stage Door, 1937

Goodbye

"Nothing says goodbye like a bullet."

—Elliott Gould as Philip Marlowe

The Long Goodbye, 1973

Gusto

"Live! Otherwise you got nothing to talk about in the locker room."

—Ruth Gordon as Maude

Harold and Maude, 1972

Hitchhiking

"The limb is mightier than the thumb."

—Claudette Colbert as Ellie

It Happened One Night, 1934

History

"If history has shown us anything it's that you can kill anyone."

—Al Pacino as Michael Corleone

The Godfather, Part 2, 1974

Hollywood

"Nobody's happy in Hollywood."

—Jack Carson as himself

It's a Great Feeling, 1949

Housekeeping

"Two single men living alone should not have a house cleaner than my mother's."

—Walter Matthau as Oscar Madison

The Odd Couple, 1968

Humor

"There's a lot to be said for making people laugh.... It isn't much, but it's better than nothing in this cockeyed caravan."

—Joel McCrea as Sullivan

Sullivan's Travels, 1941

Innuendo

"Love flies out the door when money comes innuendo."

—Groucho Marx as himself

Monkey Business, 1931

Intuition

"The mind isn't everything."

—Ingrid Bergman as Dr. Constance Peterson

Spellbound, 1945

Inventions

"In Italy for thirty years under the Borgias, they had warfare, terror, murder, bloodshed. They produced Michelangelo, Leonardo da Vinci, and the Renaissance. In Switzerland they had brotherly love, five hundred years of democracy and peace, and what did they produce—the cuckoo clock!"

—Orson Welles as Harry Lime

The Third Man, 1949

Kissing

"Many lovers come to railroad stations to kiss without attracting attention."

—Marlene Dietrich as Shanghai Lily

Shanghai Express, 1932

Love

"Love is like the measles. You only get it once. The older you are, the tougher it gets."

—Howard Keel as Adam

Seven Brides for Seven Brothers, 1954

Manners

"Bad table manners, my dear Gigi, have broken up more households than infidelity."

—Isabel Jeans as Aunt Alicia
Gigi, 1948

Maturity

"You can't stay seventeen forever."

—Ron Howard as Steve
American Graffiti, 1973

Marriage

"Marriage is like a dull meal, with the dessert at the beginning."

—Jose Ferrer as Toulouse-Lautrec
Moulin Rouge, 1952

Media

"If the headline is big enough, it makes the news big enough."

—Orson Welles as Charles Foster Kane
Citizen Kane, 1941

Men

"There are no great men, buster. There are only men."

—Elaine Stewart as Lila
The Bad and the Beautiful, 1952

Money

"It's no trick to make a lot of money, if all you want is to make a lot of money."

—Everett Sloan as Bernstein
Citizen Kane, 1941

Mortality

"You sing into a little hole year after year and then you die."

—Bing Crosby as himself
The Big Broadcast of 1933, 1933

Motherhood

"Alligators have the right idea. They eat their young."

—Eve Arden as Ida Corwin
Mildred Pierce, 1945

Murder

"You shouldn't keep souvenirs of a killing."

—James Stewart as John "Scottie" Ferguson
Vertigo, 1958

Nature

"Nature, Mr. Allnut, is what we are put into this world to rise above."

—Katherine Hepburn as Rose Sayer
The African Queen, 1951

Optimism

"Tomorrow is another day."

—Vivien Leigh as Scarlett O'Hara
Gone with the Wind, 1939

Pain

"Of course it hurts. The trick is not showing that it hurts."

—Peter O'Toole as T. E. Lawrence
Lawrence of Arabia, 1962

Paternity

"If you lose a son it's possible to get another. There's only one Maltese Falcon."

—Sydney Greenstreet as Kasper Gutman
The Maltese Falcon, 1941

Patriotism

"No bastard ever won a war by dying for

his country. He won it by making the other poor dumb bastard die for his country."

—George C. Scott as General George Patton

Patton, 1970

Pessimism

"The morning after always does look grim if you happen to be wearing last night's dress."

—Ina Claire as Grand Duchess Swana

Ninotchka, 1939

Pragmatism

"Nobody's perfect."

—Joe E. Brown as Osgood

Some Like It Hot, 1959

Politics

"Politicians, ugly buildings, and whores all get respectable if they last long enough."

—John Huston as Noah Cross

Chinatown, 1974

Relativity

"Time is a watch wound by some sucker."

—Sydney Greenstreet as Dutchman

Malaya, 1949

Religion

"God always has another custard pie up His sleeve."

—Lynn Redgrave as Georgy

Georgy Girl, 1966

Reversals of Fortune

"I've been rich and I've been poor. Believe me, rich is better."

—Glória Grahame as Debby Marsh

The Big Heat, 1953

Risk

"A man's got to know his limitations."

—Clint Eastwood as Harry Callaghan

Magnum Force, 1973

Safety

"Women and children can be careless but not men."

—Marlon Brando as Don Vito Corleone

The Godfather, 1972

Sanity

"We all go a little mad sometimes."

—Anthony Perkins as Norman Bates

Psycho, 1960

Science

"Science is sometimes frighteningly impersonal."

—Vincent Price as Dr. Warren Chapin

The Tingler, 1959

Seduction

"When women go wrong, men go right after them."

—Mae West as Lady Lou

She Done Him Wrong, 1933

Shipboard Romance

"They say a moonlit deck is a woman's business office."

—Barbara Stanwyck as Lady Eve Sidwich

The Lady Eve, 1941

Show Business

"You can lose everything else, but you can't lose your talent."

—Bette Davis as Baby Jane

What Ever Happened to Baby Jane?, 1962

SMOKING

"Smoke good."

—Boris Karloff as the Monster

The Bride of Frankenstein, 1935

SOLITUDE

"Even a turtle doesn't like to be alone."

—Yoshiro Uchida as Toshio

Gammera the Invincible, 1965

SPORTS

"Charlie don't surf."

—Robert Duvall as Colonel Kilgore

Apocalypse Now, 1979

STATISTICS

"Statistics show there are more women in the world than anything else—except insects."

—Glenn Ford as Johnny Farrell

Gilda, 1946

SURPRISES

"No matter who you get married to, you wake up married to someone else."

—Marlon Brando as Sky Masterson

Guys and Dolls, 1955

TEAMWORK

"It's even better when you help."

—Lauren Bacall as Slim

To Have and Have Not, 1945

TEARS

"Tears are only good when a fella can see 'em."

—Thelma Ritter as Molly

Lucy Gallant, 1955

TRAVEL

"One can feel nostalgia for places one has never been."

—Greta Garbo as Queen Christina

Queen Christina, 1933

TRUST

"Man who trust woman walk on duck-weed over pond."

—Alan Ladd as Neale Gordon

Calcutta, 1947

TV

"That's all television is, my dear. Nothing but auditions."

—George Sanders as Addison DeWitt

All About Eve, 1950

VIRILITY

"It's not the men in your life that count, it's the life in your men."

—Mae West as Tira

I'm No Angel, 1932

VIRTUE

"Greed, for lack of a better word, is good. Greed is right. Greed works."

—Michael Douglas as Gordon Gecko

Wall Street, 1987

WOMEN

"Women should be kept illiterate and clean, like canvases."

—Roscoe Karns as Phil Whitaker

Woman of the Year, 1942

WRITING

"Audiences don't think somebody sits down and writes a picture. They think the actors make it up as they go along."

—William Holden as Joe Gillis

Sunset Boulevard, 1950

Leslie Caron from the book *Hollywood Candid*

CROSSWORD

REEL WRITERS

by Emily Cox and Henry Rathvon

ACROSS

1 *As You Like* It screenwriter; author of *The Admirable Crichton*

5 Dylan who screenwrote *The Three Weird Sisters*

10 *The Fly* screenwriter; author of *King Rat*

11 *M*A*S*H* screenwriter (Jr.) or *Gullible's Travels* humorist (Sr.)

12 *The African Queen* screenwriter; *A Death in the Family* author

13 *Marie Antoinette* screenwriter who penned *The Last Tycoon*

15 Book found in a pew

16 Writer portrayed by Streep in *Out of Africa*

19 Anthony Hopkins' writerly role in *Shadowlands*

22 *The Misfits* screenwriter who wrote *The Crucible*, adapted by Sartre for film

25 1991 movie based on a William S. Burroughs' book

27 Epic film about the author 3 Down

29 Screenwriter of 1973's *Rhinoceros*, featuring Gene Wilder and Zero Mostel

30 1990 Oscar-winning animated short on the theme of equilibrium

31 Subject of the 1938 film *The Unashamed*

32 Sleeping sacks in Westerns

DOWN

1 *The Day of the* ___, 1973 movie based on a Forsyth bestseller

2 Attribute of many a hero

3 John who wrote *Ten Days That Shook the World*

4 Animosity

6 *Black Beauty* or *The Red Pony*
7 *One Flew Over the Cuckoo's Nest* extras?
8 Grating in vocal tone
9 How the eyes of a zombie appear
14 *Corridors of Power* author C.P.
17 Christie book and movie *Death on the* ___
18 Analysis of a verse's meter
20 Cited as similar
21 Drugged or drunken state
22 Ghastly, as *Dracula* or *The Raven*
23 Never-ending
24 Movie guides
26 Workplaces for writers
28 Indistinctly pronounce, or insult

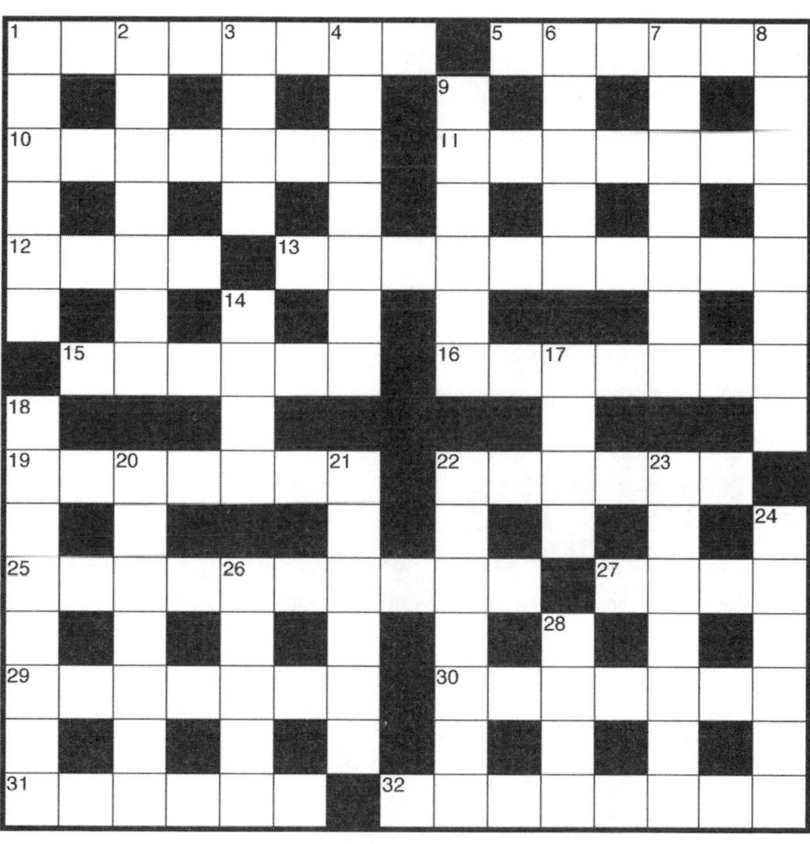

SOLUTION ON PAGE 315

CONTRIBUTORS

RAFAEL ALBERTI was born in 1902 in El Puerto Del Santa Maria, Spain. In 1939, in the wake of the Spanish Civil War, he went into exile in France and Argentina, finally settling in Italy. His books of poetry include *Cal y Canto, Sobre los Angeles, Verte y No Verte, Capital de la Glória, Entre el Clavel y la Espada, Pleamar, A la Pintura, Retornos de lo Vivo Lejano,* and *Baladas y Canciones De Parana.*

RUSSELL BANKS is the author of the novels *Rule of the Bone* and *Cloudsplitter*, among others, and *The Angel on the Roof: New and Selected Stories*. Two of his novels, *The Sweet Hereafter* and *Affliction*, were adapted as prize-winning films. He lives in the Adirondack Mountains in upstate New York.

ANNE BEATTS

ANNE BEATTS is a TV writer-producer who won two Emmys as a writer for the original *Saturday Night Live*. She also created and produced the critically acclaimed CBS sitcom *Square Pegs*. She was the first woman contributing editor of *National Lampoon* and has been published in *Esquire, Playboy, Vogue, Premiere*, and many other publications. In 1997-98, her humor column "Beatts Me!" appeared weekly in the Sunday *Los Angeles Times*. She co-edited the best-selling *Saturday Night Live* (Avon, 1977), *Titters: The First Collection of Humor by Women* (Macmillan, 1976), and *Titters 101* (Putnam's, 1984), and co-authored *The Mom Book* (Dell, 1986). Her work has appeared on Broadway in *Gilda: Live* and the Tony-nominated rock-and-roll musical *Leader of the Pack*. She is a frequent reader on the Hollywood poetry circuit.

KERA BOLONIK is a freelance writer and editor, whose feature articles and book reviews have appeared in *Salon.com, The Village Voice*, and *New York*. She lives in Brooklyn, New York.

PATRICIA BOSWORTH was an actress for ten years, appearing on Broadway, on TV, and in films. In 1966 she began writing articles on the theater and movies for *New York* magazine. Since winning a Doubleday Fellowship in writing at Columbia, she has been articles editor of *Woman's Day*, senior editor of *McCalls*, managing editor of *Harper's Bazaar* and a regular contributor the The *New York Times, Esquire,* and *Town & Country*. Her best-selling book, *Montgomery Clift: A Biography,* was called "one of the best books of the year" by the *New York Times Book Review*.

MARK CALDWELL teaches English at Fordham University. His most recent book is *A Short History of Rudeness: Manners, Morals, and Misbehavior in Modern America* (Picador USA).

RON CARLSON

RON CARLSON is the author of five books of fiction, most recently the collection *The Hotel Eden*; his new novel, *The Speed of Light*, will be published later this year. He has been awarded a National Endowment for the Arts Fellowship in Fiction, a Pushcart Prize, and the Ploughshares Cohen Prize. He is a professor of English at Arizona State University and lives with Elaine Carlson and their two sons in Scottsdale, Arizona.

The color photographs of WILLIAM EGGLESTON first came to public attention in the mid-1970s, most forcefully in the 1976 exhibition *William Eggleston's Guide*, which originated at the Museum of Modern Art, New York City, and traveled to five other U.S. museums. Eggleston, born in 1937, has been a lecturer in Visual and Environmental Studies at Harvard University and has received grants from the Guggenheim Foundation, the National Endowment for the Arts, and the Arts Survey. He makes his living as a photographer in the Mississippi-Tennessee region and in Washington, D.C.

F. SCOTT FITZGERALD published his first novel, *This Side of Paradise*, in 1920. His masterpieces include *The Beautiful and Damned*, *The Great Gatsby*, and *Tender Is the Night*. He died of a heart attack in 1940 at the age of forty-four, while working on *The Love of the Last Tycoon*.

PHILIPPE GARNIER, a French writer based in Los Angeles, is a regular contributor to *Libération*, as well as a book scout and translator for various publishers in France. His last documentary was *Boetticher Rides Again*, released in 1996. His four published books include a 1984 biography of David Goodis. *They Made Me a Screenwriter* is adapted from a chapter of *Honi Soit Qui Malibu*, published in 1996 by Editions Grasset.

DAVID GATES has twice been nominated for the National Book Critics Circle Award, for the novel *Preston Falls* and for the short story collection, *The Wonders of the Invisible World*. He is also the author of the novel, *Jernigan*.

DANIEL HALPERN is the author of eight collections of poems, the editorial director of the Ecco Press, and a recipient of fellowships from the Guggenheim Foundation and the National Endowment for the Arts, as well as a 1993 PEN Publisher Citation. He is the author of *Halpern's Guide to the Essential Restaurants of Italy* and, with Julie Strand, of *The Good Food: Soups, Stews & Pastas*. For twenty-five years he edited the international literary magazine *Antaeus*, which he founded in Tangier with Paul Bowles. He has taught in the graduate writing program of Columbia University, at The New School for Social Research, in and the writing program at Princeton University.

ANNETTE INSDORF is a professor and director of undergraduate film studies at Columbia University, and was chair of the Graduate Film

ANNETTE INSDORF

Division from 1990 to 1995. Previously, she taught at Yale, where she received her Ph.D. in English. Her books include *Francois Truffaut; Indelible Shadows: Film and the Holocaust*; and *Double Lives, Second Chances: The Cinema of Krysztof Kieslowski*, recently published by Talk Miramax/Hyperion.

TAMARA JENKINS is the director of *Slums of Beverly Hills*, a semi-autobiographical coming-of-age story set in the seventies. Winner of a Guggenheim Fellowship for filmmaking, Jenkins has written and directed several programs for public television. She attended the Sundance Institute Screenwriting and Filmmakers Lab.

STEVEN KATZ is a screenwriter living in New York. His film *Shadow of the Vampire* opened on December 29, 2000.

DAVID LEAVITT

DAVID LEAVITT is the author of several novels and story collections, including *Family Dancing*; *The Lost Language of Cranes*; *A Place I've Never Been*; *Arkansas*; *The Page Turner*; and *Martin Bauman*. He divides his time between Italy and Los Angeles.

FRED G. LEEBRON's novels are *Six Figures* and *Out West*. His work has received Michener, Fulbright, Stegner, and Pushcart prizes, and new stories of his are in *TriQuarterly* and *DoubleTake*. He lives in Gettysburg, Pennsylvania, with his wife and two children.

FRED G. LEEBRON

DAVID LEHMAN's most recent book is *The Last Avant-Garde* (Anchor Doubleday). He also wrote *The Daily Mirror* (Scribner), which comprises 150 of the poems from his experiment of writing one poem every day. In 1988 he launched, and is now the series editor of, *The Best American Poetry*. He is the author of three poetry collections: *An Alternative to Speech* (1986), *Operation Memory* (1990), and *Valentine Place* (1996). The poems included here are from the forthcoming *The Evening Sun*. Among his critical books are: *The Line Forms Here* (1992) and *The Big Question* (1995). He is the general editor of *Michigan Press Poets on Poetry Series*, and teaches at Bennington, Columbia, and the New School for Social Research.

JONATHAN LETHEM lives in Brooklyn. His most recent novel is *Motherless Brooklyn* (Doubleday).

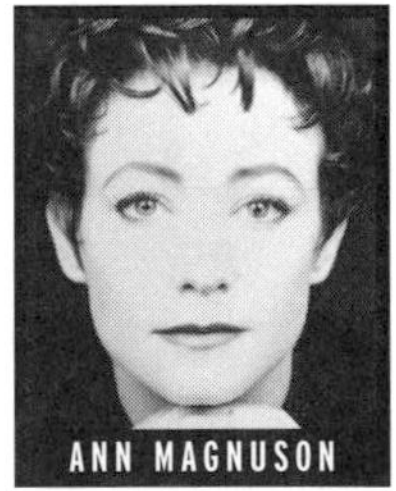
ANN MAGNUSON

ANN MAGNUSON is an actor and writer living in Los Angeles. She has appeared in numerous plays and movies, including the films *Desperately Seeking Susan*, *Tequila Sunrise*, *Friends and Lovers*, *Tank Girl*, and *Clear and Present Danger*.

Her television credits include *The Drew Carey Show*, *Caroline in the City*, and *Happy House*, a.k.a. *The Ann Magnuson Show*.

LOU MATHEWS's novel, *L.A. Breakdown*, about illegal street racing, was picked by the *Los Angeles Times* as one of the best books of 1999. His first full-length play, *The Duke's Development*, is a finalist in this year's National Repertory Theatre Foundation's play competition. He lives a half-mile below the Hollywood sign in Beachwood Canyon (called Pinyon Canyon in Nathanael West's *Day of the Locust*).

LOU MATHEWS

CHRISTOPHER MERRILL's most recent books are *Only the Nails Remain: Scenes from the Balkan Wars* (nonfiction) and the translation of Ales Debeljak's *The City and the Child*. A new collection of poems, *Brilliant Water*, is forthcoming from White Pine Press.

OGDEN NASH was born in 1902 in Rye, New York. Educated at St. George's School and Harvard, he came to New York, where he worked as a copywriter for Doubleday, and later joined the staff of *The New Yorker* magazine. Famous for the wit of his humorous verse, he was the author of nineteen volumes of poetry, including *Everyone but Me and Thee* (1962) in which "Viva Vamp, Vale Vamp" appeared. Ogden Nash was elected to the American Academy of Arts and Letters in 1950. He died in 1966.

FRANK O'HARA was raised in Grafton, Massachusetts, and went to Harvard, where he studied music and met John Ashbery. An editorial associate at *Art News*, he was later appointed assistant curator of the Museum of Modern Art and became a part of the New York art scene of the 1950s and 1960s. During his lifetime, he published four books of poems: *A City Winter*, *Meditations in an Emergency* (from which the poem "To the Film Industry in Crisis" comes), *Second Avenue*, and *Lunch Poems*. He died in July 1966 in an accident in the dunes on Fire Island.

Born and raised in Hollywood, VICTORIA PRICE received double honors in theater and art history from Williams College in Massachusetts. Her biography/memoir of her father, *Vincent Price*, was published in 1999 by St. Martin's Press. Currently a contributing writer and editor to the *St. James Encyclopedia of Popular Culture*, she also writes for A&E's *Biography* series.

JON RAYMOND is the managing editor of *Plazm* magazine, an arts and culture quarterly originating in Portland, Oregon. He once made a feature-length movie based on the syndicated daily comic strip *Crock*, which played one time before receiving a cease and desist order. He currently lives in Brooklyn.

RACHEL RESNICK's first novel, *Go West Young F*cked-Up Chick*, was published by St. Martin's Press last year. So far, the book has not been optioned. Resnick acted as consulting editor on this issue of *Tin House*. She lives in Topanga, California. Check out her web site at: www.rachelresnick.com

RACHEL RESNICK

BARNEY ROSSET was the owner of Grove Press from 1951 to 1986. There, he publishing D. H. Lawrence's *Lady Chatterley's Lover* and Henry Miller's *Tropic of Cancer*, and later founded the *Evergreen Review*. He published his friend Samuel Beckett's *Waiting for Godot* (1954)—the first American publisher to put him into print—and later published more than twenty other volumes by Beckett, including his last work, *Stirrings Still*, which Beckett dedicated to Rosset. He currently heads Foxrock, a press named for the Dublin suburb where Beckett was born. Rosset has received numerous awards, including a 1988 PEN American Center Publisher Citation.

DAVID ST. JOHN's most recent collections of poetry are *Study for the World's Body: New & Selected Poems* (HarperCollins), which was nominated for the National Book Award in Poetry, and *The Red Leaves of Night* (HarperCollins), nominated for the *Los Angeles Times* Book Prize. He recently received an award in literature from the American Academy of Arts and Letters. He lives in Venice, California.

DAVID ST. JOHN

CHRIS SOLOMINE got his B.S. in film from Syracuse University and his M.A. in creative writing and literature from University of Illinois at Chicago. He adapted Homer's *Odyssey* and André Malraux's *The Royal Way* for the screen with Russian director Andrei Konchalovsky. His screenplays include Dostyoevsky's *Last Night* and *Run It Back*. He lives in New York and Los Angeles and is currently working on a contemporary film adaptation of *The Brothers Karamozov* as well as the novel that's been in his desk for nearly a decade.

DEANNE STILLMAN is a widely published and anthologized writer. Her work has appeared in The *New York Times* (*Magazine*, *Book Review*, *Arts & Leisure*, *Travel*); The *Los Angeles Times* (*Magazine* and *Book Review*); *Salon.com*; and *Slate*, among others. She is a former columnist at *Buzz* magazine. Her plays *Pray for Surf*, *Star Maps*, and *Inside the White House* have won prizes in festivals around the country. Her book *Twentynine Palms: A True Story of Murder, Marines, and the Mojave* will be published in spring 2001 by William Morrow.

DEANNE STILLMAN

MARK STRAND, a former poet laureate of the United States, is the author of nine volumes of poetry, including most recently *Bliz-*

zard of One, which won the Pulitzer Prize in 1999. His books have brought him numerous awards and prizes, among them a MacArthur Fellowship. He is the translator of several books, including *The Owl's Insomnia* by Rafael Alberti, which includes the poem reprinted here. His latest anthology is *The Making of a Poem: A Norton Anthology of Poetic Form*, which he co-edited with Eavan Boland.

DAVID TRINIDAD's most recent book of poems, *Plasticville*, was published in 2000 (Turtle Point Press). His other books include *Answer Song* and *Hand Over Heart: Poems 1981–1988*. He teaches poetry at Rutgers University, and directs the Writers at Rutgers series. He is a member of the core faculty at The New School's M.F.A. Writing Program.

MIA TAYLOR

MIA TAYLOR is a free lance writer. She formerly worked in script development. She lives in Hollywood, near Sunset Boulevard.

KATHERINE VAZ is the author of the novel *Saudade* (St. Martin's Press, 1994), the first contemporary novel about Portuguese-Americans from a major publisher. The Library of Congress chose her second novel, *Mariana*, as one of the Top 30 International Books of 1998. Her collection *Fado & Other Stories* won the 1997 Drue Heinz Literature Prize.

KATHERINE VAZ

XAVIER VILLAURRUTIA was a Mexican poet and playwright who founded the first experimental theater in Mexico in 1928. A mentor to Octavio Paz, he also influenced other young Mexican poets, notably Ali Chumacero.

BRUCE WAGNER

BRUCE WAGNER wrote the novel *I'm Losing You* (Villard) and directed the film of the same name. His third novel, *I'll Let You Go*, will be published in 2001, also by Villard. He recently directed the digital feature *Women in Film* for Killer Films/The Independent Film Channel.

ELIOT WEINBERGER's most recent books are *Karmic Tales*, a collection of essays, and *Unlock*, a translation of the poetry of Bei Dao. He is also the translator of *Nostaligia for Death* by Xavior Villarrutia, which appeared in 1993.

J	M	B	A	R	R	I	E		T	H	O	M	A	S
A		R		E		L		G		O		A		T
C	L	A	V	E	L	L		L	A	R	D	N	E	R
K		V		D		W		A		S		I		I
A	G	E	E		F	I	T	Z	G	E	R	A	L	D
L		R		S		L		E				C		E
	H	Y	M	N	A	L		D	I	N	E	S	E	N
S				O						I				T
C	S	L	E	W	I	S		M	I	L	L	E	R	
A		I				T		A		E		T		U
N	A	K	E	D	L	U	N	C	H		R	E	D	S
S		E		E		P		A		S		R		H
I	O	N	E	S	C	O		B	A	L	A	N	C	E
O		E		K		R		R		U		A		R
N	U	D	I	S	M		B	E	D	R	O	L	L	S

Crossword solution, from p. 309

PHOTO CREDITS

NO, BUT I SAW THE MOVIE
p. 11 Hollywood Theater
Photo by Bill Stanton
p. 12 and p. 18 A scene from *The Sweet Hereafter* and a photo of the film's director, Atom Egoyan
Photos by J. Eisen/Fine Line ©2000 Fine Line Features
p. 15 A scene from *Oscar and Lucinda* ©1998 Twentieth Century Fox
p. 16 Sigourney Weaver in *The Ice Storm* ©1998 Twentieth Century Fox

ANDRAS HAMORI INTERVIEW
p. 27 Andras Hamori takes a bubble bath Photo by Liam Daniel
p. 28 A scene from Istvan Szabo's *Sunshine* Photo by Peter Sorel ©1998 Twentieth Century Fox
p. 40 Agota and Vinterberg Photo courtesy of Thomas Vinterberg

HITCHCOCK/NABOKOV
P. 48 Hitchcock © Bettmann/Corbis
p. 48 Nabokov © Hulton Deutsch Corbis

WE ARE NOT FRIENDS
p. 56 Nicole Kidman and Tom Cruise © Reuters NewMedia Inc./Corbis

JERRY STAHL INTERVIEW
p. 63 Jerry Stahl and Ben Stiller Photo by Scott Del Amo ©1998 Artisan Entertainment
p. 64 A scene from *Permanent Midnight* Photo by John P. Johnson © 1998 Artisan Entertainment
p. 65 Ann Magnuson collects herself Photo by Rocky Schenck
p. 66 Stahl and Arty Nelson, writer/director of *Down with the Jones* Courtesy Jerry Stahl collection
p. 71 Alf Photo by John P. Johnson © 1998 Artisan Entertainment

LET US NOW PRAISE FAMOUS MEN
p.76-91 All celebrity look-alike photos by William Eggleston

LOST & FOUND
p. 96 Buster Keaton in *Film* (1964) Photo by Steve Schapiro/TimePix
p. 101 Anton Pavlovich Chekhov © Austrian Archives/Corbis

MASTER AND MARGARITA
p. 115 Stalin © Panet Art
p. 116 Bulgakov Photo Courtesy Ardis Publishers
p. 118 Kremlin Tower and Gate © Hulton-Deutsch/Corbis
p. 121 Joseph Stalin © Hulton-Deutsch/Corbis
p. 124 Roman Polanski © Bettmann/Corbis

DEFENDING THE SEARCHERS
p. 145 John Wayne with John Ford © Bettmann/Corbis
p. 149 John Wayne with Howard Hawks © Bettmann/Corbis

ALEX COX INTERVIEW
p. 158 Alex Cox Photo by Tom Collins
p. 161 Sid Vicious © S.I.N./Corbis

DIANE ARBUS
p. 177 Photo of Diane Arbus Courtesy of Patricia Bosworth Collection

TODD HAYNES INTERVIEW
p. 214 Todd Haynes Photo by Markus Hansen

THEY MADE ME A WRITER
p. 235 Robert Tasker in Rowland Brown's *Quick Millions*
p. 227, 234 Robert Tasker, 1936
p. 226 Ernest G. Booth

LOST AMONG THE PINAFORES
p. 243 A Scene From *Howards End* Photo by Derrick Santini. ©1992 Sony Pictures Entertainment

STUDIO OPTIONS DESERT ...
p. 261 Joshua Tree ©Joseph Sohm; ChromoSohm Inc./Corbis

THE MAN WHO WAS MADE ...
p. 272 and 275 Women wearing Holy Ghost Festival capes. Photos by Michael Trudeau

AN "I" FOR AN "EYE"
p. 289 Photo by Bob Waldman
p. 290, 297, 298, 299 Movie stills from *Quills* By David Appleby © Fox Searchlight
p. 293 and 295 Scenes from *The Unbearable Lightness of Being*

PORTFOLIO
p. 47 Photo of Rita Moreno
p. 225 Photo of Marlon Brando
p. 307 Photo of Leslie Caron
Photos by Murray Garrett from *Candid Hollywood*, courtesy of Harry N. Abrams

HEAD SHOTS ON CONTRIBUTOR'S NOTES
pgs. 310-315
Anne Beatts by Lynn Goldsmith;
Annette Insdorf by Andre Baranowski;
David Leavitt by Jerry Bauer;
Fred Leebron by Tom Levy;
Ann Magnuson by Len Prince;
Rachel Resnick by Marc Hanauer;
Deanne Stillman by Martin Sugarman;
David St. John by Milly Bendall;
Mia Taylor by Teal Minton;
Katherine Vaz by Michael Jang

CONTINUITY STILLS
All continutiy shots courtesy of John Divola from his book *Continuity* (Smart Art Press & Ram Publications)

RSUB

The Tin House Martini

Pour 1/2 oz of Pernod into a cocktail shaker and swirl until it coats the inside of the shaker, pour off any excess. In countries where it is still legal, such as Portugal and Spain, absinthe can be appropriately substituted for Pernod.

Splash two eye-dropperfuls of Cinzano dry vermouth into the bottom of the shaker, and again swirl it about, then pour off the excess.

Pour 4 to 4 1/2 oz of Tanqueray gin into the shaker, add ice, and with a ridiculously long-handled silver mixing spoon, stir exactly twenty times.

Pour the drink into a very well-chilled martini glass then add three small cocktail olives, or two large ones, sans toothpick.

The flavors of olive and Pernod commingle so deliciously, that at least one of the olives should be consumed after the drink is finished. You see, sometimes consolation can be found in the bottom of a martini glass.

. . . .

The Tin House martini was developed for *Tin House* magazine by Mr. Greg Connolly, bartender at the Four Seasons restaurant in New York City, who has also been known to call it "The Best Martini in the World." Order The Tin House Martini at the Four Seasons bar, or use this recipe to educate your favorite bartender about this inspired improvement on the standard gin martini.